THE ART OF NARRATION IN
WOLFRAM'S *PARZIVAL* AND
ALBRECHT'S *JÜNGERER TITUREL*

ANGLICA GERMANICA SERIES 2

Editors: Leonard Forster, S. S. Prawer and A. T. Hatto

Other books in the series

THE ART OF NARRATION IN
WOLFRAM'S *PARZIVAL* AND
ALBRECHT'S *JÜNGERER TITUREL*

LINDA B. PARSHALL

CAMBRIDGE UNIVERSITY PRESS

CAMBRIDGE

LONDON   NEW YORK   NEW ROCHELLE

MELBOURNE   SYDNEY

CAMBRIDGE UNIVERSITY PRESS
Cambridge, New York, Melbourne, Madrid, Cape Town,
Singapore, São Paulo, Delhi, Tokyo, Mexico City

Cambridge University Press
The Edinburgh Building, Cambridge CB2 8RU, UK

Published in the United States of America by Cambridge University Press, New York

www.cambridge.org
Information on this title: www.cambridge.org/9780521169202

First published 1981
First paperback edition 2011

A catalogue record for this publication is available from the British Library

Library of Congress Cataloguing in Publication data
Parshall, Linda B
The art of narration in Wolfram's Parzival and
Albrecht's Jüngerer Titurel.
(Anglica Germanica: Series 2)
Bibliography: p.
Includes index.
1. Wolfram von Eschenbach, 12th cent. Parzival.
2. Albrecht von Scharfenberg, 13th cent. Jüngerer
Titurel. I. Title. II. Series.
PT1688.P3   831'.2'0923   79-21146

ISBN 978-0-521-22237-2 Hardback
ISBN 978-0-521-16920-2 Paperback

CONTENTS

v

ACKNOWLEDGEMENTS

I am indebted to many friends and colleagues for their help and encouragement. Thanks are due foremost to Professor A. T. Hatto whose contributions are past recounting. His interest and moral support have been constant since I first began the study in 1970 as a Ph.D. thesis under his tutelage at Queen Mary College, University of London. Professor Kenneth Northcott of the University of Chicago first formed my approach to medieval literature. Professor C. S. Jaeger of Bryn Mawr College kindly read and criticised the manuscript in its early state. His comments and those of Professor M. O'C. Walshe were especially helpful.

Through the various stages of research and writing I have received assistance from several institutions. Generous support from the American Association of University Women and the Deutscher Akademischer Austauschdienst made possible a year abroad in 1978-9. The Portland State University Foundation provided a subvention to assist with publication costs. I am particularly grateful to the libraries of Queen Mary College, the Warburg Institute, the Germanic Institute and Senate House of the University of London, to the British Library, and the Portland State University Library. My greatest debt is to my husband Peter who has never hesitated in his encouragement and willingness to read yet another version.

INTRODUCTION

The late thirteenth-century poem, the *Jüngerer Titurel*, is an important monument in the post-classical phase of the Middle High German poetic tradition. Its considerable popularity and influence attest to the significance of this lengthy work for our understanding of developments in the courtly romance form. Although writing two generations after Wolfram von Eschenbach, the author poses as Wolfram, adopting not just Wolfram's name and subject matter but also much of his vocabulary and style, his mannerisms as a narrator, and even the few details of personal history that Wolfram betrays in his writings. Yet in spite of the imitation there is much in the formal structure, narrative technique, and insistent moralistic tone of the JT which identifies it as the product of a later era. The relationship between the JT and Wolfram's works is thus especially revealing not only of changes in the art of narration in the thirteenth century but of attitudes towards literature and its tradition.

The overwhelming success of the JT offers an interesting perspective on the literary reception of Wolfram, indeed on the history of literary reception and criticism in general.[1] For not only was the JT imitated repeatedly over the subsequent two centuries, but it was also already accepted as Wolfram's work before the end of the thirteenth century[2] and hailed in the fifteenth as 'das haubt ob teutschen puechen'.[3] The author's impersonation was still accepted in the Romantic period when rekindled enthusiasm for the JT held it to be one of the greatest products of the German Middle Ages and the apex of Wolfram's career. This acclaim was finally dampened when Karl Lachmann identified it not as Wolfram's work but as the 'langweiliges, todtes, und geziertes Werk' of a follower.[4] Lachmann's authority plunged the JT into a lasting disrepute from which it has only recently begun to recover.

1

The poem which stimulated all this attention remains, for both practical and aesthetic reasons, largely unfathomed, though substantial strides have been made over the last fifteen years. The JT's episodic plot is unusually involved and difficult to summarise. Basically, the tale is built on the tragic love story of Tschinotulander and Sigune, drawn mainly from the texts of Wolfram's *Titurel* fragments and *Parzival*. This central plot is framed by the history of the Gral, with Titurel's youth and the founding of Munt Salvasch serving as a preface, and an abbreviated version of Parzival's adventures as a conclusion. The JT's heavy reliance on Wolfram as a source for characters and plots as well as a model for style has been demonstrated.[5] In addition there is considerable elaboration of plots and descriptions drawn from other poems, encyclopedias, bestiaries and so forth, along with decisive influence from the medieval rhetorical tradition.[6]

Study of the historical aspects of the JT is complicated by uncertainties concerning its author, date, and geographical provenance. The narrator initially identifies himself as Wolfram von Eschenbach and maintains this disguise until near the end of the work. Finally, in stanza 5883, he reveals himself as 'Albreht', without reference to his earlier misrepresentation. In addition, seven so-called 'Hinweisstrophen' have been inserted at two separate points in the text. These refer to the fact that the JT is not by Wolfram, though they do not actually name Albrecht.[7]

Various theories have been presented ascribing parts of the JT to Wolfram himself, to an unnamed second poet, and to a continuator named Albrecht. But it is now generally accepted that the entire JT is essentially the work of the single poet who names himself Albrecht. Scholars first sought to identify him as Albrecht von Scharfenberg, a poet mentioned by the fifteenth-century author Ulrich Füetrer in his *Buch der Abenteuer* as one of the greatest German poets,[8] but equation of these two Albrechts remains unsubstantiated.[9] It appears that the author of the JT will not be identified with any certainty until further documents are uncovered. Thus we can only presume that the work is the sole surviving example from the pen of an otherwise unknown poet named Albrecht.

There is sounder evidence for dating the JT. Richard of Cornwall (died 1272) is named in stanza 2946 as still living, and this seems to provide a *terminus ante quem* for at least the first half of the poem. The only other internal evidence is an inserted reference stating that Wolfram has been dead for fifty years.[10] A quotation from the JT in one of the sermons of Berthold von Regensburg (died 1272) has been cited as external evidence for a *terminus post quem*. However, Berthold's surviving sermons are later reworkings by his successors from notes and memory. Hence, this in isolation cannot be regarded as a reliable criterion.[11] The most persuasive theory is offered by Erich Petzet who uses the JT text and a fragmentary dedication poem extant in only one copy to substantiate his dating of 1270–5 for the poem's completion.[12] Although the precise relationship of this '*Verfasserfragment*' to the epic is unclear, it can reasonably be considered as Albrecht's work, probably written after most of the JT was complete. Petzet's argument can be summarised as follows: Albrecht's original patrons abandoned him late in the work (see JT 64 and 5767–8). He then wrote a short poem (the Heidelberg fragment) identifying himself as author of the JT and dedicating his work to Ludwig der Strenge (Ludwig II – 'duc loys et palatinus', VF 20), in hopes of winning him as a patron. This was done between the death of Richard of Cornwall (2 April 1272) and the election of Rudolf of Hapsburg (1 October 1273), during which period Ludwig was considered a possible successor to Richard's throne. Albrecht's appeal failed (JT 5883), and he finished the poem about 1275, presumably without support.[13] This hypothesis has been convincingly supported by de Boor's recent work on Albrecht's original patrons.[14]

The JT's geographical provenance is likewise uncertain. It has traditionally been localised in Bavaria.[15] However, more

3

recently Walter Röll in a detailed analysis of JT manuscripts argues that the strong shadings of Middle German in Albrecht's language place the work further to the north, perhaps at Wittenberg.[16] De Boor's proposal that Albrecht was born in Bavaria but then worked further north satisfies both views.[17]

A considerable number of extant manuscripts further attest to the popularity which the JT enjoyed throughout the later medieval and Renaissance periods. From a total of eleven complete manuscripts and forty-six fragments known to Wolf, two are placed in the late thirteenth century, twelve *ca.* 1300, thirty-two in the fourteenth century, and nine in the fifteenth. There is also an incunabulum version printed at Strasbourg in 1477.[18]

The JT's vast length, the number of manuscripts, and confusion over textual recension have posed major obstacles. The first modern printing was K. A. Hahn's 1842 publication of a manuscript in Heidelberg (Cod. Pal. Germ. 383), now not considered one of the best.[19] In 1941 Werner Wolf undertook a full critical edition. Volumes 1 and 2 (1955; 1968) have appeared, but Wolf's edition was interrupted by his death which left the final volume including some 2000 stanzas in preparation. In spite of this, and in spite of the faults demonstrated by Röll, Wolf's edition is indispensable.[20] Its inaccuracies may render certain types of linguistic investigation difficult if not impossible. However, matters of content, literary sources, and narrative technique can readily be explored on the basis of Wolf's carefully prepared text and even, with caution, Hahn's transcription.

Conrad Borchling's *Preisschrift* of 1895 is the first major study of the JT and its relationship to the works of Wolfram von Eschenbach. Borchling examines the JT text in detail, concentrating on factual content and stylistic analysis, and convincingly shows that it is derived in large part from *Parzival, Willehalm,* and the *Titurel* fragments. Borchling's single-minded demonstration of the JT's dependence on Wolfram, however, led him to neglect many interesting

aspects of the work and to undervalue Albrecht's achievement. Some of this was made good in the following decades
by other scholars, though in general the JT's reputation was
still marred. Wolf's edition and his associated scholarly contributions thus represented a milestone in the revaluation of
Albrecht's work.[21] Until recently, interest in the JT centred
on textual and stylistic aspects, identification of sources or
analysis of the poem's philosophical and religious content.
Little was done to elucidate features such as narrative and
descriptive technique, character portrayal, or depiction and
motivation of action. With the appearance of Hanspeter
Brode's comprehensive dissertation in 1966, however,
Albrecht's poem was put to a broader kind of scrutiny and
emerged clearly as a work needing to be examined on its own
merits rather than as a poor reflection of Wolfram.[22] Hedda
Ragotzky's book on *Rezeptionsgeschichte* devotes a major
chapter to Albrecht's impersonation of Wolfram and draws
sound conclusions about the role of tradition in Middle High
German poetry and specifically about the Wolfram 'Rollen-
bild'. Both she and Brode have made major strides towards a
broader understanding of Albrecht's achievement, and their
work is fundamental to the present study.[23]

The recent move to reappraise Albrecht's JT is part of a
general trend towards a broader perspective in medieval
literary studies. The application to older literature of critical
modes developed in the study of modern works has brought
new insights and values to the field. The analysis of narrative
technique is a case in point. A short time ago it was still
necessary to argue the validity of this approach to medieval
romance. But as Peter Haidu recently noted:

> The news has perhaps begun to leak out beyond the pur-
> lieus of medievalism that these texts, far from being either
> naive, sentimental stories akin to fairy tales or rather heavy
> moralizing allegories, can instead be seen as confident,
> complex and most likely entirely self-conscious manipula-
> tions of the elements of fiction.[24]

The likelihood that a poet such as Wolfram von Eschenbach was consciously ironic, that he recognised and exploited distinctions among author, narrator, and reciter, or that within his tradition he commented on his tradition – these and related insights have opened up new interpretive vistas to current scholarship. Recent Wolfram studies have given credence to the notion of intentional fictionality within a traditional medieval framework, a perspective that can be extended to Albrecht as well. Although there is a tendency in this kind of approach to isolate the work from its historical context, the importance of tradition must maintain a central place here. Indeed, a quotient of self-consciousness may render the medieval poet's relationship to traditional forms more crucial as well as more complex. Certainly for Albrecht tradition was paramount, and for him it represented an inspiration, not a hindrance.

1. DESCRIPTIVE TECHNIQUE: THE STRUCTURE OF ENVIRONMENT

PARZIVAL AS A MODEL OF FORM

Defining an artist's relationship to the tradition in which he was working is certainly a primary objective in the study of medieval works of art. In courtly romances and epics we are often aided by direct references to sources, cited as part of the necessary 'validation' of a tale.[1] It is rare, however, to find a poet analysing his artistic relationship to his model or commenting on the goals of his own art.[2] Albrecht does both, discussing his debt to Wolfram's poems and elucidating his own poetic aspirations. His commentary – delivered in the guise of Wolfram von Eschenbach and more directly when Albrecht himself speaks out – expresses a consciousness of his place in an on-going tradition as both critic and creative artist. Thus Albrecht offers a particularly rich perspective on the understanding of innovation and tradition that obtained in late thirteenth-century German literature.

Our first glimpse of Albrecht's intention occurs in the JT prologue which echoes in content and vocabulary the prologues of Wolfram's *Parzival* and *Willehalm*. At the end of the prologue[3] the narrator sets forth his objective:

86 Der von Provenzale   und Flegetanis parlûre
   heidenisch von dem grale   und franzoys tûnts kunt
                                         vil aventûre.
   daz wil ich diutsch, gan iz mir got, hie kunden.
   swaz Parzival da birget,   daz wirt zu liehte braht an
                                         vakel zunden.

Here Albrecht's narrator, speaking as Wolfram, refers specifically to the story of *Parzival* and its sources, authenticating in the traditional way the tale he has undertaken. Through a metaphor of light (continuing the imagery of Wolfram's prologue), the narrator states his intention to clarify the obscurities in *Parzival*. Having identified himself and the objective of

7

his work, he goes on to explain that public demand has brought him to this undertaking.

87 Ich bin so vil gevraget   von edeler diet der mere,
    daz michs durch not betraget,   wer der edel, reine,
                                       kŭsche waere,
    der solcher selden vrucht da was der bernde.
    immer selic hie si waren,   und dort was si got selbe
                                       selden wernde.

The relationship which the narrator here establishes with his public[4] is quite uncharacteristic of Wolfram's poetry, indeed of earlier thirteenth-century works in general.[5] There is no sense of an audience as an immediate presence, fictional or otherwise. The demand which he faces is rather an accumulated response made over time, much the sort of demand that brings a modern-day scholar to revise a previous work. Albrecht's Wolfram poses as an author of acknowledged stature and authority who sets out to fulfil the promise of his earlier career.

The very fact of Albrecht's enterprise as well as its popular success indicates a continued interest in the tale of Parzival and sustained admiration of Wolfram's poetic genius. Clearly there was an audience eager to know the full story of the Gral, and Albrecht did not regard himself as attempting a forgery but rather as the continuator of Wolfram's opus.[6] Albrecht's sense of his own discipleship is most clearly expressed in the *Verfasserfragment* where he defends his impersonation and treats directly the challenges facing a follower. He draws an analogy between his literary ambition and the construction of a temple in Venice left unfinished at the death of its original builders.[7] The episode offers a parable on the venerable nature of art and the individual artist's responsibility to his own artistic tradition.

VF 2 Venezaer vil riche   ein tempel hant erbouwen.
    von den, die meisterliche   gestein kunden graben
                                       und erhouwen,

der nam den ende vil und muosten sterben:
ir werc daz edel tiure   liezen sie dar umbe niht
                    verderben.
VF 3 Ander sie da namen   ze meister disem tempel.
die muosten eben ramen.   ir wage maez gaben sie
                    exempel
uf elliu ort und worhten sam die erren.
ist witze, swer daz minner   lobt, swenn er hat
                    gebrechen an dem merren?[8]

Here Albrecht asserts his characteristically medieval view of
the artist's purpose as the perpetuation of an established
pattern. That the story of Titurel, Tschinotulander, and
Sigune was left incomplete justifies his efforts, for Wolfram's
art should not be lost to the world just because he died before
finishing it (VF 4).

The choice of an architectural metaphor is revealing in
several ways. First, the scope of Albrecht's undertaking was
comparably immense. At the time of this dedication he had
written over 5000 stanzas and had still to deal with large
sections of material. Secondly, a temple is especially appropriate to the central image in the JT – the Gral temple, itself
incomplete in the sense that its full story remained unfinished. Thirdly, the comparison with architecture suggests
a concept of poetry as a monumental, formal construction,
an attitude which is true to Albrecht's understanding of his
art.[9] For him the wholeness of a work of art is what allows it
to stand on its own, apart from its creator. The importance
of Wolfram's poetry demands its continuation even if by a
lesser master (VF 10). For in Albrecht's view it is in the nature
of art always to improve: 'Alle edliu kunst sich bezzert unde
waehet' (VF 14, 3). Thus Albrecht sees his work as a further
step towards an artistic ideal: 'kunst diu edel hoehste,   dast
rein getiht' (VF 14, 4). He did not suffer in the role of
Epigone![10]

In the text of the JT, Albrecht again considers the importance of totality and continuity in a literary creation. He is

conscious of the structures of *Parzival* and *Willehalm* and is distressed because he feels that each is marred by incompleteness – one with an unsatisfactory ending, the other with a weak beginning:

5910 Ez iehent die merke richen   daz mich an vrevden
                                           pfendet.
    iz si wunderlichen   ein bvch geanevenget vñ daz
                                     ander gendet.
    sant wilhalmes anevanc si betovbet.
    vñ parcifal ze letste   nach ir beider werdicheit
                                     berovbet.

Albrecht magnifies the urgency of his task. By finishing his own poem, ostensibly completing the *Titurel* fragments, he is also providing *Parzival* with a proper conclusion and thus granting it its rightful claim to glory. For *lob*, essential to a great work, can only come when the work has a satisfactory ending.[11]

5900 Ez wart nie lop gerichet   wan daz mit lob sich endet.
    swaz von den eren slichet   ze letzt daz wirt an wirde
                                     gar geschendet.
    swaz grozer wirde hat ein anegenge.
    nimt iz ein swaches ende   sin eren don der klinget
                                     niht die lenge.

The emphasis on conclusions reflects something in addition to an aesthetic concern with formal unity, for the references occur shortly after Albrecht's first complaint over loss of patronage (5767–8) and his confession that he is not Wolfram but 'Albreht' (5883). Thus he is making a personal appeal for support to finish his tale, a commitment which he hails as a Christian mission:

5909 Sit alle dinc bekronet   sint mit gvtem ende.
    mit werdicheit bedonet   wirt ditz bvch zeletst svnder
                                     wende.
    wil iz got nach kristenlichen eren.

vñ daz bi himel trone   kan taegelich daz hofgesinde
    meren.
5911 Daz vns an disem bvche   alsam iht hie gelinge.
vñ daz dehein vnrvche   vnendelich von endicheit
    iht bringe.
altissimvs der geb vns rehten ende.
vmb daz vor allen dingen   sol kristenheit zv gote
    valden hende.

Albrecht did in fact manage to bring his tale to a close, though presumably not on the scale he had hoped. Merely 300 stanzas follow his discussion of endings. In this relatively short space he attempts to tie up the vast material of his narrative, explaining all that was left unclear in *Parzival* as well as rounding out various sub-plots.[12] Given Albrecht's denunciation of 'ein swaches ende' it is disturbing to discover at the close of the JT how abruptly he hastens the many strands of his plot to conclusion. Albrecht carries out his objective, but in such a mechanical way that we must seek an historical explanation for it. Judging from his remarks in the text itself and from the closing portions of the narrative one is compelled to assume that he finished out of a sense of obligation much more than inspiration. In all likelihood this was due to circumstances beyond his control. No doubt he never managed to find another patron willing to support his efforts.[13]

Admittedly Albrecht's glorification of proper conclusions near the end of his own work must be seen as partly self-serving. Yet beyond his personal aims and despite his haste in tying the plot together, it is overwhelmingly evident that formal completeness and refinement were of tremendous importance to him. This is reflected in every aspect of his literary aesthetic – in the poem's overall structure, the construction of particular episodes, the treatment of motifs, even in the individual stanzas. Most striking is Albrecht's style, particularly his mannered language and complex stanza, which are modelled on Wolfram's late style in *Titurel*. The stanza which Wolfram employed in these fragments is related to that of the *Nibelungenlied* but rendered more elaborate and supple in Wolfram's hands, achieving an extraordinary blend of lyricism and dramatic power. In the JT the stanza becomes still more elaborate and intricate.[14] In contrast to Wolfram's, it is also less flexible. Whereas Wolfram allowed for some variation in rhythm, length of line, and rhyme, almost every one of Albrecht's stanzas follows a strict and highly demanding pattern. All four lines end in feminine rhymes. The first, second and fourth are long with a caesura, the third shorter. There is a feminine rhyme at the caesurae in lines one and two, and in nearly all cases a feminine rhyme at the caesura in the fourth line in addition to a regular metric scheme.[15] This emphasis on intricate structure, on strict adherence to formal pattern, results in a kind of stylised language which bends itself to fit the pattern, often creating what seem to be incomprehensible circumlocutions. Indeed, Albrecht's JT has long been regarded as virtually unreadable.[16] This assessment is partly deserved, for Albrecht's meaning is often camouflaged behind his rhetorical virtuosity. Word order is seldom normal; involved paraphrases using nouns and prepositions are substituted for adjectives; and participial forms are relied on heavily. This leads to occasional ambiguities for the reader.[17] Furthermore, Albrecht enjoys deft word play: repetitions of *wirt* and *wirde*, the counter-balancing of *anegeng* and *ende*, or oxymorons such as *vnendelich von endicheit* are typical of his use of language.[18]

This intricate verbal manoeuvring is based largely on Wolfram, who himself has been accused of having a dark, unclear style. But Albrecht takes the *ornatus difficilis* considerably further. In the guise of Wolfram, Albrecht intends to continue and perfect the style and clarify the content of the master's works. For one of Albrecht's stated objectives as Pseudo-Wolfram is to straighten out that which is bent: 'ich wil die krumb an allen orten slichten' (20, 3). The choice or words alludes to Wolfram's defence of his own narrative technique in the bow metaphor, and Albrecht plays again on this image in the *Verfasserfragment* (7 and 8). Given the difficulty of Albrecht's language, there seems to be a paradox in the obscurity which results from his emphasis on well-defined forms. Yet Albrecht's language is, in fact, relatively precise, if complex. Though we may find his text at times unfathomable, this was not the case for his closer contemporaries.[19] It is significant that Albrecht's goal was not to 'straighten out' Wolfram's style – that he strove to refine and consummate – but to straighten out the significance of the text. *Krump* and *sleht* are not terms of stylistic criticism but refer to narrative technique, in other words to a poet's straightforwardness in transmitting the matter and meaning of his tale. Gottfried's criticism of Wolfram as '*des hasen geselle*' as well as his praise of Hartmann's '*cristallinen wortelin*' reflects a similar perspective.[20]

That Albrecht exalted the model of Wolfram's language is made clear in the dedication poem where he praises Wolfram above all German poets:

VF 4, 3 ich waen des wol, daz muoter ie getrüege
      den lip uf tiuscher erde,   der mit getiht an worten
                                 waer so clüege.
VF 5   Und waer aber iemen lebende,   so cluoc an richer
                                    witze,
      dem waer doch niemen gebende   daz zehende lop.
                                sin sin was solher spitze,
      daz er diu wort ergruop so wunder waehe,
      daz ez noch gaebe stiure,   swer sinniclichen uf sin
                                  forme saehe.

Albrecht implies surprisingly that the very excellence of the style renders it susceptible to imitation by a diligent student. His choice of metaphor is remarkably plastic. The act of creation is paralleled to an artist incising a design on a stone. A sharp instrument, the poet's *sin*,[21] engraves the words into a permanent artefact for others to emulate.[22] Like the temple metaphor, Albrecht's image stresses the visual quality of language, further enhanced in the final line by the use of *forme* and *sehen*. As the temple in Venice stood incomplete, yet betraying its final form, so Albrecht views the works of Wolfram as an enduring structural guide. By using such metaphors to describe a literary tradition, Albrecht is projecting his model as if it were an image on a page. Wolfram claims to be unlettered, refers to oral sources, and seems to deliver his poem to a listening audience. Yet Albrecht has read Wolfram's works. It is their written form which provides the basis for his own creation. And it is to a reader more than a listener that his own poem is directed.[23]

Albrecht's consciousness of his own style is apparent from several other statements in the JT which demonstrate a concern with rhetorical elegance.

1632, 2 nu han ich zit noch sinne,   daz ich diu wort so
                                                 sůze kunde kleiden
            mit geblůmter kunst vil zuhte riche,
            als si zehove gelerent   sprechen mit gewonheit
                                            hoveliche.

Language decoratively arrayed is taken as appropriate to the chivalrous world of his tale. This view is not unique to Albrecht but reflects the tendency to linguistic elaboration common in later thirteenth- and early fourteenth-century German poetry.[24] Yet *'geblůmte kunst'* seems to capture the essence of Albrecht's stylistic aspirations.[25] Though no doubt reflecting the influence of rhetorical traditions, it betrays a personal perspective which unites both formal and moralising objectives. The goal of *'kleiden mit geblůmter kunst'* invokes the visual aspect of poetry in commending elaborate style as constituent to language of the highest quality, the ideal level towards which poetry should strive. That it is equated with the language of the court reflects Albrecht's idealisation of the courtly realm. Furthermore, this language is distinguished not just by technical virtuosity or sheer beauty, but by its resultant moral effect:

897, 2 ob ich daz sunderlichen   geprǔven kunde mit
                                     geblǔmten worten,
    so mocht ein menlich herze linden sere.

Thus formal aspects of poetry are granted intrinsic merit
essential to the proper transmission and interpretation of the
maere. The *wort* is not just external but implies the internal
sin as well. Through his '*geblǔmte kunst*' Albrecht performs
the loftiest kind of exegesis on Wolfram's works, elevating
them and the JT to new heights.

Albrecht's approach to language as form is aptly, and from
our point of view ironically, distilled in the central motif of
the story of Tschinotulander and Sigune which he inherited
from Wolfram. The object of the hero's quest, the object filling a role comparable to the Gral in *Parzival*, is a leash covered
with jewels which form the words of a story. Indeed, it is the
story itself that is sought. The visible, precious quality of
words is succinctly captured in this image. Furthermore, the
leash, materially precious, becomes the object of a quest
because the story inscribed on it is not read to completion –
emphasis again on the importance of conclusions. That such
a tangible object should serve as the central motivation of
Albrecht's narrative is characteristic. In *Parzival* the Gral, a
state of mind much more than of matter, is likewise an elusive goal. But its material nature – like the written messages
inscribed fleetingly on its surface – is far from tangible. This
distinction is symptomatic for nearly all aspects of either
poet's narrative technique.

Inspired by a delight in linguistic complexity already apparent in Wolfram's works, Albrecht has created a new poetic
form in which structural aspects are of paramount value. The
arabesques of Albrecht's language, the rich pattern of his
stanza, and the complex interweave of motifs in his plot are
part of a new aesthetic in which form both defines meaning
and is meaning. Albrecht's achievement can be understood on
its own terms as a glorification of language, especially written
language, and what it can attain. To judge the JT by the

standards of oral presentation which still dictated the aspirations of Wolfram is to do Albrecht a disservice. For Albrecht is not composing just for the transitory experience of listening but primarily for the more leisurely, contemplative activity of reading. Albrecht is building a temple of language.

ARCHITECTURE AND SPACE

Descriptive technique is an aspect of narrative style that has only recently been a matter of interest for students of medieval German literature.[26] It is not the subject described which is of so much concern here, but the author's approach to that subject. In the context of architectural descriptions Albrecht's Gral temple has long been recognised as a *tour de force*. Yet the vast amount of research devoted to it has focused on specifics of content, literary sources, and the temple's possible relation to actual buildings.[27] These approaches overlook the particularly revealing questions of technique in the poet's treatment of his subject. For instance, within the process of telling one can usefully distinguish the narrator's perspective from that of the characters and that of the audience. Is there a pattern in those aspects typically emphasised? How are descriptions integrated into the narrative?

Architectural representations in *Parzival* and the JT offer a rich field for comparison, not least because of the prominence of Munsalvaesche in both poems: in *Parzival* as a symbolic setting, in the JT as an emblematic backdrop. In addition to the castle of Munsalvaesche and the temple of the Gral, both poems contain other architectural descriptions which, as will be shown, consistently reflect each poet's perspective. It is convenient to begin with the architecture at Munsalvaesche, for Albrecht's treatment of the castle and his famous Gral temple are based on the information given in *Parzival*.

In Wolfram's *Parzival* the young hero unknowingly enters the realm of the Gral, and the audience or reader is no more aware than he of the journey's destination.[28] The castle of the Gral or Munsalvaesche (first named in line 251, 2 by Sigune) is initially called a *hûs* by an unidentified fisher-king (225, 22). Neither the audience nor Parzival is prepared for the grandness of the structure which appears before the young knight's eyes:

226, 13   dâ was diu brükke ûf gezogen,
            diu burc an veste niht betrogen.
            si stuont reht als si waere gedraet.
            ez enflüge od hete der wint gewaet,
            mit sturme ir niht geschadet was.
            vil türne, manec palas
            dâ stuont mit wunderlîcher wer.[29]

This description is surely intended as a literal projection of Parzival's experience. Those facts are given which are noticeable from his vantage point: bridge, soaring towers, great halls, and fortifications – the impression of an impregnable fortress. The line 'si stuont reht als si waere gedraet' captures the beholder's amazement before an unexpected sight, and the audience is brought to share this reaction. The home-spun charm of the simile also serves to indicate the hero's naïveté, for Wolfram captures Parzival's spontaneous reaction as though the narrator were actually present beside him.

Parzival's initial view of Gurnemanz's castle is presented in a similar fashion: towers peek one by one over the horizon and Parzival – more naïve than in the above scene, for Gurnemanz's is, after all, his first castle[30] – imagines them to be springing up as though they had been sown (161, 23–30). The metaphor is again simple and, in keeping with Parzival's lack of familiarity with civilisation, appropriately natural, agricultural. Although this image appears in Chrétien's poem, Wolfram has invested it with poignancy and humour by isolating it as a first impression and expanding on the comic aspect. Chrétien goes on to describe the exterior and interior of the castle, thereby lessening the impressionistic effect on which Wolfram capitalises to emphasise the hero's *tumpheit* (162, 1).[31]

A delightful variation on a character's first impression of
an architectural structure is given as Gawan approaches
Logroys in Book 10:

508, 1   An der bürge lâgen lobes werc.
                  nâch trendeln mâze was ir berc:
                  swâ si verre sach der tumbe,
                  er wând si liefe alumbe.

The mistaking of a man-made object for an organic property
is reminiscent of Parzival's initial response to Gurnemanz's
castle and to Munsalvaesche, as is the association of Gawan
with a *tumber*. This need not be a specific reference to
Parzival, though the parallels are suggestive (see below pp.
183ff.). Certainly there is a text-enriching echo here since the
alert audience, recalling the naïve Parzival of Books 3 and 4,
is led to reflect on how far the now-absent hero has progressed.

    Gawan's first glimpse of Clinschor's castle is likewise pre-
sented on approach (534, 20ff.), although the perspective is
not so consistent. Some aspects are seen from a distance and
others from close at hand, yet the impression of actuality is
maintained through the personal identification with the protagonist, the listener's feeling of participation heightened by
the emotional tenor of the opening lines:

534, 20   eine burg er mit den ougen vant:
                  sîn herze unt diu ougen jâhen
                  daz si erkanten noch gesâhen
                  decheine burc nie der gelîch.

Wolfram's description does not linger over specific aspects of
the scene, for the details would only be distracting to his
mode of presentation. Instead each listener is left to his own
imagination to fill out Gawan's reflection. Even the improbable discernment of four noble women amidst the four
hundred peering out of the windows passes by smoothly. An
audience's expectations do not require an entirely logical

depiction of space but are fulfilled by Wolfram's relation of space to dramatic action.[32]

Returning to our first example, further physical details are included in the description of events following Parzival's arrival at Munsalvaesche. He is conducted to a grassy courtyard untrampled by tournaments (227, 8ff.), to a private room (227, 25), and, after having washed, is taken to meet Anfortas. Their meeting occurs in a large hall which is described at some length just as Parzival enters:

229, 23   si giengen ûf ein palas.
             hundert krône dâ gehangen was,
             vil kerzen drûf gestôzen,
             ob den hûsgenôzen,
             kleine kerzen umbe an der want.
             hundert pette er ligen vant
             (daz schuofen dies dâ pflâgen):
             hundert kulter drûffe lâgen.
230, 1   Ie vier gesellen sundersiz,
             da enzwischen was ein underviz.
             derfür ein teppech sinewel,
             fil li roy Frimutel
             mohte wol geleisten daz.
             eins dinges man dâ niht vergaz:
             sine hete niht betûret,
             mit marmel was gemûret
             drî vierekke fiwerrame:
             dar ûffe was des fiwers name,
             holz hiez lign alôê.
             sô grôziu fiwer sît noch ê
             sach nimen hie ze Wildenberc:
             jenz wâren kostenlîchiu werc.

Once more we share the protagonist's first impression of a scene. Parzival is initially struck by the glow of a hundred chandeliers; then he notices couches covered with quilts, carpets, and lastly great blazing fireplaces.[33] The audience thus absorbs an impression of the room simultaneously with the hero. A vivid, unified image is evoked, not fragmented by details, and the audience partakes of Parzival's confusion and wonder as he enters this atmosphere of splendour. The narrator's reference to Wildenberc (230, 13–14) does not disrupt the continuity of the experience but, like the similes discussed above, provides a comparison to Parzival's experience which is accessible to the audience, bringing the scene closer. The contrast between their world and this magnificence is surely intended to amaze, just as Parzival is amazed by the contrast with what he has previously seen. The narrator's references to the immediate world of his listeners have been regarded as disruptive attempts to cultivate the audience's interest in their entertainer rather than his tale. On the contrary, such comparisons give the audience a more concrete sense of the literary realm, and the narrator serves as a credible authority mediating between the real and the literary worlds.[34]

When Parzival is introduced we are given a vivid description of his host's attire as Parzival might see it (231, 1–14), then in the ensuing account of the presentation of the lance we are once again left with the vague and mystified impressions of a newcomer (231, 15 – 232, 4). Neither the motivation nor the meaning of the event is revealed. Although left in suspense along with the hero, we are nevertheless able to envision further aspects of the scene because of the way figures are described moving within the hall during this and the subsequent ritual of the Gral. Through this movement various architectural details are brought into focus though not actually described. They are not presented as objects of intrinsic interest but serve rather as background elements to define the space.[35] Filled with the movement of its inhabitants, the great hall expands and takes shape in each listener's imagination. As a three-dimensional space alive with commotion and atmosphere, it is an integral feature of the tale, woven tightly into the developing action.

Albrecht, in his introduction of Munt Salvasch[36] in the JT, employs an entirely different descriptive technique. As we have seen, Albrecht assumes that his audience is familiar with the Gral story and accordingly abandons the element of suspense. Titurel, having been chosen by God to receive the Gral, sadly bids farewell to his parents and is conducted by angels to Foreist Salvasch. A single stanza relates how he fights against many heathens on his way there (297), and this is directly followed by an introduction to the vast forest. Although we are told that Titurel has travelled here, we are given no details of his course or the length of his journey to suggest the distance covered. The Foreist Salvasch exists in its own time and space.

298 Foreist Salvasch vil irre   was aller menschen sinne.
     nicht halber mile virre   kunde sich vor dick vorrichten
                                                nieman drinne.
     sehzic mile der walt was zallen siten,
     ein berc, von dem enmitten   alumbe waren drizic mile
                                                zeriten.
299 Der berc was so behalten,   den kund ot nieman
                                                vinden,
     wan des di engel walten   wolten, daz er sich da solt
                                                gesinden.
     sus fůrten sie nu Titurel den werden
     aldar mit sanges done,   den er vernomen selten het uf
                                                erden.

The location of Munt Salvasch at the centre of a wilderness extending thirty miles in each direction is taken from Book 5 of *Parzival*, where Sigune passes on this information to her cousin (250, 20-4). Significantly it is the narrator who relates it here, and he gives an account of the magnificent plants and trees filling the wood, clearly Edenic in character (300-1). The narrator providing this exotic setting remains conspicuously present to summarise events. Titurel himself does not participate in the experience of his physical surroundings; he simply arrives at Munt Salvasch, and the angels soon bring others to join him so that he will not be alone in this strange place (302, 2-3). It is pointed out that, though in the realm of the Gral, Titurel is not 'da heime', for 'bi got ist unser heim zer zeswen hende' (302, 4). Albrecht's narrator is omnipresent as explicator of his tale and interpreter of its moral significance for the Christian society he is addressing. Here he expands on the subject of Titurel's virtue, weaving this into a discussion of the need for fortifying virtues in general and Munt Salvasch in particular.

The controlling force of the narrator persona is typical of the JT. From Titurel's arrival in the Gral realm he has cleverly led us through a short sermon on virtue as an introduction to the fortress built on Munt Salvasch:

310 Palas, turne wite   und ander werde vesten,
    als taegelich man mit strite   der burge hûten sold
                                         von argen gesten.

Here Albrecht has nearly quoted *Parzival* (226, 18-19, see above, p. 17), but unlike Wolfram he does not relate the description to his hero's experience. Rather the facts are supplied from an objective point of view for the reader's information. These two lines are followed directly by a moralising aside reiterating the need for fortification against evil:

310, 3 si sint vil ark, di gest, di unser lagent,
     und slichent in diu herze.   wol in, di iz mit wer da
                                         gein in wagent!

An allegorical interpretation of the fortress is thus clearly suggested, with *unser* continuing the homiletic tone. The narrator goes on to speak even more directly to his audience, asking if he need tell them in detail about the virtuous people who came to live in the Gral realm, since after all they are known already from *Parzival*.

The moralising commentary is clearly not intended as support for the narrative action, aimed at heightening our identification with the protagonist or augmenting our participatory sense of the physical or spatial aspects of a scene (like Wolfram's comparison with Wildenberc, for example). Rather, the comments in the JT lead away from the story line and the narrative time by introducing new subject matter as factual embellishment or general moralisation, passages tangentially evoked by the narrative content. To a certain extent these comments themselves become the subject matter. In this instance they suggest an allegorical reading of the castle's fortifications as a lesson on the need for bulwarks against attacks on virtue. Albrecht is taking no chances. He does not allow his audience to become too involved in the narrative *per se* and overlook its relevance to their own lives. His narrator is continually present to draw the general meaning from the particular instance, thus controlling one's perception of the *maere*.

The narrative content remains continuous behind the commentary, however, strengthened by periodic allusions to Wolfram's works. After an account of the Gral's generosity and the richness of Salvaterre, the story of the castle is taken up again:

318 Der bu do was geschehende   an der burc mit vesten,
    also sint daz was sehende   Parcifal, dem si geviel zum
                                         besten.
    ob alliu her mit hazze da wern lebende,
    daz si in zu drizic jaren   ein halbez brot her ab niht
                                    weren gebende.

Once again Albrecht paraphrases part of Wolfram's first depiction of Munsalvaesche (*Parzival* 226, 20–2). Such subtle evocations of the *Parzival* text help to substantiate the authenticity of Albrecht's Wolfram-mask.[37] In addition, direct reference to Parzival's visit to the castle reminds the reader of the important position which this building holds in the original story. The castle's construction in the JT is thus located in an historical continuum leading into *Parzival*. Yet the castle itself is scarcely integrated into the narrative action of the JT but stands as an isolated backdrop, a sort of tableau.

Though the narrator continues the subject of Munt Salvasch, he gives no further details about the fortress. In fact, he speaks of his hesitation in undertaking a description of such a richly fashioned structure:

319 Solt ich daz allez erbowen   mit worten der geziere,
    waz stein da wart gehowen   von bilden riche tusent
                                              stunt wol viere,
    ich wen, in drizic jaren wirz nicht vol worchten.
    doch můz ich ůchz hie kunden: des heb ich an in
                                              sorklichen vorchten.

The imagery reflects the discussion of poetic form in the Heidelberg *Verfasserfragment* where the same metaphor of constructing a magnificent edifice out of words appears. Albrecht declines to undertake such a project here, however,[38] since his verbal rendering of the castle would take thirty years to complete (the same time required for the building of the Gral temple! See below, p. 31). Rather he turns to a discussion of the linguistic significance of the name Salvaterre and ends this section with another reference to *Parzival*, thus avoiding a repetitive account of the *palas* and the events that took place there, while reinforcing the fiction of his identity as Wolfram. He also explains Parzival's failure to pose the crucial question as stemming from *zuhtrich ein valte*, a plausible explanation given Wolfram's emphasis on his hero's *tumpheit*.[39]

328 Wie dem palas waere   zem gral und der gezierde,
    des habt ir vor daz maere,   wie man da Parcifalen
                                              kondiwierde
    durch fragen bi dem trurigen wirte,
    des in zuhtrich ein valte   me danne unbescheidenheit
                                              verirte.

It is typical of Albrecht's narrative technique that the fortress of Munt Salvasch should remain isolated from the narrative action. As we shall see, this is true for the Gral temple as well. That Albrecht does not indulge in reciting at least some of its physical characteristics, especially the richness of its decoration, is not in keeping with his normal tendency. But this is easily explained since his next subject is the temple of the Gral. It would have been anti-climactic to invest time and attention in other aspects of the castle just prior to conceiving one of the most elaborate architectural descriptions in the history of literature.

The long description of the temple which Titurel builds for the Gral (329–439) is distinctly set off from the 'action' of the plot, clearly distinguishing it from the depiction of Munsalvaesche in *Parzival*. It must be kept in mind that we are not comparing two depictions of the same building here, for Wolfram only mentions the temple as part of the complex of buildings at Munsalvaesche, whereas for Albrecht it is a focal point. This change of emphasis is of course significant in itself, just as, in dealing with the Gral as an object, Wolfram describes the ceremony and Albrecht the temple. What then is the significance of the Gral temple within the JT as a whole? What are the poet-narrator's demands on his readers or listeners? What conclusions can be drawn from Albrecht's emphasis on an elaborately described and partly allegorised temple as opposed to the ineffable, symbolic vision of Wolfram's Munsalvaesche?

The idea for Albrecht's Gral temple seems to derive from a single reference near the end of *Parzival*:

816, 13   si bâten den von Zazamanc
                 komen, den diu minne twanc,
                 in den tempel für den grâl.
                 er gebôt ouch an dem selben mâl
                 den wîsen templeisen dar.
                 sarjande, rîter, grôziu schar
                 dâ stuont. nu gienc der heiden în.
                 der toufnapf was ein rubbîn

25

von jaspes ein grêde sinwel,
dar ûf er stuont: Titurel
het in mit kost erziuget sô.

The only physical aspect of the temple mentioned by Wolfram is the ruby baptismal font.[40] In the last line quoted above, the pronoun *in* seems to refer to the font. This could, however, be taken as a reference to the *tempel* of line 15. Such an interpretation would account for Albrecht's notion that the Gral temple was erected by Titurel.

There are two further allusions in *Parzival* to the resting place of the Gral. The first occurs when Parzival returns with Cundrie to Munsalvaesche. He and Feirefiz are led to Anfortas's room where the ailing king lies suffering. Before Parzival poses the question which will heal his uncle, he asks where the Gral is, turns towards it, and genuflects three times (795, 21–5). The second reference to the Gral's location occurs in Wolfram's description of preparations for a ceremony:

807, 16   den [the Gral] truoc man zallem mâle
der diet niht durch schouwen für,
niht wan ze hôchgezîte kür.

Since the Gral is seldom brought forward, the implication can be drawn that it otherwise remains in the temple where Feirefiz is baptised.

This scant information available in Wolfram's *Parzival* served as a springboard for Albrecht's elaborate description of the Gral temple, covering 112 stanzas.[41] The whole section is clearly set off from the surrounding narrative, introduced by a stanza recalling Parzival's visit to Munsalvaesche (quoted above, p. 24) and concluding with the temple's dedication.[42] The account begins with the building's construction and the precious materials used (329–36). The foundation of the temple is a hill of solid onyx (337–8). On this polished surface the temple's architectural plan miraculously

appears (339–40). Here Albrecht begins his description of
the building itself, an impressive catalogue of fantastic structural and decorative elements, the whole ablaze with jewels
and carved ornament.[43]

Differences are already apparent in the attitudes of Wolfram
and Albrecht towards description. The specific detail and the
very fact that so many stanzas are devoted to an edifice are
strikingly unlike the technique of *Parzival*. In order to look
more closely at Albrecht's descriptive technique, a number of
stanzas should be examined in greater detail.

341 Sinwel als ein rotunde   nach aventiur gehŏre,
    wit und hoch. er kunde   geprŭfen wol zwen und
                      zweinzic kŏre,
    uzen her dan unde fur geschozzen
    ieglich kor besunder.   so richer kost einen armen hete
                      verdrozzen.

342 Uf erin sŭl gewelwet   wart ditz werch so spehe.
    an vrouden ungeselwet   wer min herze, ob ichz noch
                      gesehe,
    ein tempel also rich uberal begarwe.
    da schein uz rotem golde   ieclich edel stein nach
                      siner varwe.

343 Da sich di gewelwe reifent   nach der swibogen
                      krumbe,
    von sŭlen ubersweifent   sach man manich riche list
                      daran alumbe,
    wol ergraben, mit weher kunst gewieret.
    von berlin, von korallen   wart daz werk gein richer
                      kost gezieret.

344 Uber al di pfiler obene   ergraben und ergozzen
    vil engel hoch zelobene,   als si von himel weren dar
                      geschozzen
    in vrouden vluge und also lachebaere,
    daz noch ein Waleis tumbe   gesworen het, daz er bi
                      lachen waere.

345 Vil bild in richem werde   ergozzen, ergraben, erhowen,
    als der kunic begerde,   crucifixus unde unser vrowen,

von hoher kunst mit richer kost gereinet,
daz ich da průfens můz gedagen.   ich han much
                                   solcher kunste niht vereinet.
346 Doch můz ich prüfen mere: di altaer waren riche
vil wol nach gotes ere   gezieret schon und also
                                   meisterliche,
dar nach und als der richeit was begunnen.
sold ichz besunder průven,   so wer mir not, und wer
                                   ich baz versunnen.
347 Aller zierde wunder   trugen di altaere:
uf ieclichem sunder   kefse, taveln, bilde kostebaere
stůnt, dazů uf alln ein rich ziborje,
mit gesmelze waehe gewieret,   vil heiligen bilde dar
                                   an mit schöner glorje.
348 Saphirus hat di edele,   daz er des menschen sunde
tilget ab der zedele   und hilfet im zugot mit wazzers
                                   unde,
daz uber sich zu berge da kan fliezen.
des steines kraft die tugent git,   daz man die sunde
                                   mit riwen kan beriezen,
349 Ob man den rechten weste,   wan sie sint drier hande.
der selbe wer der beste   und volliclichen wert wol
                                   hundert lande.
man sicht ouch mangen sine kraft verliesen,
swenne man siner wirde   zu rechte haltnusse niht kan
                                   erkiesen.
350 Got selb in einem saphire   Moysi mit schrift was
                                   gebende
aller sunden fire.   swer nach der selben lere noch
                                   wer lebende
al der gebot, der fumfe sint gezweiet.
sus vil der höhsten tugende   sich an dem saphire
                                   mangerleiet.
351 Durch daz di altersteine   uber al saphire waren.
sint er von sunden reine   den menschen tůt, so kund
                                   in nicht beswaren,

er kertz ot ie zem besten aller dinge.
ob er iz hohe koufen   solt, iz het in doch gewegen
ringe.
352 Samit, der grûne gebete,   gesniten uber ringen,
ob iedem alter swebete   fur den stoup, und swen der
priester singen
wolt, so wart ein bort al da gezucket.
ein tube einen engel brachte,   der kom uz dem
gewelbe her ab geflucket.

The description of the temple building begins with general
information about its structure: it is circular, large, and high,
with twenty-two side-chapels.[44] The dome rests on bronze
pillars, the arches are decorated with rich carvings and smiling
angels. Having begun with an account of the original construction process, Albrecht has progressed via the general
exterior to details of the interior, concentrating on the
abundance of ornament and decoration. His cataloguing of
various features is objective; he presents an account, not a
first-person visual impression. The mention of the reaction of
a 'Waleis tumbe' (344, 4) is an allusion recalling *Parzival* as a
text, not the ongoing actions of a character (after all, Parzival
has not yet been born!). Similarly the phrase 'als der kunic
begerde' (345, 2) seems isolated and out of place, a reminder
of the narrative frame within which the temple description
has been placed: its construction by Titurel. Yet the discon-
tinuous effect of the allusion underscores the secondary
nature of such narrative detail.[45] Already in the first few
stanzas the temple description has taken on a momentum of
its own, and references to the *maere* seem superimposed.

Albrecht next tells of the many altars (346–7) covered
with decoration and bearing reliquaries, panels, ciboria, and
holy images. The following three stanzas discuss the miraculous qualities of sapphire, beginning with its ability to cleanse
man of his sins. This excursus is explained in the following
stanza (351) where we learn that the altars are made of
sapphire because of the stone's particular properties.[46] Next

we are told that a velvet canopy hangs over each altar to keep the dust away – an incongruously practical and mundane note in such a setting!

This summary of barely one-tenth of the temple description allows for some general conclusions about Albrecht's technique. He has assembled an overwhelming amalgam of details. The narrator begins in an orderly progression with the construction of the temple, but the narrative strands seem to dissipate. An overview of the complete sequence, much abbreviated, indicates this more clearly: construction materials, foundation, columns topped with sculpted angels, sculpture, altars of sapphire, a velvet canopy, doves and angels, jewelled windows, roof, God as the source of all this, the gratitude of the Gral society, jewels in place of glass, main dome representing heaven, an astronomical clock, statues, no paintings, side-altars, orientation towards the east, other choirs, the single altar and miniature temple in the centre, portals leading to *palas* and *dorpter*, an organ with singing birds, sculpture of the Last Judgement, choirs, nave, delight of the Gral society, lack of a crypt, lighting, accoustics, lighting of the altars, every inch covered, gratitude of the Gral society, choir screen, vaulting, exterior relief frieze, buttresses with gargoyles, exterior walls, towers, windows and towers, main tower, bells, interior floor, and Christian dedication.

Albrecht's description is non-linear; it follows no obvious path but is in its own way impressionistic. The overriding effect is an abundance of decoration, a *horror vacui* of fantastic proportions:

415, 2 ... nu merket selbe, da was ot niender laere
    spanne breit der tempel uz und inne.

Neither within the description of individual elements nor through their arrangement in his narrative does Albrecht maintain continuity. He repeatedly interjects learned discussions or allusions, moralisations, or references to the Gral society (whose members seem quite out of place).[47] In contrast to the

30

visual images which Wolfram conveys by associating description with a single observer, Albrecht springs omnisciently
from one vantage point to another. The elements within his
description are difficult to link together coherently, either as
a 'narrative' of the temple's construction, a step-by-step
guided tour, or as a technical description. The Gral temple in
the JT stands isolated from the story's action and beyond our
grasp. The dazzling complexity of this temple is as much the
reflection as it is the creation of Albrecht's rhapsodic
language.

Splendid isolation is no doubt exactly the impression
Albrecht desired to achieve. He has taken care to separate the
temple from his story in other ways as well. For instance, the
narrative time in which it is first located seems to fluctuate.
Prior to describing the temple Albrecht informs us that the
Gral no longer resides in Salvaterre but has been transported
to India, the land of true Christians (325), thus distancing the
audience from 'sharing' the experience of its construction.
References to *Parzival* likewise remove the sense of simultaneity. Within the description there is only one direct reference to time. This is in a stanza telling of the miniature
temple which stands at the centre of the larger one and houses
the Gral. Here we are told: 'daz werc wart alz volbracht in
drizic jaren' (383, 4), an ambiguous reference which could
apply to either one or both temples. Then, following the
temple description and the *Marienlob*,[48] the story line is again
taken up when the narrator informs us that four hundred
years later Titurel was still serving 'got und werden vrowen'
(440). This is not an easily conceivable chronology, but lifts
the already mysterious Munt Salvasch into a magical realm
where our time no longer exists. Occasional references to
Titurel or the inhabitants of Munt Salvasch gesture towards
locating the Gral realm within an historical continuum. Nevertheless, the account remains in a sort of undefined past. It is
the narrator persona who provides an intermediary for the
audience, but his comments enhance the temple's remoteness.

They serve to remind us of its distance from him and us, and are certainly never convincing in implying an eye-witness account (compare 342, 345, 346). For all its detail, the elaborate structure of the Gral temple in the JT remains temporally as well as spatially indeterminate.

The ambiguous nature of this temple description is reflected in the reactions of nineteenth- and twentieth-century scholarship. Albrecht's architectural fantasy has been both criticised and acclaimed, felt to embody the late Romanesque style or admired for its Gothic qualities. It has served as the model for actual buildings and been held to reflect a mystical experience of space rather than a physical structure.[49] What was the intended response?

This is a difficult question, not least because of the tension in Albrecht's description between the density of material objects and the supernatural aura of the temple itself. Lessing's comment on the proliferation of detail in Albrecht von Haller's poetic language speaks to the point: 'Ich frage ihn nur, wie steht es um den Begriff des Ganzen?'[50] Lessing goes on to draw a distinction between narrative poetry and painting, which offers insight into the impact of Albrecht's descriptive technique. For Albrecht does describe the physical aspects of the temple, and though the structure is unmistakably symbolic, he repeatedly integrates it into the matter of the tale (as opposed to the purely allegorical *Marienlob*, for instance). Lessing points out that 'die Zeitfolge ist das Gebiete der Dichtung' (p. 129), and, as we have seen above, Albrecht's temple hovers rather uncertainly within a chronological frame. Wolfram's descriptive elements, on the other hand, unfold in time. Not dissimilar to Homer's portrayal of Achilles' shield,[51] Wolfram's descriptions evoke an intense visual experience, though one that remains ineffable. The elusiveness as well as the symbolic impact of Wolfram's Munsalvaesche is achieved by not describing details. Albrecht, in contrast, elevates the Gral temple to a level of abstraction through, rather than in spite of, the proliferation of detail.

32

Albrecht is interweaving an ideal Christian vision into his narrative matter. Or perhaps better, he is weaving his narrative into an ideal Christian vision. For while his temple is linked to action, its description seems capable of standing alone. Yet rather than giving an impression of brilliant space, the temple seems finally burdensome in its decor, busied with mechanical apparatuses – though, significantly, not with people. Prosaic notes obtrude, such as the dust canopies or the display before each portal of the stones used in it with accompanying explanations of their mysterious powers – learned didacticism of a sort within this realm as well. The numerous mechanical devices seem likewise uncomfortably worldly and technical, yet were clearly not so for Albrecht's contemporaries.[52] Rather they too partook of the hermetic qualities of the jewels and precious stones which fill the temple with mystery.

Albrecht's employment of so much material to transport his audience to an ethereal realm is a paradox which cannot be resolved from the perspective of narrative continuity. Nor can it be explained as a consistent allegory.[53] Rather the poetic monument itself embodies Albrecht's achievement, and its overwhelming effect resides in the process of assimilation demanded of any reader or listener. Although individual elements are described and often moralised as they are introduced, the structure as a whole slips inevitably away as the details pile up. Albrecht's circuitous progression adds to the confusion so that finally one is left with a mass of rich and beautiful objects which seem to swim before one's inner eye. As Frankl points out (p. 182), Albrecht's desultory description stimulates the imagination and creates a far deeper impression of the incomprehensibility of the structure than more straightforward reportage would do. So we are left with a strange and impressive blend of magical technology and mystical theology captured in poetic form. The temple becomes part of the reader's own experience rather than something connected with the lives of Albrecht's characters; it is the result of interaction between reader and text. Indeed, the Gral temple space cannot be visualised as part of the story, nor does it need to be, for it does not function as a setting for action but remains apart, only reappearing once more at the very end of the poem, and then briefly, when it and all of Munt Salvasch are miraculously transported through space to the east (6163–4).[54] The temple description is a symbolic evocation of the Gral's importance within the story and of Christian virtue within the world at large.

Although the Gral temple is the most conspicuous instance of Albrecht's use of architecture in the JT, other passages show the same tendency to develop a complex structure from the outline given by Wolfram, to remove it from the narrative action and invest it with a religious aura.[55] Sigune's hermit cell, for instance, is first mentioned in Book 9 of *Parzival*:

435, 2   diu âventiure uns kündet
                daz Parzivâl der degen balt
                kom geriten ûf einen walt,
                ine weiz ze welhen stunden;
                aldâ sîn ougen funden
                ein klôsen niwes bûwes stên,
                dâ durch ein snellen brunnen gên:
                einhalp si drüber was geworht.

Typically for Wolfram this brief description is given through Parzival's eyes. The hero is riding in search of adventure and happens on the lonely hermitage. In an aside the narrator tells us that the devout hermitess is Sigune whose life is spent in mourning her lost love. Sigune's exemplary devotion to the dead Schionatulander inspires a diversion for which Wolfram excuses himself before plunging back into the story with Parzival's approach to the hermitage:[56]

436, 26   über ronen âne strâzen
                Parzivâl fürz venster reit
                alze nâhn: daz was im leit.
                dô wolter vrâgen umben walt,

ode war sîn reise waere gezalt.

437, 1   Er gerte der gegenrede aldâ:
'ist iemen dinne?' si sprach 'jâ'
do er hôrt deiz frouwen stimme was,
her dan ûf ungetretet gras
warf erz ors vil drâte.
ez dûht in alze spâte:
daz er niht was erbeizet ê,
diu selbe schame tet im wê.
er bant daz ors vil vaste
zeins gevallen ronen aste.

In these lines Wolfram includes a few more details about the
building and surroundings. Now the audience is aware that
the hermitage is newly built over a swift stream in an isolated
area, is little-frequented, and has a window. As the action
progresses we learn there is an outside bench, for Sigune bids
Parzival sit there (438, 10-11). We also learn that the stream
below the hermitage springs from a nearby rock, for Sigune
says Cundrie habitually ties her mule there (442, 19-20).
These details are all incidental; they form an integral part of
the depiction of action. This narrative technique creates a
strong visual impression of the scene in the listener's mind, for
each progressive action is linked with mention of some aspect
of the setting, and thus the whole space is made dynamic.

Albrecht's presentation of this small building exemplifies
the care with which he approaches Wolfram's narrative. He
begins with Sigune's wish to give up all worldly riches and
have only a *kloster* for Tschinotulander:

5437 Der gerte ich niht mere   von der vil richen pfrv̆nde.
      Danne daz in gotes ere   ein kloster rich in dirre
                                               wuste stvnde.
      Dar inne ich bvzzet die grozzen schvlde mine.
      Tschionatulander   din svnde bvzze min sele fvr die
                                               dine.

35

The narrator later tells how this cell came to be built:

5463 Kvndrien bat sie werben   zv bowen ir eine klovsen.
      Die lie des niht verderben   erlichen hiez der kvnic
                                               sie da behovsen.
      Zv montsalvatsch bi eines velsen orten.
      Vber einen klaren brvnnen   die klovse gesegent wart
                                               mit reinen worten.
5465 Kvndrie tegeliche   nv mohte dar niht riten.
      Ez was der virre so riche   daz sie nu zal der wochen
                                               must erbeiten.
      Daz zil ir an dem samztage wart gesprochen.
      So braht ir kundrie   swes sie gar bedorfte al durch
                                               di wochen.
5466 Sigvn begert die virre   durch in gesinde des grales.
      Daz man si nv iht irre   an ir gebet des pflag sie
                                               svnder twales.
      Danne vnder weiln was sie etwenne klagende.
      Sie kunde wol bedenken   daz er ir riet gebet fvr
                                               weinen tragende.

Thus far Albrecht's discussion of the building's location is carefully based on information in *Parzival*. His explanations for the extreme isolation of the hermitage and for Kundrie's rare visits follow quite naturally from Wolfram's text, as does Sigune's desire for solitude. The cell is blessed by Bishop Boniface (the Gral temple too was dedicated by a bishop) and named 'Klousent Fontsaluacie'. The name is an allusion to the name of Trevrizent's hermitage in Wolfram's *Parzival*, 'Fontane la Salvatsche' (452, 13), serving again to link the JT with its prototype on yet another level, testing the reader's memory and subtly extending the dimension of the present episode.

In the following stanzas Albrecht's narrator continues his discussion of Sigune's cell. He describes the lavish paintings which decorate her walls, executed in accord with Sigune's request.

5467 Sigvn des niht entwalen   durch keine sache wolde.
      Die klovsen hiez sie malen   von lasvr vnd ovch von
                                    rotem golde.
      Von pvlleweiz cynober paris rote.
      Niht menschen grᵉvn ot lovter   gar smarag var gel
                                      swartz in rehter lᵉote.

There is no suggestion of such murals in Wolfram's text. Albrecht seems to have added this section out of his predilection for architectural embellishment which can sanctify a humble cell and provide a textual context for moralisation.

He begins by reminding us of the penitent function of contemplating Christ's life, then turns to the interior of the cloister and a description of the individual painted scenes. The introductory stanza (5469) sets the scene with mention of the crucifix as primary symbol of Christ's suffering. Then each scene is described briefly, beginning with the Annunciation (5470) and Nativity (5471).

5469 Daz crvcifix entwichen   moht ir nie vz dem mvte.
      Wie reine minneclichen   vns cristen crist erlost mit
                                      seinem blvte.
      Daz wart geschaffet vor mit ordenunge.
      E daz in die klosen   qvam die klagerich die klare die
                                      iunge.
5470 Vnd wie die ware minne   vz fronem himelriche.
      Mit trewenrichen sinne   den vogt der engel zoch
                                      gewalticliche.
      So daz in gabriel der magde kvndete.
      Dvrch reinekeit ir kevsche   die sie des heiligen geistes
                                      gar entzvndete.
5471 Vnd dar nach wie sin iugende   geleit wart in ein krippe.
      Daz ir die ware tugende   da gap vnd er vns menschen
                                      wart gesippe.
      Der aller engel schar beschvf so klare.
      Vil liehter danne die svnne   der wolde hie demut
                                      liden offenbare.

The sequence continues (through 5482) with a list of scenes all of which are taken from the life of Christ.[57] As in the stanzas quoted above, there is no sense of a visual impression conveyed. Only the traditional iconic elements of each scene are noted; when details are given, such as the names and lands of the three kings, they have no visual referent. There are occasional reminders that paintings are being discussed (such as 'Dar nach sie des niht irten   sie malten fvrbaz schone', 5474, 1) yet these do not enable us to visualise them as such. Instead such references seem incongruous, rather like the references to Gral knights in the temple description. More consistent are the moralising asides, primarily on the virtue of *diemüete*. Emphasis falls on the *lêre*: 'Die tagezit die sibene die wurden ir der waren minne ein lere' (5478, 2). Finally the narrator moves away from Sigune's painted chapel to complete what has become his sermon (5483–91). Sigune's feelings of piety and repentence are shown to be evoked by the symbolic meaning of Christ's life which in turn is underscored by the narrator's comments. That the crucifixion both begins and ends the discussion of decor stresses the redemptive power of Christ's sacrifice, his suffering for man's sins, and the significance for Sigune, indeed for all mankind. Through her sorrow Sigune is raised to exemplary status. Lichtenberg (p. 46) speaks of Sigune's cell as a *Grabkapelle,* 'denn die Betrachtung der Passion Jesu ist neben dem Trauer um Schionatulander der Lebensinhalt Sigunes, einer Leidverwandten der Gottesmutter'. Albrecht makes this connection clear:

5487 Dvrch Schionatulander   qvam sie von erste in rewe.
Vnd ihesus crist der ander   des tot den klagt sie ovch
                                                                     mit gantzer trewe.
Die mac wol zv der engel schar gewisen.
Wan ir vil grozze trewe   lie got zv reht vf rehten
                                                                     acker risen.

As before, Albrecht has not overtly contradicted the facts

given by Wolfram, yet his additions alter the spirit of the scene. In *Parzival* Sigune's life is solitary, humble, and ascetic:

437, 16   diu klôs was freuden laere,
dar zuo aller schimpfe blôz:
er vant dâ niht wan jâmer grôz.

The elaborate and costly decor described by Albrecht seems inconsistent with this sombre, pious atmosphere. Albrecht is aware of the discrepancy, for he hastens to emphasise Sigune's personal poverty and self-denial (5437, 5486). The richness of the decor is, like the ornamentation in a church, a sign of God's glory, not man's. The narrator's emphasis on the orthodoxy of Sigune's piety and the strong religious turn of his moral didacticism further reflect this view.

Albrecht delights in describing artistic ornament and architecture, yet he is unconcerned with projecting an effective visual or spatial impression of these fundamentally visual subjects. A physical object is approached by way of its particular features which are inventoried in great detail. Yet these elements are never quite recomposed for us; they remain isolated from one another and finally from the context of the narrative. The Gral temple and Sigune's hermitage, though firmly rooted in the physical realm, are ultimately poetic contrivances for which a significance is suggested by the story's content but whose impact resides in the symbolic and moralised level of the narrator's commentary and in the very splendour of Albrecht's linguistic achievement. Architectural descriptions temporarily usurp the narrative foreground of the JT and gradually become transformed into poetic visions which linger as emblems in the reader's imagination.

Although unsympathetic, Lessing's words are descriptive of Albrecht's technique: 'Ich höre in jedem Worte den arbeitenden Dichter, aber das Ding selbst bin ich weit entfernt zu sehen' (p. 25). For part of Albrecht's intention is surely that the reader be constantly aware of the poetic structure being erected. We must appreciate the artifice and be moved by it to dwell on the moral commentary being addressed to us.

An emphasis on form for its own sake, ornate elaboration, and grandiose scale are evident on every level of Albrecht's poetry: in the visual pattern of a poetic line, the verbal play of 'geblůmte kunst', in the monumental scale of the poem itself. Particularly manifest in Albrecht's description of the Gral temple, elaborate description takes precedence over internal motivation or relation to action – form becomes independent of content. Likewise the temple's very ornateness reflects the value placed on an ornate poetic style, and its physical and conceptual elusiveness reflects the esoteric attraction of Albrecht's language.[58] The Gral temple description offers a symbolic ideal within a literary work which itself strives to be a model of its kind.

2. CHARACTERISATION: SECONDARY ROLES AS NARRATIVE CONTEXT

The vast chronological and geographical scope of Albrecht's *Jüngerer Titurel* embraces the whole of Wolfram's *Parzival*. On a nominal level the two works are consistently linked, with all of *Parzival*'s main characters, as well as a majority of secondary characters, incorporated into Albrecht's elaborate plot structure.[1] This close relationship makes it possible to pose a number of questions concerning important differences in the methods of characterisation used by each poet. In what manner are characters presented and developed? To what extent are particular characters consistent within the course of each poem – as independent personalities, in their relationships with other characters, and in their roles within the overall narrative progression? To what extent are Albrecht's characters consistent reflections of their prototypes? Most important, these matters need to be examined in context, within the developing narrative itself. This is true not only for Wolfram, whose narrative technique is self-avowedly a process of gradual unfolding, but also for Albrecht, whose formal emphasis relies on an intricate network of themes.

It has long been recognised that one of Wolfram's greatest strengths is the genuineness of his characters, particularly figures who play secondary roles but are nonetheless sketched with amazing vividness.[2] Among the several such characters in *Parzival* there are three who also appear in secondary roles in the JT and offer a convenient comparison. These are Jeschute, Orilus, and, tangentially, Lähelin. Though fertile subjects for analysis they have been generally neglected in studies of Wolfram's characters.[3] Their counterparts in the JT have not been investigated at all.

WOLFRAM'S JESCHUTE, ORILUS, AND LÄHELIN

The rich narrative texture of Wolfram's *Parzival* engages its audience with an impression of immediacy and participation.

The experience of the poem has been compared to the sensations of a stranger arriving in a small unfamiliar town:

> From day to day people cross our path and gradually faces become familiar. Some of the inhabitants may be relatives, a number become acquaintances, a few become friends, while many remain strangers, except in appearance. Our knowledge of all of them will grow through meetings and conversations and will be extended by what is told by third parties, while such gossip will speak of many people whom we may never meet. But since the circle is a small one, restricted geographically, we will become more and more aware of ties of blood, friendship, and business existing between its members, and imperceptibly we will recognize a network of bonds, which, no matter how multi-stranded it may seem to us, we will assume to have even more strands reaching away into regions beyond our knowledge.[4]

This aptly characterises the kaleidoscope of impressions which strike the audience of *Parzival*. Events seem to unfold before one's eyes, people and scenes are glimpsed and then lost from sight only to reappear later, recognisable yet altered by the events of the intervening time which, though unreported, thus acquires a reality of its own. Yet we are not allowed to wander aimlessly through this world, for in spite of apparent randomness our progress is carefully guided by the poet. The conversations overheard and characters encountered all have their place in the unfolding tale of Parzival. Intricate thematic patterns link far-flung episodes of the poem into a unit, reflecting forwards and backwards and strengthening the narrative fabric. In the world of Wolfram's tale, even minor figures are thus of primary importance for the coherency and depth of background they help to provide.

The relationship between Orilus and Jeschute functions as a sub-plot in *Parzival*. These characters appear only twice in the foreground of the action, yet their story forms a concise unit in itself, and one that is particularly meaningful in that it marks significant stages in Parzival's progress. Jeschute is first seen in Book 3 when Parzival, having barely left the protected isolation of his upbringing, happens unexpectedly on a luxurious tent. Its visual impact is related just as it comes into Parzival's view (129, 18-26). The following lines show the young adventurer already inside the tent. Although in Chrétien's poem Perceval is said to enter the tent (on horseback!) under the mistaken assumption that it is a church,[5] no explanation is given in the German version for the hero's action. This modifies the overtly comic aura of the French tale and suggests the motive of simple curiosity, one easily shared by the audience. That Parzival's actual approach and entry are not described, further increases the impact of what he discovers there, since we have not been prepared for it by any sort of introduction.

129, 27	duc Orilus de Lalander,
	des wîp dort unde vander
	ligende wünneclîche,
	die herzoginne rîche.
130, 1	glîch eime rîters trûte.
	si hiez Jeschûte.

In this short passage the listener has stepped into the shade of the tent with Parzival and shares his surprise and wonder. Though the woman is identified by name for the audience, this information does not elucidate the scene but adds to its allure.[6]

Sensuous images abound in the next few lines as a tantalising vision confronts us:

130, 3	Diu frouwe was entslâfen.
	si truoc der minne wâfen,
	einen munt durchliuhtic rôt,
	und gerndes ritters herzen nôt.
	innen des diu frouwe slief,

43

der munt ir von einander lief:
der truoc der minne hitze fiur.
sus lac des wunsches âventiur.
von snêwîzem beine
nâhe bî ein ander kleine,
sus stuonden ir die liehten zene.
ich waen mich iemen küssens wene
an ein sus wol gelobten munt:
daz ist mir selten worden kunt.

   ir deckelachen zobelîn
erwant an ir hüffelîn,
daz si durch hitze von ir stiez,
dâ si der wirt al eine liez.
si was geschicket unt gesniten,
an ir was künste niht vermiten:
got selbe worht ir süezen lîp.
och hete daz minneclîche wîp
langen arm und blanke hant.

Through this barrage of impressions the audience gazes on a lovely apparition along with the poem's hero. The atmosphere is charged with eroticism, intensified by images of smouldering fire: parted lips *durchliuhtic rôt* and hot with *der minne hitze fiur*, white limbs uncovered to a suggestive degree, a warm, lovely body shaped by God himself.[7] The effect of this description is ambiguous. The woman is asleep, innocent of provocation. Indeed, her modesty is so great that she would have covered herself had her husband been present (19–20).[8] At the same time she is amorousness itself, challenging and battle-ready: 'si truoc der minne wâfen', and 'sus lac des wunsches âventiur'. The association of battle terminology with love is common, but Wolfram counters this topos with the vision of a sleeping Venus,[9] a paradoxical coupling of aggression and vulnerability that heightens the sensual impact of the scene. Both Parzival and the audience are taken unawares by this sudden confrontation. Delivered orally – especially by a sophisticated reciter – the dramatic potential would be even greater.[10] The scene is at once more mysterious than in Chrétien's story where it is explained that the woman is alone because her attendants are out picking flowers (672-6).[11] It is also potentially more seductive, for we, like Parzival, are given quite a bit of time to contemplate Jeschute. In Chrétien's tale the duchess, who is not described, is awakened by the stumbling of Perceval's horse (677-80), but Wolfram allows an extended gaze beginning 36 lines before she awakens.

What is the young hero to make of this? How will he respond? The audience has been cleverly led to associate with Parzival; the narrator himself has drawn a comparison (130, 14-16) suggesting clearly what *he* might do under the circumstances if given such a chance. And the hero appears to follow the expected course, though in a highly unchivalrous manner:

130, 26   der knappe ein vingerlîn dâ vant,
            des in gein dem bette twanc,
            da er mit der herzoginne ranc.

Reference to the allure of the *vingerlîn* is a hint (as is *knappe*, perhaps) that Parzival's objectives are not conventional, and is established in the following lines which banish the once heady atmosphere;

130, 29   dô dâhter an die muoter sîn:
            diu riet an wîbes vingerlîn.
131, 1   ouch spranc der knappe wol getân
            von dem teppiche an daz bette sân.

Only now has the narrator explained Parzival's rash behaviour: the lad is attempting to follow his mother's instructions! This is a significant change from *Perceval* where the hero explains his intentions at once, and the duchess is awake from the moment he enters the tent (682ff.). Certainly the ring is part of Parzival's motivation, yet how are we to interpret the preceding description of Jeschute? Is Wolfram merely indulging us in this ravishing vision, or is the scene viewed through

45

Parzival's innocent eyes as well? The carefully maintained ambiguity suggests that both are intended. For the description is coincident with Parzival's first view of Jeschute, and one is swept along by the woman's enchanting image just as Parzival himself must be. Wolfram's narrative mode suggests a genuine erotic response on Parzival's part while insisting on his total naïveté in such matters.[12] That the young hero is too chaste to know even how to recognise the suggestiveness of the situation is part of the humour. As Peil has put it, 'Parzival kämpft, wo eigentlich ein anderer Krieg geführt werden sollte' (p. 172). The audience is involved in the play of dramatic irony, recognising the discrepancy between the innocent motivations ascribed to Parzival and the impulsive aggressiveness of his actions. The irony is complicated in that the listener is repeatedly led to misread Parzival's behaviour.

The narrator maintains his tongue-in-cheek attitude throughout this section, constantly alluding to a possible second reading through puns and non-sequiturs. Jeschute's chasteness is stressed in the same breath as the account of her compromising position:[13]

131, 3   Diu süeze kiusche unsamfte erschrac,
         do der knappe an ir arme lac.

The battle metaphor in Jeschute's remarkably controlled response – her first words to Parzival – is appropriately susceptible to a sexual interpretation, and here it is she herself who delivers the pun (compare 139, 17). She is indeed chaste and sweet, but she is neither naïve nor hysterical.

131, 8   ... 'wer hât mich entêret?
            junchêrre, es ist iu gar ze vil:
            ir möht iu nemen ander zil.'

Parzival scarcely gives her time to protest (131, 11–13), and the ensuing struggle between the two develops the enticingly ambiguous battle metaphors still further (131, 14–21), until the narrator's culminating observation, 'doch wart dâ ringens vil getân' (21). The next two lines are totally unexpected:[14]

46

131, 22   der knappe klagete'n hunger sân.
                     diu frouwe was ir lîbes lieht.

But Jeschute seems in control as she responds with justifiable irony:

131, 24   si sprach 'ir solt mîn ezzen nieht.'

Her comment is perhaps called for by the narrator's odd sequence of remarks in the preceding lines – a report of Parzival's hunger followed by reference to Jeschute's beauty.

There is a consistent pattern in Wolfram's recasting of his model. As a character Parzival is rendered more direct and unpremeditated, less conventionally polite (though Perceval's politeness is formulaic and thus nearly insulting, albeit unconsciously), and generally more ingenuous. He enters the tent unannounced, lunges for the ring as soon as he sets eyes on it, and abruptly declares his hunger. This blunt, seemingly instinctive manner is implied by the intentional ambiguity of the mode of narration which either withholds the reasons for Parzival's behaviour until after his actions have been described, or disregards motives altogether. For instance, Chrétien gives a reasonable account of Perceval's great hunger; the effect of Wolfram's silence is more suggestive and humorous. Parzival does not have his prototype's sense of etiquette. He fails to ask Jeschute to share his meal, nor does he bid her farewell. Furthermore, Chrétien's polite hero is even somewhat cavalier, remarking that the duchess's lips compare favourably with those of his mother's chambermaids (723–8). All of this indicates a disarming lack of worldliness on Parzival's part, a naïveté which partly excuses his ineptness.[15]

We are reminded that, for all of Parzival's shortcomings, he is nonetheless *wol geborn* (132, 15). Though this may seem an ironic epithet for the narrator to apply here, it is in fact fully consistent with the picture portrayed. For while Wolfram's changes emphasise Parzival's naïveté and *tumpheit*, they also emphasise his goodness. An example is Wolfram's omission of the mother's warning not to offend or force any woman,[16] so that Parzival is not explicitly disobeying her advice. He does what he is told, though a tendency to over-literal interpretation traps him in humorous moments (not fording the muddy brook). There is a kind of moderation in Wolfram's narrative, however, which tones down the comic aspect in Perceval's proclivity towards exaggeration. Chrétien's hero kisses the unwilling duchess many times[17] – again quite contrary to his mother's advice. His misdeeds are both greater and less serious than Parzival's. For Parzival at times betrays a sensitivity which in spite of his foolishness hints at responsible action. He does respond to Jeschute's entreaties, for instance. When she says he must go, he takes himself off at once:

132, 15   dô sprach der knappe wol geborn
         'wê waz fürht ich iurs mannes zorn?
         wan schadet ez iu an êren,
         sô wil ich hinnen kêren.'

Parzival does not understand what is wrong and is unafraid of her husband, yet he goes because he senses his staying would bring harm to *her*.[18] Thus we see that Wolfram, for all the doubles entendres and humour of his presentation, is meticulous in his treatment of Parzival, showing us a young man whose inborn nature, his *art*, is essentially blameless, whether or not his actions are in accord with social convention.

And what of the woman who may have ignited a spark in Parzival's young heart? Wolfram has presented her differently from Chrétien as well. He has rendered her more beautiful and has set the scene for her appraisal in a much more suggestive way. He has also given her a stronger personality. She neither weeps nor laments, but addresses her assailant with irony, even humour (131, 24–30). While he eats she remains silent, growing more uncomfortable, until she tells him simply that he ought to return her ring and brooch and take his leave, lest he incur her husband's wrath. She makes no mention of her own wretchedness, nor does she weep helplessly until her husband returns, as does her counterpart in Chrétien's poem.

Thus far the scene has been Parzival's, Jeschute a stage in the hero's progression towards awareness. But now, as Parzival rides off, the narrator remains with Jeschute, awaiting the predicted anger of her husband. In the sections devoted to the main hero, it is unusual for Chrétien or Wolfram to digress from the hero's path. Here, the perspective allows the audience to observe Jeschute suffering under her husband's jealous rage, thereby condemning Parzival's foolish behaviour. Yet Wolfram expands the scene considerably beyond Chrétien's version, developing a sense of individuality in the characters of Jeschute and Orilus while revealing significant aspects of their relationship as man and wife.

In six lines recounting Orilus's return to his tent the reader seems to re-enter the scene at his side, viewing the 'evidence' through the husband's eyes (132, 29–133, 4). He immediately notices the trampled grass and tent ropes, and upon seeing his wife *al trûric* assumes she has shamed him by taking a lover. The complexity of his reaction is disclosed in the ensuing exchange, while the narrator limits his introduction to the epithets *wert, erkant,* and *stolz* (133, 3–5).

133, 5   dô sprach der stolze Orilus
          'ôwê frowe, wie hân ich sus
          mîn dienst gein iu gewendet!
          mir ist nâch laster gendet
          manec rîterlîcher prîs.
          ir habt ein ander âmîs.'
          diu frouwe bôt ir lougen
          mit wazzerrîchen ougen
          sô, daz sie unschuldic waere.
          ern geloubte niht ir maere.
            iedoch sprach si mit forhten siten
          'dâ kom ein tôr her zuo geriten:
          swaz ich liute erkennet hân,
          ine gesach nie lîp sô wol getân.
          mîn fürspan unde ein vingerlîn

nam er âne den willen mîn.'
'hey sîn lîp iu wol gevellet.
ir habt iuch zim gesellet.'
dô sprach si 'nune welle got.
sîniu ribbalîn, sîn gabilôt
wârn mir doch ze nâhen.
diu rede iu solte smâhen:
fürstinne ez übele zaeme,
op si dâ minne naeme.'

Unlike his prototype in Chrétien's poem, Orilus asks no questions but abruptly accuses his wife of being unfaithful. His first concern seems the dishonour this brings to him. He does not enquire about Jeschute's condition, though obviously she is unhappy. Indeed, her tears seem only to confirm his suspicions, though she cries now for the first time – at being wrongly accused. Orilus is preoccupied with his own feelings and wounded vanity and does not heed her words. He is already convinced.

Here the temptation to psychological interpretation is great, not merely because the scene lends itself so willingly, but because of the changes Wolfram has made on his model. In Chrétien's story the duke questions his lady with courtesy, generous in his responses until he hears of the kiss (788–810). In Wolfram's tale Orilus's self-righteousness, though certainly allowable within the context of the chivalric code,[19] is exceptionally violent given the lack of evidence. In fact, the kiss is never mentioned to Orilus, whereas in *Perceval* it continues to be the focal point.[20] Rather, Orilus's lack of confidence in Jeschute seems to hint at an insecurity about himself which is reflected more as the scene progresses. Jeschute helps confirm his suspicions by her honest description of Parzival's appearance (133, 18). Though couched in an account of an apparently mad youth who took her ring and brooch, it is only her praise of Parzival's beauty that draws a reaction from Orilus. He is not interested in symbols but in her affections. Later he himself cites her admiration of Parzival's beauty as the reason for his jealousy (271, 4–5). This underscores the psychological impact of Wolfram's change of emphasis from the legally more significant kiss to Jeschute's feelings.

Jeschute's attempts to reason with him are remarkably logical in contrast with Orilus's *idée fixe*, but in assuring him that a woman of her rank would not stoop to such a lover, again she unwittingly touches his wounded self-esteem.[21] This is evident in even the first few lines of his lengthy reply.

133, 29 aber sprach der fürste sân
     'frouwe, ich hân iu niht getân:
134, 1   irn welt iuch einer site schamn:
     ir liezet küneginne namn
     und heizt durch mich ein herzogin,
     der kouf gît mir ungewin.
     Mîn manheit ist doch sô quec,
     daz iwer bruoder Erec,
     mîn swâger, fil li roy Lac,
     iuch wol dar umbe hazzen mac.
     mich erkennet och der wîse
     an sô bewantem prîse
     der ninder mag entêret sîn,
     wan daz er mich von Prurîn
     mit sîner tjoste valte.
     an im ich sît bezalte
     hôhen prîs vor Karnant.
     ze rehter tjost stach in mîn hant
     hinderz ors durh fîanze:
     durch sînen schilt mîn lanze
     iwer kleinoete brâhte.
     vil wênc ich dô gedâhte
     iwerr minne eim anderm trûte,
     mîn frouwe Jeschûte.'

Orilus continues his monologue for another 46 lines, following his initial defensive remarks with a detailed account of his many victorious battles. There is nothing in Chrétien's version to suggest such an impassioned speech. Indeed, li Orgueilleus follows his jealous outburst with an immediate turn to the mundane – he sits down and eats. This underscores the ridiculous in his behaviour which surfaces both here and in the later scene in *Perceval*. Wolfram's Orilus, in contrast, is not a comic figure.

Orilus's tirade is a natural extension of Wolfram's narrative technique, however, functioning on more than one level within the poem. First it emphasises Orilus's great skill and ferocity as a warrior, so that his threat to avenge himself on Jeschute's attacker increases in impact. Secondly, many of the names mentioned by him are or will be familiar to the audience, weaving the narrative texture even more tightly. The irony is heightened by the gradually disclosed interrelationships among characters. Erec, Jeschute's brother as well as the hero of Hartmann's poem, is himself known for a lack of *mâze* in balancing knightly valour and *minne*. The parallelism is later strengthened by the similarities between Jeschute and Enite, who both ride after their husbands. Galoes (134, 24) is known to the audience as Parzival's uncle. The laughter of Orilus's sister Cunneware (135, 15ff.) will acknowledge the same youth on whom Orilus seeks revenge. And finally Parzival will show himself to be the dragon here predicted (137, 18–19).[22] The dramatic irony is thus intense throughout Orilus's boastful speech, for the attentive audience already recognises some of his misconceptions, and if familiar with the story will appreciate the still unrevealed connections.[23] This is certainly so with Orilus's most portentous statement – his boast of having just killed a knight. For his victim was Schionatulander, about whose death Parzival hears in the very next scene from his cousin Sigune. We, like Parzival, are challenged to connect the various threads of Wolfram's narrative.

There is yet a further implication in Wolfram's addition of this monologue, and that is the light it sheds on Orilus as a character. The very intensity of his harangue suggests an insecure reaction. This he expresses himself in suggesting that Jeschute resents having lost rank in marrying him. His claim that he is hated by all the knights of the Round Table is likewise shown to be mistaken. On the other hand, he has fought many battles and won, and he has fought them for Jeschute's sake. The intensity with which he has served his lady is consistent with his extreme behaviour in this scene and reflects the importance of his love for Jeschute as a motivating force. Though not explicitly stated, Orilus's devotion to his wife is made clear here and in the later scene (see below). He recognises his rights as a husband, but also his feelings as an *amî* (133, 10). In denouncing her, he too is punished. As he denies himself the pleasures of her love, his words are filled with nostalgia, and echoes of the initial description of her loveliness resound as well:[24]

136, 1   ich ensol niht mêr erwarmen
        an iweren blanken armen,
        dâ ich etswenn durch minne lac
        manegen wünneclîchen tac.
        ich sol velwen iweren rôten munt,
        [und] iwern ougen machen roete kunt.

Wolfram's narrator does not openly interpret Orilus's state of mind but lets his behaviour and his words speak for themselves. As a character Orilus is psychologically convincing, and the audience, though aware of his misinterpretations, must also sympathise with his ardour. He is not condemned. What he tells of his knightly exploits befits his current passion, however, and suggests a lack of moderation. For Orilus's sense of service is extreme, both in the ferocity of his battles and in his denunciation of his wife. Orilus has often killed his opponents, and though Wolfram makes no comment here, the taking of life has been shown to be one of the poet's central concerns, a flaw in the chivalric code. As a warrior Orilus is not a positive model.[25] Similarly there is implicit criticism of Orilus's rigid interpretation of duty between husband and wife. His strict adherence to the rules of chivalry leaves him deaf to Jeschute's pleas, unable to recognise her love or express his own in human (as opposed to conventional) terms. Wolfram grants him the right to treat her as he does, but he does not sympathise with it (see 264, 1–19; below p. 63). His sympathy lies with Jeschute, and the careful, tender depiction of Orilus's final forgiveness demonstrates how much the poet's sympathy also lies with the reality of Orilus's love for his wife and not with the code which blocks his sincere emotions.

In keeping with her demeanour in confronting Parzival, Jeschute attempts to reason with her husband (136, 11–22). She has been wrongly accused without being allowed any defence, yet she accepts this injustice with dignity.[26] Her attitude towards Orilus is sharply contrasted with his towards her, for she is totally selfless. Her concern is with him; she overlooks her own misfortune for the sorrow she now feels at his misery. Wolfram's narrator puts special emphasis on her extraordinary attitude by ending the scene with a commentary which recalls and verifies the content of her short speech to which he adds his own personal admiration:

137, 20   al weinde sunder lachen
               diu frouwe jâmers rîche
               schiet dannen trûreclîche.
               sine müete niht, swaz ir geschach,
               wan ir mannes ungemach:
               des trûren gap ir grôze nôt,
               daz si noch sampfter waere tôt.
               nu sult ir si durch triwe klagn:
               si begint nu hôhen kumber tragn.
               waer mir aller wîbe haz bereit,
               mich müet doch froun Jeschûten leit.

Orilus and Jeschute ride off, and the narrator turns back to follow the adventures of Parzival. They disappear momentarily from sight, but they have achieved a kind of reality in the listener's imagination and will be easily recognised when they reappear in Book 5. In a short dramatic episode Wolfram has presented two characters with individual strengths and weaknesses, has bound them intricately into the fabric of his story, and has touched on several of the profound questions of his narrative: the warrior's guilt, the relationship of husband and wife, the value of *mâze*. One is struck by the vividness of the vignette. How has Wolfram achieved it?

An analysis of the point of view reveals that, as narrator, he has refrained from overt narrative comment or interpretation with the exception of his admiration for Jeschute's beauty (130, 14-16), Parzival's motivation in taking Jeschute's jewels (130, 29-30), and the analysis of Jeschute's attitude towards Orilus (137, 23-6). Wolfram has described neither of the characters in physical detail. The strong visual and atmospheric image of Jeschute lying asleep in the tent, coinciding as it does with Parzival's experience, seduces the listener's imagination. In fact, only a few details of Jeschute's appearance are related. Of her costume we are told almost nothing, of her horse's saddle only enough to recognise it when it reappears later (see below p. 57ff.). Orilus is not described at all, either in physiognomy or in attire. No further objects or settings are described except as they occur in the delineation of action (e.g. the tent ropes). In general the poet allows the characters to tell their own story through action and dialogue. The verbal exchanges are surprisingly natural,[27] the mode of expression or behaviour convincingly apt to each character. Jeschute speaks and moves with composure and reserve. Orilus reveals his intemperate nature through dialogue and action, while accusing his wife of immoderation (136, 24-5) – yet a further instance of Wolfram's irony.

The extensive use of irony in this section is perhaps the most telling feature of Wolfram's narrative mode, for it reveals an attitude towards his audience at once concerned with pleasing and challenging. Irony, especially 'dramatic irony', lends extra levels of enjoyment and participation to the pleasure of vicarious experience. One is both alongside the characters and superior to them, looking down with a broader perspective, seeing their folly, regretful or amused at things imperceptible to them. Yet Wolfram's ironic play extends to the relationship between narrator and audience, and the challenge comes in having to discover much of it for oneself. The narrator does not offer his comments neatly labelled. Neither does he interpret the characters for his listeners. This demand for active participation is a distinctive aspect of Wolfram's narrative technique.[28] As narrator Wolfram does not lead us to easy judgement of characters. He defends Jeschute's innocence and goodness to which her own behaviour attests, but only after misleading us with the opening description. As for Orilus, we are given no direct help but must draw our own conclusions. In general Wolfram's narrator refrains from omniscient analysis independent of the plot structure, but instead incorporates his few observations into a continuous, dramatic account of character action and interaction. By this means the characters make a vivid impression; they seem distinct individuals reacting naturally to events and to each other, motivated by their intrinsic emotional and psychological states. One is compelled to wonder what will become of them.

The first encounter with Jeschute and her exchange with Orilus form an integral part of the *Parzival* narrative and an independent dramatic episode. We have seen Parzival invade the lives of these people, disrupting their normal pattern of existence. The vignette ends with Orilus and Jeschute riding away from the audience's view. As the narrative progresses, their place in courtly society and the intricate ties binding them to Parzival are gradually revealed to us, though Parzival himself never associates statements he hears about a certain Orilus and Jeschute with his first amorous adventure. They remain nameless for him; he remains the mysterious Red Knight for them.[29]

The second episode devoted to Orilus, Jeschute and Parzival occurs in Book 5 after Parzival's failure at Munsalvaesche. Considerable time has elapsed and Parzival has changed in many ways. He has perfected the attributes of a chivalrous knight, he has married a beautiful woman, and he knows much more about his own ancestry from two conversations with his cousin Sigune. In fact, his first encounter with Jeschute was followed immediately by his first meeting with Sigune, when she named Orilus as her beloved's killer (141, 9). Then, totally unaware of his near encounter with that man, Parzival vowed to seek vengeance on him. Now Parzival's second encounter with Jeschute is immediately preceded by his second encounter with Sigune, and this time the moods are reversed. In the first instances his behaviour was condemned by Jeschute while Sigune praised him. Here Sigune condemns him, whereas he redeems himself with Jeschute.

As in the previous case, the scene is introduced through Parzival's eyes:

256, 11   er kom ûf eine niwe slâ.
          wandez gienc vor im aldâ
          ein ors daz was wol beslagen,
          und ein barfuoz pfäret daz muose tragen
          eine frouwen die er sach.
          nâch der ze rîten im geschach.
          ir pfärt gein kumber was verselt:
          man het im wol durch hût gezelt
          elliu sîniu rippe gar.
          als ein harm ez was gevar.
          ein bästîn halfter lac dar an.
          unz ûf den huof swanc im diu man.
          sîn ougen tief, die gruoben wît.
          ouch was der frouwen runzît
          vertwâlet unde vertrecket,
          durch hunger dicke erwecket.
          ez was dürre als ein zunder.

sîn gên daz was wunder:
wandez reit ein frouwe wert,
diu selten kunrierte pfert.

257, 1   Dâ lac ûf ein gereite,
smal ân alle breite,
geschelle und bogen verrêret,
grôz zadel dran gemêret.
der frouwen trûrec, niht ze geil,
ir surzengel was ein seil:
dem was sie doch ze wol geborn.
ouch heten die este und etslich dorn
ir hemde zerfüeret:
swa'z mit zerren was gerüeret,
dâ saher vil der stricke:
dar unde liehte blicke,
ir hût noch wîzer denn ein swan.
sîne fuorte niht wan knoden an:
swâ die wârn des velles dach,
in blanker varwe er daz sach:
daz ander leit von sunnen nôt.
swiez ie kom, ir munt was rôt:
der muose alsölhe varwe tragen,
man hete fiwer wol drûz geslagen.
swâ man se wolt an rîten,
daz was zer blôzen sîten:
[nantes ieman vilân,
der het ir unreht getân:]
wan si hete wênc an ir.

He first sees the tracks of two horses, one poorly shod,
and then a lady riding one of them, a nearly starved nag with
a hemp bridle and an unadorned saddle. This description
echoes Orilus's earlier words; it is the incarnation of his
threat:

137, 1   'iwer zoum muoz sîn ein bästîn seil,
iwer phert bejagt wol hungers teil,

iwer satel wol gezieret
der wirt enschumphieret.'

Riding this pitiful creature is a *frouwe wert* whose pure white
skin shines through her torn garments, and whose mouth is
red as flame. The similarities with Parzival's first view of
Jeschute in the earlier episode are evident. Once more we are
shown the scene through the hero's eyes, and again emphasis
is given to physical beauty, though the eroticism is subtler,
the humour more obvious.[30]

There are other changes besides the lightening of tone. It
is now clear that Parzival apprehends this woman's loveliness,[31] whereas in the previous scene it was ultimately unclear whether he was aware of her beauty. He has learned
much since then and can now recognise female loveliness and
a *frouwe wol geborn*, treating her with proper respect.
Although it is not explicitly stated, we may assume that
Parzival gradually recognises Jeschute as the woman whose
ring and brooch he took, though he is not aware of the consequences of his folly.[32] This is suggested in his assurance that
since becoming a knight he has wronged no woman (in fact
he wronged both his mother and Jeschute before that time).

258, 17   'jane wart von mîme lîbe
            iu noch decheinem wîbe
            laster nie gemêret
            (sô het ich mich gunêret)
            sît ich den schilt von êrst gewan
            und rîters fuore mich versan.'

It is possible to see his statement here as a sign that he remem-
bers his former encounter – at least vaguely. Wolfram leaves it
ambiguous, hinting through the description of Jeschute –
which identifies her for the audience – and Parzival's words,
but never pinpointing a moment of realisation for the hero.
Later in the scene it is clear that Parzival has recognised
Jeschute, yet exactly when this recognition occurred is not
related. For her part, Jeschute identifies Parzival immediately

as a result of his inborn beauty (258, 1-4), the same quality
he sees in her. In Chrétien's text the duchess knows Perceval
at once (3782f.) though no reason is given. Perceval does not
recognise her until her husband's angry speech rehearses the
earlier scene (3835ff.). This logical explanation is conspicuously missing from Wolfram's story.

Jeschute accuses Parzival of having assailed her, but her
words show she is consistent in her patience and kindness
(258, 5-14). Her polite speech betrays little anger; rather she
speaks with humility of her fate, wishing him joy in spite of
the sorrow he has caused her. Her continued selflessness and
submission are made clear through her actions and words.
She refuses the assistance that Parzival offers, concerned as
before for *his* safety.

259,11   'welt ir uns toetens machen vrî,
           sô rîtet daz i'u verre sî.
           doch klagte ich wênec mînen tôt,
           wan daz ich fürhte ir komts in nôt.'

The scene has thus far been filled with allusions to the previous encounter. The structure of the episode is similar;
Parzival comes unexpectedly upon Jeschute; Jeschute is presented in both cases through vivid sensuous images; explicit
details reappear. Thus Wolfram has linked this scene with the
foregoing one, making it clear that during the intervening
time Orilus and Jeschute have not mended their relationship.
Orilus's unabated anger is related by Jeschute (259, 19-26),
who also tells Parzival that her husband is riding alone just
ahead of them.

The encounter between Parzival and Jeschute forms a
neatly structured unit. The scene is set with a lengthy descriptive passage, and their actual conversation, given in some
detail, is framed in commentary by the narrator who insists
again on Jeschute's virtues (257, 26-30; 260, 6-11). The following narrative unit centres on Orilus. As Parzival arms himself, Orilus is warned of his presence by the neighing of

Parzival's charger (260, 16–21). This detail adds a spatial dimension to the scene and demonstrates Wolfram's ability to enliven his narrative through acutely observed incidental details. In addition, the symbolic implication here is unmistakable – Parzival's stallion bending and neighing towards Jeschute's mare underscores the erotic basis of the conflict among these three people.[33]

Orilus's violent reaction to the whinny epitomises his state of mind:

260, 22   daz ors warf er mit zornes site
            vaste ûz dem stîge.

As Orilus whirls around to face Parzival, Wolfram begins a lengthy description of the duke's appearance. Thus the audience's first visual impression of this knight coincides with Parzival's. During the previous encounter with Jeschute, Parzival did not see Orilus – nor did the audience. Now he materialises as an elaborately dressed, fully armed warrior ready to charge.

260, 24   gein strîteclîchem wîge
            hielt der herzoge Orilus
            gereit zeiner tjost alsus,
            mit rehter manlîcher ger,
            von Gaheviez mit eime sper:
            daz was gevärwet genuoc,
            reht als er sîniu wâpen truoc.
261, 1   Sînen helm worhte Trebuchet.
            sîn schilt was ze Dôlet
            in Kailetes lande
            geworht dem wîgande:
            rant und buckel heten kraft.
            zAlexandrîe in heidenschaft
            was geworht ein pfellel guot,
            des der fürste hôch gemuot
            truoc kursît und wâpenroc.

It is obvious that such an account is not intended to represent Parzival's view of Orilus, for it is too detailed and contains much historical material concerning the origins of various pieces of armour (the initial description continues through 262, 13). Forgoing any description until this point, however, is a very effective dramatic tool, for both hero and audience experience the excitement and shock of the warrior's charge, and the *retardierendes Moment* increases suspense while the outcome hangs in the balance. In addition the description is charged with dramatic irony, as was Orilus's long tirade in the earlier scene. Here each item of his equipment binds him to Parzival's world. Thus the elements in the long account form a symbolic statement, stressing not only the quality of Orilus's armour but the still unrecognised connections between him and Parzival.[34] At the same time Wolfram's description delivers a visual impact because of the prominence given to one aspect of Orilus's equipment, the startling dragons on his armour (262, 4–13).[35] Rather than becoming lost in the web of detail, the dragons provide a focus of attention. The scene is powerfully projected as the battle proceeds (262, 23–263, 30), filled with the blazing friction of metal on rich armour and flashing dragons' eyes.

As the horses charge towards each other Wolfram decelerates his narrative by altering his point of view.[36] First he reminds his audience of the quiet presence of Lady Jeschute who anticipates and fears the outcome of this well-matched joust:

262, 27   diu hielt dâ, want ir hende.
            si freuden ellende
            gunde enwederm helde schaden.

These lines evoke several responses. The audience is pulled back from Orilus as the whole scene comes into view. The tense, isolated figure of Jeschute reinforces the actuality of the event and the prospect of tragedy. Her remarkable capacity for forgiveness is again stressed in her concern for both of these men who have wrongfully caused her misery.

Next the figure of the narrator moves into the foreground, summarising Orilus's reasons for punishing Jeschute: Orilus believes himself cuckolded and disgraced, and as husband he has the authority to punish his wife as he sees fit (264, 1–19). This intrusion takes the place of li Orgueilleus's long explanatory speech in Chrétien's tale. Here the audience is informed while uncertainty about Parzival's knowledge is maintained, thus heightening the dramatic irony. The narrator is also given an opportunity to pass judgement: 'mich dunket si hân bêde reht' (264, 25). The suspense is increased by the narrator's quandary, and the audience is led to consider the ethical ambiguities of the situation. Which of them is most in the right? Parzival is excused by his ignorance; Orilus is exercising his legal rights. The narrator does not help us to decide. Instead, having retarded his narration through commentary and description, he relates Parzival's somewhat comic defeat of his opponent.

265, 12   der begreif ouch in dô sunder twâl
           unt zucte in ûz dem satel sîn:
           als ein garbe häberîn
           vastern under de arme swanc:
           mit im er von dem orse spranc,
           und druct in über einen ronen.

Now Orilus, likened to a sheaf of oats, speaks with Parzival for the first time. In the ensuing conversation (if it can be termed thus, the victor having pinned his foe over a fallen tree!), Orilus's excessive pride becomes manifest. He refuses to forgive Jeschute for the despair and disgrace he believes she has brought him, and he tries without success to bribe Parzival with promises of land and fealty.[37] At last Orilus consents to a reconciliation. He formally forgives his wife, and at his command she springs to kiss his blood-stained face (268, 16–24, quoted below, pp. 64–5). This perfunctory reunion concludes the scene.

The modifications on Chrétien's model have led to a portrayal of Orilus and Jeschute as consistent characters and
attest to Wolfram's reliance on irony for adding dimension to
his narrative. Unlike the sudden and total capitulation of li
Orgueilleus in *Perceval*, Orilus's pride and anger remain impla-
cable even in defeat, and it is only the threat of losing his life
that leads him to give his wife a formal pardon. The inadequacy of this gesture is shown in the following scene when
his forgiveness is genuine. Wolfram also manages to imply
Jeschute's presence in the background, and her concern for
both men is echoed by the narrator's indecision. Orilus's
defiance of his victor, his submission and reluctant pardon of
Jeschute come alive through dialogue and depiction of action
with scarcely any commentary on the narrator's part.

The concluding section involving these three characters
takes place at the cave of the hermit Trevrizent, the coincidence of location another example of Wolfram's irony. Freely
returning the ring he had purloined, Parzival swears on a relic
casket that Jeschute is innocent. Orilus now forgives her
fully and welcomes her back into his heart:

270, 5   die gâbe enpfienc der degen guot.
              dô streich er von dem munde'z pluot
              und kuste sînes herzen trût.
              ouch wart verdact ir blôziu hût.
              Orilus der fürste erkant
              stiez dez vingerl wider an ir hant,
              und gap ir an sîn kursît:
              die was von rîchem pfelle, wît,
              mit heldes hant zerhouwen.

This passage depicts the lovers' actual and complete reunion.
The contrast between this kiss and the previous one under-
scores the contrast between Orilus's total forgiveness of
Jeschute here and his earlier superficial gesture:

268, 16   'wol her, ir sult geküsset sîn.
          ich hân vil prîss durch iuch verlorn:

waz denne? ez ist doch verkorn.'
diu frouwe mit ir blôzem vel
was zem sprunge harte snel
von dem pfärde ûf den wasen.
swie dez pluot von der nasen
den munt im hete gemachet rôt,
si kust in dô er kus gebôt.

In both cases the blood on Orilus's face recalls the fight just
lost and emphasises his stature as a mighty warrior. The
depiction of each kiss is subtly rendered to enhance our
awareness of the psychological state of Orilus and Jeschute.
In the first reunion Orilus stands (one imagines him im-
mobile) with bloodied face, orders Jeschute to come to him,
and passively accepts her kiss. She springs at his command.
The text gives no hint, however, that either character is convinced by this reconciliation.

The second kiss is described with equal subtlety. Here it is
Orilus who kisses Jeschute. Before doing so he wipes the blood
from his mouth. Wolfram's virtuosity shines forth in these
small details which capture Orilus's real awakening – it is he
who now makes the gesture, both actually and figuratively.
He kisses her, wiping away beforehand the stain of conflict,
for her sake. Orilus's love for Jeschute is emphasised by such
images, by the words *herzen trut*, by the return of the ring to
Jeschute's finger, and by Orilus's solicitous gesture of covering his wife's nakedness with his ragged cloak.[38] Jeschute
wears rags again, but this time of a different sort. Orilus's
love for his wife is great enough to overcome even his pride,
for now recognising her righteousness he rejoices at his defeat
since it has restored his happiness (270, 25 – 271, 9).

That the gestures involved in the reconciliation have legal
implications as well does not detract from their significance
as personal statements. Wolfram has made the kiss into a
central image. Yet it is central in a way very different from
Chrétien's tale in which Perceval's kisses spark li Orgueilleus's
kiss, whereas the latter two kisses – one legalling binding, the

kiss, whereas the latter two kisses – one legally binding, the next emotionally – are imbued with symbolic and psychological force. The image continues in the following scene, with Jeschute's passive role emphasised by enjambment (273, 29–30). That this marriage has been not only saved but strengthened is reflected by the aura of tranquillity which pervades the final reconciliation (272–3).

Thus the dramatic tale of Jeschute and Orilus, initiated and resolved by Parzival, is happily concluded. In this instance Parzival has functioned as a humanising influence, a Gawan-like 'Katalysator der Menschlichkeit'.[39] For although Parzival's *tumpheit* is the cause of misfortune, the rashness and immoderation of Orilus's jealous anger suggest a lack of trust, or better, an inadequacy in the chivalric code which defines Orilus's relation to his wife, that Parzival serves to uncover. Thus Parzival acts as a catalyst, bringing problems to a crisis point and ultimately resolving them fully. As he, still unrecognised, disappears again from Orilus's and Jeschute's lives, he leaves them in a new harmony. Orilus has changed, for he has lost much of his overweening pride. His moderation is evident in his speech to Parzival and in his behaviour at Arthur's court (274–9). He is now capable of admiring, without envy or hatred, a knight greater than he (276, 19ff.). But Wolfram takes care to show Orilus not totally transformed; he remains unchanged in appearance and undaunted in spirit. Preparing to ride to court he dons a full suit of armour – one imagines the same elaborate trappings in which he faced Parzival – and springs with panache onto his fully outfitted charger! Orilus is still the noble, valiant warrior he was (*valsches vrîe*, 274, 30; *küene*, 275, 5; *werde degn*, 275, 10). The changes wrought have been his personal gain.

Both the first and second encounters of Parzival with Jeschute and Orilus are independent dramatic units, though intricately bound with the rest of the narrative not only by Parzival's role but by many thematic and motival elements as well: Orilus's killing of Schionatulander, the ring and brooch,

Trevrizent's cave and the sword, Orilus's Gral horse, and the unrecognised family ties. Within the *Parzival* narrative as a whole, Jeschute and Orilus are minor characters who elucidate a step in Parzival's 'education'. Wolfram's mastery is evident in the harmonious integration of this sub-plot into his main story, in the sustained dramatic irony, and in his characterisation of the two as distinctive figures who challenge the imagination.

In relating these episodes Wolfram's narrator has generally avoided interpretation. He recounts the action and captures the visual impression of different scenes as though he were a powerless bystander. As with architectural descriptions, a visual image is projected by association with specific action and with characters' emotional reactions rather than with physical detail. The dramatic effect of Wolfram's narrative is heightened by the simultaneity of his description: the audience is taken into the scene, listens to the dialogue, views the action as it progresses, and often seems to experience through the senses of the characters.

Orilus and Jeschute do not appear in active roles anywhere else in the narrative, but are merely referred to by other characters or by the narrator. However, there are two further subjects connected with them in Wolfram's text which are important in studying Albrecht's treatment of Orilus and Jeschute. These are Orilus's defeat of Schionatulander and the characterisation of Orilus's brother Lähelin. Schionatulander's death is referred to by Orilus and later by Sigune in her conversation with Parzival (see above pp. 52 and 57). Once again the audience is directly involved in the unfolding narrative, piecing together information along with (and, as here, ahead of) the hero. Sigune explains that Schionatulander fought to defend Parzival's lands from being usurped by Lähelin and was ultimately killed by Orilus. Rather than condemning her lover's killer, however, she blames herself for urging Schionatulander into danger (141, 16–24). She seeks vengeance neither here nor in her subsequent meetings with

Parzival; she first sends him deliberately on the wrong path and later asks only that Anfortas be healed. In Book 9 she names Orilus once more in speaking to Parzival of her deep mourning (439, 30).

Orilus's brother Lähelin appears only once in the foreground of action in *Parzival*, but he is mentioned nineteen times and comes to stand as the very figure of a formidable warrior.[40] His first brief appearance in Book 2 (79, 13ff.) characterises him only with conventional knightly traits. Defeating him comes to represent a major goal for the young Parzival through Herzeloyde's parting words of advice to her son:

128, 4   'der stolze küene Lähelîn
dînen fürsten ab ervaht zwei lant,
diu solten dienen dîner hant,
Wâleis und Norgâls.
ein dîn fürste Turkentâls
den tôt von sîner hende enphienc:
dîn volc er sluoc unde vienc.'

Parzival accepts the challenge and vows to avenge his father and himself. The image of Lähelin here is distinctly evil, for he has not only killed one of Parzival's vassal princes but has killed and captured his subjects. It is shortly after this that Parzival hears about Lähelin from Sigune; and he later wonders aloud if his first opponent (Ither) is the Lähelin of whom his mother had spoken (154, 25). From Trevrizent Parzival learns that Lähelin once entered the Gral realm, killed a Gral knight in a joust, and then took his victim's horse (473-4). Parzival too rides a Gral horse, which leads Trevrizent to ask if he might be that same Lähelin.[41]

In Wolfram's *Parzival* Orilus is not directly associated with Lähelin's deeds, though a connection is suggested by Sigune's relation of Schionatulander's death to the defence of Parzival's lands. The two brothers remain essentially distinct, with Orilus carefully portrayed as a proud, passionate man whose passionate man whose strengths and weaknesses are gradually revealed through intimate scenes, while Lähelin – far less individualised – stands for fierce valour and aggressive knighthood.

ALBRECHT'S JESCUTE, ORILUS, AND LEHELIN

In the JT, Jescute, Orilus, and Lehelin play more prominent roles than do their prototypes in *Parzival*. They appear in a greater number of scenes, and their actions are repeatedly linked with Tschinotulander's progress. They are nonetheless secondary figures who disappear from the narrative for long stretches, coming to the fore in three main episodes, one near the beginning and two in the last third of the text.[42] Primarily involved in Tschinotulander's story, they outlive him and hence serve to join his tale with that of Parzival.

The plot involving these characters centres on the hound's inscribed leash. This motif appears in *Parzival* where Sigune names Orilus as Schionatulander's killer and implicates the leash in causing his death (141,16), and in *Titurel II* where the story of the *brackenseil* begins. In the *Titurel* fragment an idyllic woodland scene is interrupted by a baying hound wearing a long, jewelled leash. Schionatulander captures the hound and brings it to Sigune who begins reading the inscription on the collar. She discovers the hound's name, 'Gardevîaz', and a story of young love. Before Sigune can finish reading, however, the hound breaks away. Schionatulander attempts to retrieve it but loses its track, and Sigune, desolate at not being able to finish the story, vows to withhold her love from Schionatulander until he has returned the hound with its leash to her (165–6). Schionatulander promises to undertake the search (167).

This fragment of 39 stanzas and the scant related information in *Parzival* provide the core material for the central plot of the JT – an epic quest for the inscribed leash. In Albrecht's tale three couples vie for its possession: Ekunat and Clauditte,

69

Tschinotulander and Sigune, and Orilus and Jescute. In the JT Orilus wins the dog in a joust and retains it throughout the major part of the text. The enmity between him and Tschinotulander increases until their final confrontation resulting in Tschinotulander's death, the scene immediately preceding Parzival's first encounter with Jeschute in *Parzival*. Wolfram does not associate Orilus with the *brackenseil*, but in the JT Orilus's involvement with the leash begins with his first appearance in the narrative, shortly following the incorporation of the second *Titurel* fragment.

In Albrecht's text, having vowed to find the hound, Tschinotulander returns with Sigune to Kanvoleis where the young hero arms himself in preparation for his quest (1222–88). As Tschinotulander begins his search, the narrator reflects on the initial chase and its near success:

1292 Zehant alda der brack entran   Sigunen mit der
                                                               strange
        und sich der talfin des versan   und lief im durch di
                                                               stimme nach so lange,
        daz siniu bein enpfiengen vil der wunden –,
        und wer er do vol loufen   ein ponder lank, er het
                                                               den bracken vunden.

The chronology here is confusing, for the narrator jumps back to the original scene of Sigune and Tschinotulander in the woods. It is not clear how much time has passed since then; it would seem more than one day considering the lengthy process of their return, the arming, farewell, and now the search, but this is not clarified.[43] The narrator continues on from the previous point when the hound became entangled in the long leash not far from Tschinotulander. Undiscovered by the young yero, it is found by King Teanglis von Theserat, who frees and then follows it in anticipation of adventure. This he finds in the shape of Orilus von Lalander (1298). No description is given here of Orilus who defeats Teanglis in an unspectacular contest (1303–4), thus becoming possessor of

70

Gardivias. Following this cursorily sketched scene, the narrator breaks in with a forecast of the woes that will result from
this duel:

1305 Des siges und des seiles   wart Orilus hie riche.
      owe Sigun, unheiles!   ich wen, ůch beiden nimmer
                                              mer entwiche
      kumber, not, dir und dem talfine,
      der da nach disem seile   ist im walde dolnde mange
                                              pine.

Within the context of the JT alone, such an unexpected
exclamation appears incongruous and shocking – additionally
so because of the narrator's emotive address to a character
not present in the scene (see below p. 217). The sentiment is
justified, however, if the reader is familiar with the Sigune
scenes in *Parzival.* Albrecht is interweaving his plot with
Wolfram's narrative and showing Orilus on the first step of a
collision course with Tschinotulander. These connections are
not explicitly stated, however. The audience must independently bring them to bear.

A major difference from Wolfram's technique is already
apparent: the narrative focus is not following the hero but
has diffused. In *Parzival* the protagonists' experiences lead us
into new realms; each stumbles (or strides confidently, in
Gawan's case) into the lives of figures who achieve definition
as he interacts with them. The audience tends to encounter
characters along with the hero. When this pattern is broken,
it is generally a case of the focus remaining for a brief time
behind the hero, as with Orilus and Jeschute, observing the
consequences of his deeds. Seldom are new characters and
situations introduced independently. In the JT, however,
characters and events are introduced in a variety of contexts
and in the absence of the main hero. Orilus is first presented
in a joust with Teanglis, and nothing in Albrecht's description
indicates his importance within the story. Yet his significance
and the significance of this battle are made clear through the

poet's interjections and the reader's prior knowledge. The full impact of the scene comes when the audience recognises this joust – between two briefly identified knights – as the initiation of inevitable conflict between Orilus and Tschinotulander, whose destinies from this point are intertwined.

With the next stanza the focus switches back to Tschinotulander; again the change in time and place is not clearly defined. After a solitary night in the forest (1307-8),[44] the young hero comes upon Teanglis, challenges, and defeats him. Tschinotulander then sends a challenge to Teanglis's lord. This precipitates Tschinotulander's debut in a formulaic encounter which is a specific echo of *Parzival*: an unknown knight engages and defeats the followers of an unknown king, who in this case is Arthur.[45] Tschinotulander kills the first two knights who challenge him; these are Yblet, a nephew of Teanglis, and Arbidol, a nephew of Orilus and Lehelin (1346-51). Albrecht emphasises the brothers' devotion to Arbidol:

1348 Der furste von Lalander   sin oheim was furware,
     und Lehelin der ander.   den beiden gie zu herzen so
                                                     der clare.

     sin vreude kund ir vreude hohe setzen,
     sin leit ir herzen serte,   sin truren kund si beide an
                                                vreuden letzen.

This death represents the second major step towards the inevitable clash between Orilus and Tschinotulander.[46] The interrelation of the characters has become more complicated, though no meeting has yet occurred. Albrecht takes care to stress the developing conflict, interjecting portents of unhappiness for Sigune (e.g. 1352, 4; 1371, 4; 1395, 3). The characters are being inexorably directed along a path of conflict by the structure of the plot. The significance of events is explained by the omniscient narrator who foresees the consequences of each development.

Thus far, little has been shown of Orilus's character except for his skill as a warrior and his strong kinship ties. This devotion to kin is further emphasised as the time comes for Orilus himself to face Tschinotulander. Orilus is taunted by a page who tries to stir him to action by recalling Arbidol's death (1371-3). Orilus does not answer this challenge at once. Rather, Arthur guesses that the unknown knight is Ither, and promises high reward to whoever defeats him.[47] After several more knights have tried and failed, the challenge to Orilus is repeated and he accepts, stating his deep-felt loss and wish for vengeance:

1392 'Vurwar ich nicht erwinde',   sus antwurt im der
                                       starke.
     'miner swester kinde   von im sin jugend lit in todes
                                         arke.
     der was ein kron ob allen jungelingen.
     des můz ich immer truren,   swie vrȯlich vogel in dem
                                       meien singen.
1393 Sin kunicliche jugende   ist immer wol zu weinen
     von werder wibe tugende.   er můz mir tiure gelten
                                       hiut den cleinen,
     e sich der tac in abent hat gewendet.
     ich wen, ouch sin amie   mȇz an ir hohen vreuden sin
                                         gepfendet!'

Albrecht's audience would, of course, recognise the truth of Orilus's prediction and, knowing the challenger to be Tschinotulander and the 'amie' to be Sigune, they would also appreciate the irony in the precision of this woeful forecast. Sigune's great sorrow would have been known from Wolfram's poem, and Orilus's words here can be added to the narrator's many foreshadowings. For the attentive audience there is perhaps another kind of irony in Orilus's boast that he will dispatch Tschinotulander so quickly. Clearly much longer than a day will pass before his threat is realised.

Although this episode is rich in character interaction, its primary function is not to demonstrate Orilus as an individual personality or to present a convincingly natural conversation, but to reiterate the bases for conflict between him and Tschinotulander. The motivation behind Orilus's failure to react to the initial taunt is left unclear, and he responds to the renewed challenge with a general statement about his feelings. In fact, no actual dialogue has taken place. Rather the reason for enmity between Orilus and Tschinotulander has been reviewed three times, and Tschinotulander's great prowess as a warrior has been stressed.

As Orilus is armed and sent off, Albrecht briefly describes his appearance:

1396 Den tracken was man sehende   an schild, an helme
                                                                                riche.
        sin ougen rubin brehende.   zimier und wapen stůnd
                                                                im keiserliche.

This is the first description of Orilus in the JT and is clearly based on the *Parzival* battle scene discussed above. The next two lines of the same stanza refer to Tschinotulander's helmet (mentioned earlier as well, 1244–8):

1396, 3 der talfin fůrt daz schapel cronebaere.
           di bůchstabe sageten,   daz Sigun noch rein und
                                                               kůsche waere.

Differences between Albrecht's and Wolfram's descriptive modes are immediately striking. First of all, in the JT stanza there is confusion about who is being described; the last two lines follow abruptly and unexpectedly, changing the focus from Orilus to Tschinotulander. Secondly, the point of view is omniscient and abstracted from the actual circumstances. Wolfram's text is consistent in both the object of description and the point of view: the focus remains on Orilus who appears as if through Parzival's eyes while the two are poised to charge each other. Though not in detail what Parzival sees, the effect is emotionally valid for the audience. In the JT, on the other hand, the brief descriptions stand apart from the narrative, the objective elements isolated from the action and even from the two characters involved. One gains no dramatic image of this scene, nor is one led to sympathise emotionally through the sharing of a personal viewpoint. The conflict is presented on a symbolic level: the confrontation of two costly helmets. That Tschinotulander's bears a written message seems appropriately in harmony with the importance of the written word in the JT.

Albrecht's description of the battle between Orilus and Tschinotulander resembles the pattern set earlier when Teanglis met Orilus (1299-1304) and Tschinotulander met Teanglis (1323-5).

1397 Wie si nu hie gebaren?   des wil ich iuch bescheiden:
    vintlichez varen   geschach nach ritters orden von
                                           in beiden.
    ir deweder dahte nicht verderben.
    si beide was wol angeborn,   ob si ritterlichen kunden
                                           werben.

1398 Diu ors zu beiden siten   si kunden wol ersprengen.
    ir mûtlichez riten   man sach, di zoume kurzen,
                                           ponder lengen.
    geriten ritterlichen wart von beiden.
    daz eine sper zubrochen   sach man di lufte gen der
                                           hôhe cleiden.

1399 Ein ander sper zu bieten   ein knappe sich niht sumde.
    der talfin kund sich nieten,   des im unpris di straze
                                           fluhtic rumde.
    Duranze wart mit nide her gedrucket,
    so daz dem uz Lalander   lip und lebn vil nahen was
                                           gezucket.

1400 Man und ors, die beide   wurden uber stozen.
    von kinde nie so leide   wart Orilus, vor zageheit
                                           dem blozen,
    sint er zeKanadice den sperwaere
    so mangem ritter vor behielt.   des begunder sich
                                           nu schamen dirre maere,

1401 Er wart gesehen erblichen,   di sin varwe erkanden,

75

der zeswe arm geswichen.　　er het in anders mit dem
　　　　　　　　　　　　　　　swert bestanden.
er hiez sich in zu herberge fûren.

The essence of these stanzas is summed up in one line: 'geriten
ritterlichen wart von beiden' (1398, 3). Repetition of *beide*
points to the closeness of the match, yet tension is not
expressed by other means. The rhetorical question and answer
of the opening line set a relaxed tone which is maintained by
the brevity of this passage and the use of conventional
imagery. The potential drama in the encounter is not exploited, for the battle's strategic importance is external to the
specific action.

Wolfram's description of Parzival's battle with Orilus in
Book 5 of *Parzival* offers revealing similarities and contrasts.

262, 30　　diu ors in sweize muosen baden.
263, 1　　Prîss si bêde gerten.
　　　　　die blicke von den swerten,
　　　　　und fiwer daz von helmen spranc,
　　　　　und manec ellenthafter swanc,
　　　　　die begunden verre glesten.
　　　　　wan dâ wâren strîts die besten
　　　　　mit hurte an ein ander kumen,
　　　　　ez gê ze schaden odr ze frumen
　　　　　den küenen helden maeren.
　　　　　swie willec d'ors in waeren,
　　　　　dâ sî bêde ûf sâzen,
　　　　　der sporn si niht vergâzen,
　　　　　noch ir swerte lieht gemâl.

Here too the narrator is removed from the action, looking on
now from Jeschute's point of view. The image projected is
powerful, both emotionally and visually. Emotional impact
comes not only from sharing Jeschute's tension (see above
pp. 62f.), but from both men's great desire to win, and the
assurance that the two warriors crashing towards one another
represent the epitome of knightly skill. That each meets his

match is stressed by repetition of *bede*, as in the JT passage, and by Jeschute's reluctant admiration of the beauty in a joust between such well-matched champions (262, 25-6). The impressionistic quality of the visual description – horses bathed in sweat, the air lit by sparks and flames – achieves an astonishing immediacy. There is no blow-by-blow narration of movements, but the rhythm and images combine to convey a vivid sense of the pounding onslaught. The audience, totally absorbed in the moment, is not encouraged to dwell upon the broader implications of this battle for either warrior. The immediate outcome is what matters: who will win? who perhaps will die?[48]

A very different effect is achieved in Albrecht's battle description where the length of line and more leisurely meter themselves dissipate tension. The description is interrupted by summary and omniscient commentary as the battle itself is interrupted while a broken spear is replaced. The audience is not caught up in the action but learns about it from a disinterested perspective. Correspondingly the emotions of the protagonists are unimportant. Orilus's profound anger towards Tschinotulander is barely accounted for in two formulaic lines (1395, 4; 1397, 2). In fact, Orilus is presented as just one of many knights facing Tschinotulander – forty altogether, twelve of them kings (1411). It seems quite fitting that the joust should fail to resolve the conflict but should be halted by Orilus's broken arm. Tschinotulander maintains the upper hand, yet Orilus is not defeated but retires from the field without compromising himself.

Though camouflaged among many other sometimes more vividly depicted jousts (e.g. 1409), this match signals an important step in the plot, and its indecisiveness is essential to the continuation of several narrative strands. The audience recognises Tschinotulander to be the superior warrior, yet the final contest must be postponed while Orilus's arm heals. This confrontation is a prefiguration of the ultimate and inevitable duel which they must face. In the intervening time

Tschinotulander can undertake further adventure. The plot has thickened around the two knights as a series of chain reactions, essentially independent of specific character traits or individual motivation.

What would seem the sure defeat of all the knights of the Round Table is halted when Tschinotulander is recognised by Ekunat von Berbester (1417). This clearly echoes Gawan's intervention on Parzival's behalf (*Parzival*, 300f.). Here the narrative focus returns to Arthur's court with Ekunat who pleads that Tschinotulander be pardoned. All agree, with the exception of Orilus who cannot forgive Tschinotulander for Arbidol's death (1461–3). Orilus does not mention his own partial defeat, nor does the narrator. That he cannot be placated, even by the persuasive Ekunat, projects the image of a sullen, angry man. As Orilus suddenly turns heel and rides away he is compared to an angry lion (1463, 4), which perhaps aptly characterises his resentment but seems an ill-chosen image for so abrupt an exit. That he is offending courtly rules of behaviour becomes clear in the next stanza; in fact King Arthur is personally affronted:

1464 Daz mûte den kunic sere   und ouch di kuniginne,
       wan in ein sulch unere   nie wart erboten noch ein
                                  solch unminne
      gen betelicher bet, als si do gerten.

Orilus and Jescute ride off disdainfully without bidding farewell, taking the hound with them (1465). The reference to Gardivias comes as a surprise. Yet now the subject turns to the hound as Ekunat claims him (1466). While departing, Orilus manages to respond:

1467 'Den bracken ich erherte   mit scharfen swertes ecken.
       ich vant in uf der verte,   do er lief von Teserat,
                                  dem recken',
      sprach Orilus, der het sichs underwunden.

'ich wen, der hunt ist iwer nicht.   sůchet anderhalp,
                              ir habt an mir niht vunden!'

The physical dimensions of this scene are not made clear.
Ekunat seems to speak to the assembled court, while Orilus
hears his comment and responds defiantly. With this he and
Jescute drop momentarily from sight. The narrative focus
remains on the court where, after some debate, it is decided
to ask Orilus to return and discuss the problem of the leash.
Here the narrator reminds us briefly – and anachronistically –
of the still-waiting Tschinotulander (1484, 2) before recounting Orilus's ready acceptance of the bid to return. If Orilus
seems a bit hasty in acquiescing (1487–8), we must not
question, since the narrator assures us it is true. That Orilus's
desire for vengeance as well as his prideful anger are here
glossed over indicates that personal motivation is of secondary importance. Certainly for the plot to proceed he must
rejoin the court, and this provides the primary rationale.
Both Orilus's departure and return add to the complex of
thematic patterns which are maintaining tension within the
plot structure. To view the sequence as evidence of Orilus's
volatile personality would clearly be an over-reading.

Jescute's physical appearance is described for the first time
as she and Orilus head back to Arthur's court:

1489 Ir varwe clar dem velle   gap rôt, wol under blenket,
     sam trůbel rosen snelle   des morgens towik uz dem
                                                balge schrenket.
     iz was unnot. iedoch so wart enzundet
     gelich der sunnen glenze   ir lieht antluz, als sumer
                                                reise kundet.

Although the colour imagery recalls Wolfram's descriptions,
there is no trace of the sensuousness Jeschute emanates in
Parzival. Instead, the simile of a rose is reminiscent of the
fresh and innocent loveliness which Wolfram depicts in
Condwiramurs:

188, 10   als von dem süezen touwe
                 diu rôse ûz ir bälgelîn
                 blecket niwen werden schîn,
                 der beidiu wîz ist unde rôt.

After this brief appearance, Albrecht's Jescute fades again into the background. It is unclear why her description is placed at this point in the narrative. She is not specifically being seen by any other character, nor does her beauty play a role here. Curiously the stanza describing her serves as the bridge to Arthur's court, for in the following line she and Orilus have arrived there. Ownership of the leash is discussed, and it is decided that Orilus has legally won it; whoever may want it must challenge him to knightly combat. Ekunat does so at once, and he and Orilus agree to a date eighteen weeks hence. In the meantime Arthur, as judge, should keep the hound. At this point Jescute asserts herself, refusing to relinquish the leash (1500-1). The reasons for her possessiveness are not explained, nor does any character in the narrative express interest in her motives. Is it merely a whim? The audience is left with little evidence from which to interpret her actions. Perhaps she too has not finished reading the inscription, yet this is never suggested. Indeed, a search for personal motives will prove fruitless. But on a thematic level Jescute has bound herself and her husband more tightly to Tschinotulander and Sigune, becoming in this scene the counterpart of Sigune – succeeding where the latter failed. For she has and keeps the leash.

The interwoven structures of the plot develop in complexity as the competition for the leash continues. The narrative is often difficult to follow, but the narrator's omniscience allows us to oversee all the action and to interpret a given character's motivation. The reader is continually aided by *brucken* of commentary and explication. This detached perspective does not mean that Albrecht is uninterested in showing emotions or psychologically valid motives, yet he is concerned with these only as they help the plot along, in so far as they represent elements of the poetic structure he is building. As we have seen, this structure is mammoth and ideally able to stand alone, in a sense independent of any one character or even group of characters. Necessities of the over-riding pattern lead to inconsistencies in the plot and in the internal motivation of action, however. For instance, only when Ekunat tells of Sigune's plight (1504) is curiosity about the inscription aroused, though it seems unlikely that no one would have noticed the leash before this. Likewise incon-gruous is the account of Jescute reading the inscription aloud to the assembled court (see below pp. 143ff.). Its brevity seems hardly appropriate to an event of such significance but can be understood in terms of the total structure of the leash motif, in which this reading is a preliminary stage. Of impor-tance at this point is only that the tale miraculously banishes sorrow and ill will from its listeners (1506ff.). Even Orilus is affected:

1516 Zehant nu wart geworben   ein steter vride ganze,
      daz Orilus erstorben   was siner swester sun von
                                            einer lanze.
      swie zornes rich er uz geriten waere,
      des wart nu vergezzen   von dirre wunder schrifte
                                           sůzer maere.

The *deus ex machina* has made Orilus ready to forgive all, and he agrees to stay at court for the great *hohgezît*. The motivation behind this very important change of mind is thus external, fully independent of Orilus's personality. Orilus does not come to forgiveness through reasoning, nor is his mental or emotional transformation discussed by the poet. The leash has, like Peticru's bell, worked magic.[49]

The final appearance of Orilus in this section occurs over 400 stanzas later as Tschinotulander is preparing to depart for the east.[50] Throughout the jousting the young hero has taken the same oath of security from each defeated knight: a promise to accompany him to aid Akerin. Included in the large retinue is Lehelin, who is unwilling to undertake this adventure (1938). Neither is his brother Orilus happy with the state of affairs. He is described as being concerned about who will manage his lands and once more desiring vengeance on Tschinotulander (1938, 3–4).[51] Orilus also wishes to have his brother released from his pledge and offers in return to postpone indefinitely the joust with Ekunat, as long as Sigune might wish to keep the leash (1939)![52] The narrator stresses the tension of the moment with plaintive exclamations and rhetorical questions (1940, 1; 1941, 1):

1945, 3 do er [Lehelin] von siner sicherheit enbunden
           wart, wiez do ergienge?   daz vreischent noch di
                                        vremden und die kunden.

What might have happened will never be known, for neither Ekunat nor Tschinotulander can consent to such terms. Tschinotulander will continue to prove himself in knightly combat, and Ekunat will await the appointed joust.

What can be made of Orilus's actions? He is certainly consistent in his devotion to his family, but it is out of character both for him and his brother to evade battle, much less relinquish the coveted leash. Orilus's behaviour appears incongruous, and indeed, an explanation based on this character's internal motivation cannot be satisfactory. From the perspective of overall thematic patterns, however, this episode is consistent and rich. A resolution of conflict is placed tantalisingly within reach, a pattern which is repeated throughout the poem and which heightens suspense and irony for the audience. Furthermore, Orilus is showing himself consistent with his Wolframian prototype in the attempt to use bribery as a means of overcoming an unpleasant situation, for it is just this that Wolfram's Orilus resorts to in his joust with Parzival (above, p. 63). Many in Albrecht's audience would appreciate such a subtle allusion, as they would the masterful handling of thematic elements. The inconsistencies of character are not enough to disturb the structural patterns.

Looking back on this initial section of the poem we find that neither Orilus nor Jescute, nor Lehelin has been depicted in specific or individual terms. Orilus is an outstanding warrior, respected by the Arthurian court. The personal traits he manifests can be generally summarised: he is intensely protective of his kin, letting these loyalties overshadow his sense of propriety and courtesy and finally lead him to relinquish the coveted *brackenseil*. He appears proud, occasionally disdainful and impetuous, yet listens to reason and indeed yields. Jescute appears in an even less distinct light. She accompanies her husband silently, asserting herself only once in her desire to retain the hound. Her motives are left unexplained, and thereafter she fades into the background. Her physical attributes are conventional, those of a lovely lady of the court. We know nothing of her relationship with her husband. Lehelin achieves definition mainly in relation to his brother Orilus. He is beaten in an unspectacular joust by Tschinotulander and does not wish to fight in the east – both of these facts suggesting a lack of skill and courage quite unlike the formidable warrior of *Parzival*. Albrecht does not distinguish him in any way, through description, speech, action, or motivation.

It is significant that an analysis of these characters must become involved with other aspects of the narrative: the leash, battle scenes, the problem of plot motivation, and the complexity of the contextual and structural elements. This is a result of Albrecht's omniscient perspective and evenhanded treatment of the various actors in his tale. These secondary figures are not presented as fixed personalities but as variable factors, sometimes forceful, sometimes passive. Their tractability is essential, for like pawns they can be moved about according to the needs of the plot. Albrecht is not interested in providing a view into these characters' hearts, nor in viewing the action from within, through their eyes. This attitude is also seen in the lack of moralisation connected with individual action. Instead, the poet can be sensed standing outside of his story, directing it from an independent position. He is, in fact, conducting a fugue-like movement whose individual melodies are thematic strains rather than characters.[53] On the initial level of narrative sequence Albrecht often appears to lose control of his story, discarding an element such as Orilus's desire for vengeance, or the leash itself. On another level these incongruities can be seen forming a complex pattern of tensions.

In his architectural descriptions Albrecht carefully builds on the foundation supplied by Wolfram, seldom leaving out any fact present in his model. His method is similar in depicting characters. He incorporates objective facts supplied by Wolfram, such as family ties or heraldic devices and accoutrements, as well as subtler motifs such as Orilus's attempted bribe. The similarity of detail lends credence to Albrecht's tale as well as integrating it with the matter of *Parzival*. However, in Wolfram's poetry the physical descriptive factors are inextricably bound with the vital images conveyed through action and dialogue, and with the elusive yet crucial psychological ethos of each character. It is here that Wolfram excels: in conceiving and presenting the characters as living, feeling beings. Thus for Wolfram the physical beauty of Jeschute is as important a manifestation of her nature as are *wâpen* and dress for Orilus. In the JT these remain external appendages. Hence Albrecht's Jescute is lovely but lacks that very special beauty which distinguishes her counterpart in *Parzival*. Similarly Orilus bears the same heraldic device but is not the stalwart and irascibly jealous knight of Wolfram's tale. Though superficially resembling their prototypes, Albrecht's characters are different in ethos and in function, motivated in the later poem not from a consistent individual will but from the plot itself. As with architectural descriptions Albrecht incorporates Wolfram's material into a structure which is ultimately very different from its model. Both the buildings and the characters are in themselves incohesive and not easily visualised. They are not integrated experientially into dramatic action for they are structural rather than dynamic entities.

Subsequent appearances of Orilus and Jescute repeat and refine the patterns set in this first section. After failing to dissuade Tschinotulander, however, they disappear from the tale for nearly 2000 stanzas. Lehelin, on the other hand, appears several times in this section, though very briefly.[54] He is accused of *hochfart* and *ubermůt*, which Albrecht elaborates in a moralising aside on the virtues of *wol gemůt* versus the vice of *ubermůt*,[55] repeating the black and white symbolism of his and Wolfram's prologues (2404-6). Thus far within the JT Lehelin has not been shown to deserve this criticism. Rather Albrecht seems to feel comfortable judging *ex cathedra* without having to illustrate faults, and he also relies on familiarity with the Lähelin of *Parzival*. These vices and Lehelin's failure to pass the Virtue Test seem to mould him further into an emblematic character; he is gradually formed into a sinister 'type' rather than an individual. Later the narrator comments that none would mourn Lehelin if he were killed, blaming his *nides galle* (3593). A further allusion to Lehelin's lack of virtue is made as Tschinotulander saves him from death at the hands of a heathen king: 'er nam in uz dem tode,   des vergaz iedoch diu triwe sine' (4241, 4).

When the fighting in the east is finished, Lehelin's resentment of Tschinotulander has turned to hatred. His motivation repeats the earlier Orilus–Tschinotulander vendetta: vengeance for dead kinsmen. For during the battle another nephew has been killed (as was foretold, 1945; see above, n. 52). This recalls the death of Arbidol and the passionate hatred it aroused in Orilus, as Lehelin's intense mourning is reminiscent of Orilus's for Arbidol (4368). The Baruch attempts to amend the situation by asking Lehelin to surrender the leash to Sigune, promising him and his brother gold and other rewards (4386-90). Of the several questions raised by the scene, two are important for the present discussion: the assumption underlying Akerin's offer and Lehelin's reaction. The Baruch's proposal assumes that Lehelin and Orilus are interchangeable. That is, if Lehelin agrees, Orilus will give away the leash; by appeasing Lehelin, the hatred for Tschinotulander will be banished from Orilus's heart as well. Is Akerin merely a confused old man, misjudging the situation and his own influence, or is Albrecht himself equating the two brothers? The latter is unquestionably the case, in the sense that Albrecht is not concerned with the psychological identification of either personality, but with the idea or concept the brothers represent in Tschinotulander's struggle and with the way formal balance and continuity can be achieved in his tale. This perspective is likewise evident in the failure to relate Lehelin's reaction. A refusal is essential to the plot, and therefore it can be assumed that Lehelin refuses, though in fact his answer is not recounted or even mentioned. Here again Lehelin is important for the role he performs, for the *effects* of his action. Of the numerous stanzas devoted to Lehelin in this section none is intended to specify his characterisation. Rather each appearance complicates his enmity with Tschinotulander, thus identifying him with Orilus while emphasising his lack of virtue, crystallising him into a figure of evil. The juxtaposition of vice (Lehelin and Orilus) and virtue (Tschinotulander) supports the thematic network of the epic.

Albrecht's distinctive use of repeated patterns becomes especially evident in the concluding scenes concerning Orilus and Lehelin. In celebration of Tschinotulander's victorious return from aiding the Baruch another festival is held by Arthur. Lehelin and Orilus, however, mourn the deaths of both nephews and wish vengeance. A messenger reveals that Orilus has dishonourably invaded Tschinotulander's lands during the young hero's absence, killing two princes in the process. The court is shocked by this sin committed not only against Tschinotulander but against Gamuret whose lands they had been, and against Parzival for whom Tschinotulander held them in trust (4423–4).

There are discrepancies here with *Parzival* where Herzeloyde reports that Lähelin brutally conquered Waleis and Norgals but does not implicate Orilus (see above, p. 68). This is a crucial difference as far as the character of Orilus is concerned, making his actions unquestionably dishonourable and thus discrediting his standing as a respectable knight. Ekunat refuses to fight with Orilus, whose aggression against Tschinotulander's lands has broken a vow of peace, and the two brothers must bow to Arthur's judgement supporting Ekunat, but they are both embittered.

4428, 3 An eren sin die werden   hoch die frechen.
      Orilvs vnd lehelin   der mv̊t was svnder danc ir
                                    hazz nv rechen.

4429   Die flvst ir werden mage   waren sie so wegende.
      Daz alle die werlt mit wage   in die kvnige niht
                                    wer wider legende.
      Des wolten sie gewaltes haben pflihte.
      Vnd immer rewe tragende   daz sie ie erbvten kein
                                    gerihte.

4430   Sol wirde svchen ieman   sprach artvs der gewere.
      Vrlovbes sie zv nieman   da gerten wan sie dovht
                                    wie artvs were.
      Mit dem vz graswalt vnd dem vz kanadicke.
      Dem grimme rezzen lewen   waren da gelich ir
                                    ovgen blicke.

This passage echoes Orilus's previous angry departure from court. Resentful and angry, he leaves without bidding farewell; even the image of the lion reappears (above p. 78), this time applied to both brothers. Such repetitions help unify the plot of the JT, prodding the audience's memory by thematic and metaphorical allusion, with each additional motif adding to the structure. Orilus and Lehelin are not differentiated but merge into a sinister force, a challenge which must be met by Tschinotulander.

Familiar patterns are repeated in Jescute's behaviour as

well. She remains at court, refusing to give up the leash in spite of King Arthur's pleas to the contrary. Although her tenacity contradicts her presumed loan of the leash to Sigune (1868; see Chapter 3), it echoes her original refusal to relinquish it to Arthur. Her motives are not explained, there is no moral drawn from her action, but structurally her stance serves to augment the feud between Orilus and Tschinotulander. The remaining section reinforces the negative position of Orilus and Lehelin, crowned by their merciless attack on Kanvoleis and their temporary defeat by Tschinotulander and Arthur.[56]

Looking back over this part of the narrative, one is confused by the various events related and their actual importance in the plot. Within a section of 133 stanzas (4418–550) Orilus and Lehelin have appeared repeatedly, generally at a distance. Orilus's aggressive actions during Tschinotulander's absence are reported, Orilus and Lehelin depart in anger from Arthur's court, invade Waleis, and are forced to retreat after losing many of their supporters. In fact on the level of plot development almost nothing has altered, since the situation is the same at its end as it was at the beginning – namely, Orilus and Lehelin are an imminent threat to Waleis and Norgals. On the level of character depiction there has likewise been little change, since the action is generally viewed from a great distance and broadly sketched. Yet on a thematic level the point of the sequence becomes clear: Orilus and Lehelin are shown to be scoundrels, while Tschinotulander and his men are given a chance to prove their superiority as warriors (for Tschinotulander this confrontation is 'ein spil tocken', 4533, 2). One feels aware of the poet's care in arranging these matches to his main hero's advantage, continually postponing the final show-down which will necessarily end with the death of Tschinotulander. Whereas previously Orilus's wounded arm required suspension of their duel, here Lucius's challenge arrives at a decisive moment, reprieving the fatal joust and offering Tschinotulander yet another opportunity to demonstrate his prowess.

The final section treating these characters depicts Tschinotulander's personal confrontations with Orilus and Lehelin in
three episodes: Tschinotulander's penultimate and once more
inconclusive clash with Orilus, his joust with Lehelin, and his
final joust with Orilus. The scenes concerning Orilus are depicted with much more immediacy and realism, largely because
of their greater dependence on Wolfram.

At the close of the battle with Lucius (4652ff.) Tschinotulander's men are weary of battle, so the young hero resolves
to face Orilus and Lehelin alone. A short description of the
havoc wrought in the conquered lands further emphasises the
brothers' cruelty (4659-60). This serves as a prelude to the
confrontation between Orilus and Tschinotulander which is
related in some detail, beginning with an idyllic scene interrupted by Tschinotulander's arrival:

4860 Zv waleis in dem lande   des was er allez herre.
     Zv frevden er sich wande   wan er pflac der lande
                                   nahen vnd verre.
     Vnd lac zv velde mit siner trovten amien.
     In beiden frevde nahte   vnd wurden ovch an frevden
                                   gar die frien.
4861 Eins morgens da sie lagen   mit grozzer frevden fvre.
     Ez wil ein ritter wagen   mit tioste rich der rit vns
                                   durch die snvre.
     Die mere sagt ein knappe wol behende.
     Daz ist der vz graswalt   so wurd ich aller werdikeit
                                   ellende.
4862 Er ist also niht varnde   so was der knappe iehende.
     Sich ist die richeit sparende   vor disem gar mit der
                                   zimier al brehende.
     Er hat sich endecket aller kleide.
     Von graswalt des grvnen   der ist gelich der meien
                                   verwen heide.
4863 Verwappent wart da schiere   der den trachen fvrte.
     Mit richeit der zimiere   vil hohe in hie gein manheit
                                   rvrte.

89

Daz ez niht were tschionatulander.
Den west er in der wise   daz er in entsaz nach mer
                                danne zehen ander.
4864 Iescvten er nu kuste   e danne er zvm orse gienge.
Den schilt vor seiner brvste   solt er tragen daz er
                                darvf enpfienge.
Die tioste alsust bot im dar die clare.
Nv wart er in hie sehende   den der im erzeigen wolte
                                vare.

The narration here is remarkably detailed and dramatic in contrast with Albrecht's usual mode. A high degree of plausibility is achieved through attention to small details and natural dialogue. In the first two stanzas we are shown Orilus and Jescute relaxing in Waleis (Tschinotulander's rightful land), confident and happy.[57] When the idyll is shattered by a messenger who announces a knight wishing to do battle, Orilus's response seems involuntary and indicative of real apprehension, revealing a lack of confidence which belies his contented façade. Though this is not consistent with his behaviour thus far, it is effective here both as a credible psychological insight and as a fateful omen. Orilus's instinctive fear is of course justified, for Tschinotulander is the greater warrior, as the audience knows. But a joust between the two will be well-matched nonetheless and Orilus's tension increases the narrative suspense. His moment of fear passes when he is told the unknown knight is not wearing Tschinotulander's emblem,[58] so he arms himself quickly and kisses his wife as he departs.

These few stanzas contain many echoes of Wolfram's text both in content and in narrative technique. The setting itself recalls the isolation of Jeschute's tent in *Parzival* as does the couple's loving relationship (Jescute is here Orilus's 'trovte amie' as she was 'sînes herzens trût' in *Parzival*). The crack that shows in Orilus's self-confident façade hints at feelings of insufficiency similar to the insecurity suggested by his overreaction in *Parzival*, and plays subtly on the ambiguity of his position. His farewell kiss is yet another echo of *Parzival*.[59]

So far the scene has developed consistently and dramatically. The narrator maintains an omniscient point of view but moves closer to his characters than usual, allowing the momentum of their interaction to carry the plot along. He restricts his comments and lets dialogue and depiction of action suffice. In describing the ensuing battle the narrator reverts to a more distant vantage point:

4865 Vor dem pavilvne   musten sie nv tiosten.
      Von kriechen vntz an vedrvne   gesach nie man ein
                                 sper so klein zv brosten.
      Danne daz sper daz orilus da furte.
      Da mit er in den blvmen   gesaz als ob er satel nie
                                       gervrte.
4866 Nv wizzet ir wol durantze   der lie sich brechen selten.
      Daz beleip so gantze   des musten alle die mit valle
                                     engelten.
      Die da riten tioste gein dem iungen.
      Sam orilus der fvrste   mit snelheit qvam er wider
                                     dan gesprvngen.
4867 Ein swert begunde er ziehen   snellich vz der scheide.
      Der ander da niht fliehen   wolt er stunt da nider vf
                                     die heide.
      Sin orss bevalch er einem zwei mit stricke.
      Valtzone wart enblozzet   davon iescvte nam vil
                                     hertzen schricke.
4868 Der eine krei lalander   der ander graswalde.
      Des rvffes wol enpfand er   an den slegen iedoch der
                                     manheit balde.
      Was orilus mit starken slegen swere.
      Tribent siz die lenge   so wirt iescute gar
                                     vnfrevdenbere.

Though briefly described, this encounter is strongly projected on the reader's imagination. The similarities with the Parzival–Orilus battle are striking and the differences

91

enlightening. In both cases the point of view is omniscient (though in Wolfram's narration we consistently experience alongside Parzival) and little actual description of the fighting is given. Albrecht also conveys a more Wolframian sense of movement than in his other battle scenes.[60] Jescute's sudden recognition of Tschinotulander's sword, Valtzone, increases the dramatic tension and spatial reality of the scene as the reader is reminded of her presence at the battle and her fear for its outcome. Her identification of the sword amidst the fighting, though unlikely, is similar in effect to the details given as Parzival 'sees' Orilus's armour in *Parzival*. Her fear seems emotionally valid. The sudden change of focus to this figure on the side-lines is further indication that Albrecht is modelling this scene directly on his predecessor. In both cases the tension is heightened by the changed frame of reference. In Wolfram's text Jeschute is poignantly brought into focus by her nicely delineated gesture and her deep compassion for both knights. This vividness is in keeping with her central role in the conflict. In contrast, Albrecht's two brief references to Jescute are abrupt and fleeting. Her appearance here as elsewhere is too briefly sketched to leave a lasting impression, though her concern for Orilus's safety re-emerges later when she acts to halt the joust.

Before continuing with his tale the narrator shifts our attention from the scene for four stanzas, interrupting the flow of action to remark that he will not describe the match in detail, and then reviewing once more the reasons for enmity between the two men (4869–73), similar to Wolfram's disruption of the corresponding scene in *Parzival*. The battle continues briefly until Jescute realises that Orilus is losing and impetuously asserts herself by running up and flinging her arms around him (4875–7). She begs the combatants to cease (4878) and offers to give the leash to Sigune, but Tschinotulander responds that he must seek to win it by knightly contest, even though it might cost him his life (4879). The irony of this proud statement would not be lost on Albrecht's audience.

Though there are numerous specific reflections of Wolfram's text in Albrecht's portrayal of Jescute in this scene, her behaviour is fundamentally different from the Jeschute of *Parzival*. There she was passive, here she is active, even impetuous. Twice before in the JT she acted impulsively – when she refused to relinquish the leash (perhaps three times if we count her loan of it to Sigune). Here she impulsively does the opposite. Her rashness is thus consistent, though in each case her motives are left unrevealed. Here we can assume her behaviour to be motivated by love of Orilus and fear for his life. Her feelings are not analysed, however, for they are irrelevant to the immediate progress of the story. It is her actions that are crucial. Hence, in this and the previous cases it is justifiable to look for an explanation not in Jescute's 'character' but in the exigencies of the plot. Her former acts assured the continuous antagonism of Orilus-Jescute versus Tschinotulander-Sigune. Here her thwarting of the duel provides a further delay before the fatal clash, and her offer of the leash coincides with Albrecht's attempts to keep it a living force in the narrative (see Chapter 3).

Jescute's actions continue to vivify the leash motif and to provide suspense through her relentless efforts to avert the duel. In spite of the joy brought by the gold of blessedness,[61] she is now plagued by doubts about Orilus's fate and tries to cancel the need for a match with Tschinotulander by surreptitiously sending the leash to Sigune (4891–3). When Orilus discovers this he angrily accuses her of having shamed him (4899–903). Yet Jescute attributes her behaviour to a reaction to something Orilus himself said:

4905 Herre sol ich inhulden   danne iehen hie des waren.
    So lat mich vz den schulden   seit daz ich gehort bi
                                          minen iaren.
    Nie kein wort von ev alsus verzagende.
    Danne daz ich von ev horte   des was ich allen frevden
                                          wider sagende.
4906 Wan daz daz golt so reine   mir frevde hat enzvndet.

93

Die edelkeit der keine hat mir dise werdikeit
              gevrkvndet.
Der ich vil frevdenlos hie was engestet.
Von disem wort aleine was ich aller werdikeit
              entlestet.
4907 Daz wort lat vns doch horen seit orilus der kv̊ne.
Ir mvgt ez herre enboren zv fvge niht ir iahet wer ez
              der grv̊ne.
Vz graswalt so wert ir der verlorne.
Durch daz han ich die strange von mir gesant vor
            leide vnd ovch vor zorne.
4908 Frowe ir sit entschuldet ir kvnnet nach eren sorgen.
Ich wirde gein ev gehvldet tvsent libe den wolt ich
            wenic borgen.
Ob ich die gimme solt verliesen alle.
Ich west mich lieber toten danne ob ich stunde an
            werdikeit zv walle.

This dialogue is remarkably natural and gives a sense of immediacy to the exchange between Jescute and Orilus. It also
clarifies Jescute's motivation for interrupting the battle as
well as sending the leash, and thus offers a contrast to the
earlier scenes where there was no explanation for her
actions.[62] Orilus comes into clearer focus as well. Several
aspects of his tirade are reminiscent of his first appearance in
Parzival, though the pride and anger he expresses here do not
reach the emotional intensity of that lengthy monologue. This
is due in part to the formal necessities of Albrecht's long
line but also to differences in desired effect. Wolfram's
passage is marked by a crescendo of passion, as if Orilus were
speaking ever faster and with fewer restraints on his sense of
decorum and moderation. He ends with a firm denunciation
of Jeschute. In Albrecht's scene the dishonour Jescute has
brought her husband is less serious and the emotional level is
constant. In keeping with his calmer disposition Orilus allows
Jescute to explain herself and is at once won over and paci-
fied. It is not clear that Jescute is truthful in attributing her

fear to Orilus's own words, for it is easy to assume that she is herself uncertain of Orilus's ability to defeat Tschinotulander. Her words tie the scene effectively to the earlier one, however, and the ambiguity adds interest to the portrayal. In either case her explanation is the one least likely to anger Orilus or wound his pride; she in fact reinforces his self-confidence by explaining that her every action is based on his words – she certainly finds him more responsive to her logic here than in *Parzival*!

It seems clear that Albrecht has based this unit on the corresponding scenes of strife between Jeschute, Orilus, and Parzival in Wolfram's tale. He has incorporated several elements from the *Parzival* text (the kiss, the battle with Jescute as by-stander, dishonour at her hands, Orilus's anger and pride) as well as particular stylistic devices (use of dialogue, interrupted action). These reflections are especially effective here not only for the credibility they add to the figures of Orilus and Jescute but because they help integrate this episode chronologically into the *Parzival* text. Albrecht's dependence on the *Parzival* episode also explains the absence of certain elements which one might have expected – some sign of shock when Orilus recognises his opponent, or mention of his immediate reaction to Jescute thwarting the battle. These omissions indicate that Albrecht's primary intention in this scene is not to develop individual aspects of the characters involved but to motivate the larger themes of his plot while enhancing the formal continuity of the poem.

Tschinotulander's final confrontation with Lehelin verifies the lack of intrinsic interest given this figure in earlier scenes. For here Lehelin is quickly wounded by the again unrecognised Tschinotulander and then flees in humiliation along with his men (4948-50). The reader's final view of this knight is humorously grotesque as he and his followers push each other off a bridge in their hurry to escape. Thus Lehelin is dispatched as a negative element.

The occasion for Tschinotulander's final meeting with Orilus is carefully constructed to match the few geographical

details offered by Wolfram: the location in the Brizljân wood
where Parzival comes upon Jeschute and later Sigune (*Parzival*,
129, 5-6) not far from the Gral realm.[63] In Albrecht's tale
Tschinotulander returns from his battle with Lehelin to
Arthur's court where a sorrowful Sigune, arguing the model
of Enite, begs to accompany him on the rest of his adventures
(4977). When he refuses she asks that he take her to the Gral
where she can do penance and await his return. He agrees,
and as they set off on their journey the focus switches
momentarily to Orilus and Jescute and then abruptly returns
to Tschinotulander and Sigune who spend a night in innocent
conversation in the 'Precilie' wood before riding on towards
Munt Salvasch.

5006 Orilus der fvrste   die zwei gar vngesundert.
       Wol trvc mit der getvrste   des selben mich nu fvrbaz
                                 niht enwundert.
       Sin hoher mv̊t durch frevden flust in lerte.
       Daz er mit siner amien   sunder helf alein zv velde
                                   kerte.
5007 Mit einem pavilvne   gar sunder aller vorhte.
       Do daz die servidvne   geslugen vf iuncfrowen dinst
                                   in worhte.
       Daz sie in abent morgen koste brahten.
       Die liezzen sie zwei eine   so daz sie aber wider von
                                 im gahten.
5008 Der furste reit durch striten   zv walde vnd ouch zv
                                   velde.
       Iescute sin erbeiten   zv aller stunst   must ein in
                                   dem gezelde.
       Alsam erek er sie mit im niht furte.
       Iedoch dieselbe schvlde   in hie gein strite von ir
                                   straffen rvrte.

The couple are pictured in an idyllic setting. Their tent is
pitched in an isolated landscape and they are content with
each other's companionship. Orilus self-confidently pursues

adventure while his faithful wife attends him. Except for her complaint about being left behind, this scene not only echoes the earlier one in the JT (above, pp. 89ff.) but coincides closely with its counterpart in Book 3 of *Parzival*.

Appearing unexpectedly in the account of Tschinotulander's and Sigune's journey towards Munt Salvasch, these three stanzas have a desultory effect, yet they fulfil a number of functions. By alluding so explicitly to the scene of Parzival's first meeting with Jeschute, they remind us of that episode and its consequences. For it is just after Parzival's departure from Jeschute's tent that Orilus returns, fresh from defeating a young knight who is later identified as Schionatulander. Thus Albrecht is carefully reminding his audience of the fateful implications of the impending meeting. By shifting our attention so suddenly, the poet emphasises the simultaneity of action and also heightens the dramatic irony implicit in each pair's ignorance of the other's proximity and of the imminent tragedy it signals. The now quite unmistakable similarities between the couples are multiplied: both alone in apparently uninhabited country, both young and in love, both women compared to Enite. That Orilus is here blamed for his conduct towards Jescute can likewise be seen to refer obliquely to Tschinotulander. The parallels heighten the tension and the sense of tragic destiny, developing sympathy for Orilus and Jescute. Albrecht does not achieve this by portraying them in detail, for neither their specific actions nor their conversation is reported, nor does he omnisciently probe their thoughts. But through the careful orchestration of themes and motifs he shapes Orilus and Jescute into a kind of mirror-image of Tschinotulander and Sigune.

The actual meeting of Tschinotulander and Orilus occurs with no introduction by the narrator:

5017 Iedoch sie fvrbaz zogten   vnd funden schone wite.
     Vil iamers groz bevogten   sigunen wil nu hie von
                                         disem strite.

Zv rossen der geschach mit einer tioste.
Der furste von lalander   orilus hie reit mit richer
                   koste.
5018 Die richen vnd die grozzen   sie beide an manheit
                   waren.
Der hovbet nach die blozzen   begunden hie nv
                   veintlich gebaren.
Zv hovbt kunden sie die helme stricken.
Sigun ir liehten ovgen   nie bekant in also leiden
                   blicken.
5019 Da sie die orss ensprengen   so ritterlichen kunden.
Der magde hertze twengen   der schrik began sie da
                   bi den stunden.
Zv der erden viel sie vngeschriet.
Ey frow auentevre   moht ir vns haben diser mer
                   gefriet.[64]

This rather cursory rendering does not emphasise the climactic potential of this moment as dramatic narrative but rather its formal, symbolic elements. Sigune's fainting serves as a portent of disaster and also as an allusion to Jescute's presence as a spectator in previous battles.[65] Similarly the vision of Orilus, richly outfitted, bearing down on Tschinotulander, recalls again the battle in *Parzival*. His description is not elaborated nor is the action rendered with any spatial dimension, so the figure tends to hover emblematically before us. The sense of abstraction is heightened as the narrator interrupts to discuss his own sorrow in having to relate such a sad tale. Praising Tschinotulander's virtues at length, he calls on 'frow auentevr' to defend the tragic ending (5019, 4–5027). She responds that the young hero is indeed the epitome of virtue and is doomed to lose the battle only because Orilus received the magic gold (5028–30). Thus the climactic battle is clearly prepared for in structural terms, through an unprecedented concentration of allusions and thematic doubling, and in explicit terms by the narrator's hesitation and Frou Aventiure's explanation. There is no attempt to create tension or emotional identification with the characters. The action is seen not from their point of view but from the omniscient perspective of the narrator and his listeners who have known the outcome of this battle since the beginning. The mode of narration carries the audience directly to an interpretive level, pointing out the significance of the event within the plot structure and drawing broader moral conclusions. It is in keeping with this pattern that the joust itself is disposed of in less than three stanzas:

5031 Hie lit die magt erschricket   hin lief daz pfert
                                                                verlazzen.
          Die tiost wart gezwicket   mit hurte rich sie beide
                                                                niht gesazzen.
          Die sper von grozze sich mit noten spielten.
          So daz die lufte kleine   der spriezzen oben in der
                                                                hohe wielten.
5032 Sie beliben bi einander   geschirbet vnd gezirret.
          Sam doners blicke glander   sich zv tal in einen bovm
                                                                verwirret.
          Vnd also stet zvrizzen vnd gespalten.
          Der craft zv beiden siten   kvnden hie die sper geliche
                                                                walten.
5033 Der ein viel zvr erden   fvr tot mit einer wunden.

Amid flying sparks and thundering blows the fatal deed slips by in a single, perfunctory line (5033, 1). We are given no chance to contemplate Tschinotulander's fall, for attention turns at once to Orilus:

5033, 2 Der ander wol begerde   des pfaffen in dem hertzen
                                                                an den stunden.
              Mit solher not het in die tiost erschellet.
              Danne ackrines presente   sunder danc must er da
                                                                sin gevellet.

Orilus's sudden remorse comes as a surprise; at the very moment of achieving his long-desired goal, he is filled with misery and pines for the solace of confession. The somewhat improbable sequence of lines in stanza 5033 cannot give us insight into Orilus's character, but points out the gravity of his deed and befits the aura of piety which pervades the entire scene. Orilus's function here is to underscore the presentation of Tschinotulander, and of Sigune, as paragons of virtue. This becomes even more apparent in the next few stanzas as the shaken Orilus turns to Sigune and revives her.

5036, 3 Hiemit gie der edel zv der magde.
         Alsam ein einhvrne   daz da die magt veht in dem
                                           geiagde.

5037   Aber sunder schozze   so wart der helt gevangen.
         Ir zene mit vnder klozze   tet von sinem wappen
                                     ein gvldin spangen.
         Darnach ein wenic towes mit der hende.
         Davon die magt ein kleine   der craft enpfant an
                                      frevden die ellende.

With striking simplicity Albrecht captures an image of tenderness and solicitude: Orilus – called the *edel*, the *helt* – gathers dew in his hands to gently rouse Sigune.[66] The image of the unicorn and the maid, though at first incongruous at this point in the narrative, elevates Orilus's repentence as well as Sigune's extreme grief to a symbolic level. In *Parzival* the unicorn possesses beneficial magical powers,[67] and in bestiary allegorisations it is often interpreted as Christ (since legend had it that only a virgin could capture a unicorn, as only Mary could receive Christ in the Incarnation).[68] Surely Albrecht did not intend his audience to read his allusion so programmatically, yet no doubt he intended it to be recognised. Furthermore, a typological relation between Sigune and the Virgin Mary would not be inconsistent with Sigune's penance, her devotion to the images of Christ's passion, her hermitage, or her pietà-like pose in the later episode. Orilus's penitence is raised to a new level of meaning by his gesture of submission to Sigune, his compassion, and his utter repentence as he offers Tschinotulander both Waleis and Norgals if only he will live (5040-1). Within the formal structure this represents another variation on the bribery theme, and a foreshadow of his later offer to Parzival. Getting no response from the fallen hero, Orilus departs alone (5042).

The inconsistencies in Orilus's portrayal here are numerous. If he is to be seen as an individual with some continuity of attitude and personality, his sudden expression of pious remorse is unacceptable and nothing short of a miracle. He has killed many great warriors in his day (including Galoes) and has not been bothered with pangs of guilt. Thus while his extreme reaction significantly heightens the tragedy of Tschinotulander's death, it is out of keeping with the portrayal of Orilus. A further incongruity arises in that such sorrow is inconsistent with the peace of mind brought by the gold of blessedness. Albrecht might have suggested that Orilus's change of heart coincided exactly with Parzival's taking the gold from Jescute where she lay only a few miles away. This would have been too much of a coincidence, however. Rather he merely mentions Jescute's loss of the gold, pointing out that if the joust had occurred somewhat later, Tschinotulander would have been the victor (5034-5). Furthermore, Orilus's remorse does not integrate smoothly with his appearance in Book 3 of *Parzival* where he shows no trace of this emotional state. He is no longer looking for a priest and forgiveness, but in fact yearns to repeat the battle just won (*Parzival*, 135, 19-24, see p. 52 above). Elsewhere in the Wolfram text Orilus again speaks lightly of what according to Albrecht was the most tragic moment in his life (*Parzival*, 271, 8-9).

As a reflection of the tragic implications of Tschinotulander's death, however, Orilus's role assumes consistency and significance. For every aspect of Orilus's portrayal in this scene contributes to the idealisation of Tschinotulander. Orilus's remorse and sudden piety, like his fear earlier, suggest an almost involuntary insight into the gravity of his action. Tschinotulander is distinguished from all the other knights Orilus has killed in his career. Orilus's solicitude towards Sigune shows a similar awakening to new values, and the depth of her misery likewise heightens the tragic ethos of her beloved's death. Ragotzky has persuasively argued (pp. 115f.) that in his final speech Tschinotulander represents the epitome of Christian humility, assuming as his personal guilt the guilt of the world. This is supported by the depiction of Orilus. Indeed, each element of the episode elevates the tragedy of Tschinotulander's death. Orilus, however, appears as a contradictory figure. From the headstrong and essentially villainous warrior who cruelly subjugated Tschinotulander's lands, he has changed into a pious, repentant man. His defeat of Tschinotulander transforms him like a blinding revelation. Although the JT abounds with pious moralisations, the audience has not been prepared for Orilus's contrition. The discrepancies in his portrayal are left unresolved as he rides away, disappearing from the narrative for over 700 stanzas. He will reappear just once more and be finally defeated by Ekunat, at which point all signs of his remorse have vanished (see below, pp. 104f.).

For Albrecht, secondary characters like Orilus have a dual role to play, and this leads to the inconsistencies in their presentation. On the one hand Albrecht is interested in them as characters – he troubles to adopt as many aspects as possible from Wolfram's *Parzival* and thus to identify them as specific figures. He also shows them at various points in his narrative and attempts to integrate their behaviour into his plot and to motivate their action on a narrative level. That he is aware of the problems he encounters is evidenced by the many points at which he purposely avoids troublesome complications. For instance, his treatment of Orilus's feelings after killing Tschinotulander is clearly in conflict with Wolfram's text. To continue his story by relating Parzival's encounter with Jescute (which follows almost immediately within the tale's chronology), or even Parzival's second meeting with Jescute and his battle with Orilus, would entail either extensive qualification of his own narrative or open contradiction of Wolfram's. Albrecht avoids this by omitting both scenes entirely.[69] On the other hand, it is clear that Albrecht's interest in his secondary figures as personalities is limited in comparison to Wolfram. For in the JT the characters play a second role which is ultimately of greater importance: their function as supporting elements for his major themes. The inconsistencies and lapses in character only show that for Albrecht these figures have not taken on a life of their own. Neither can the audience therefore conceive of them as existing beyond their brief appearance in a given scene. Rather they come to represent more abstract values – forces, ideas. Significance resides in their 'Demonstrationswert',[70] yet they cannot be called symbols, for they are not consistently drawn on this level either; nor are they subsumed into a clear allegorical structure. Yet at times they do attain symbolic status, especially by the time of their final appearances in the text. This befits Albrecht's concern with proper endings. His work achieves closure in offering a terminating glimpse of each figure and pointing out the significance of his or her fate. Albrecht's figures do not exist beyond our seeing of them, nor can they exist beyond the end of his massive tome. Rather their ends, like that of the JT itself, must be representative statements with implications reaching beyond the subject matter at hand. Orilus's death represents the symbolic culmination of Tschinotulander's section of the story, for with Orilus's defeat the young hero is avenged, and in the course of the battle the leash is cut to pieces. Albrecht's treatment of Orilus in his final appearance, and his portrayal of Jescute's equally symbolic fate, demonstrate his treatment of these characters as themes within his vast symphony – altered each time they appear, yet always recognisable, and ultimately subordinated to the whole.

If we turn briefly to Orilus's final battle we can see how

Albrecht interlocks various themes of his narrative. The match between Orilus and Ekunat is described in vivid language using a steadily intensifying image of fire (5792–829). The technique is similar to Wolfram's means of charging the atmosphere of a scene through general effects rather than detailed observation. The passage is rich with allusions to *Parzival* and to earlier scenes in the JT, creating a complex texture of motifs. In these repetitions Albrecht is calling the themes to a formal close in a sort of grand finale. The actual battle begins abruptly (5798) and is portrayed as the confrontation between two helmets, an image recalling the Orilus–Parzival joust in Wolfram's text as well as the initial joust between Orilus and Tschinotulander in the JT.[71] Here one helmet appears alive with dragons, the other is wrapped with the brilliant *brackenseil* (5800–4). Jescute's futile attempt to halt the struggle (5805) echoes her earlier intervention between Orilus and Tschinotulander. Whereas before she actually influenced the action, here her failure expresses the finality of this match. Her fainting (5810) relates this scene to Tschinotulander's fatal joust when Sigune fainted, and like that scene recalls Herzeloyde's collapse at the news of Gahmuret's death (see above, p. 98).

At last Orilus falls, cut in two by a Gral sword,[72] and as he is destroyed, so too is the leash, the cause of the conflict. Our sense of Orilus as an individual personality is unimportant here. He is the picture of a mighty warrior, a type identified through the details of his *wâpen*. He is shown throughout the scene in a positive light, his superb skill as a knight emphasised and his virtues praised.[73] The evil Orilus who cold-heartedly took over Tschinotulander's lands is forgotten, as is the pious, shaken killer of the young hero, for these faces are no longer relevant. Orilus's death is the final expiation for Tschinotulander's. It means the close of Tschinotulander's story, and details can only be trivial. Thus in the space of two stanzas Orilus is defeated, eulogised, and disappears from the narrative. One feels again the presence of the poet bringing the narrative strands to a close. Orilus is one of these strands, intricately woven into the texture of the JT, tinted with different hues to fit the pattern of the moment.

Albrecht's narration of Jescute's fate makes concrete the increasing similarity we have observed between her and Sigune, for in describing her final year he specifically compares the two women:

5830 Iescute was nu lange   gelegen in vncrefte.
     Durch der vnselden strange   swo nach wip ir krieges
                                 sint alhefte.
     Die prvfen nach daz in wer baz zv wenden.
     Iescute vnd sigvne   von kriege wurden sus der frevde
                                 die ellenden.
5831 Seht wie sigvne klagete   mit klage iemerliche.
     Vil klegelicher sagete   iescute vnd was der k[l]age
                                 wol zwier so riche.
     daz was ir reht sigune klagt nach wane.
     Iescute von waren schulden   da von so wart sie
                                 klage nu nimmer ane.
5832 Ein kloster in prvrine   da man den fvrsten legte.
     Ob ein die klagende pine   die kuniges frvht von
                                 karnant sich wegte.
     Daz ez zv horen nieman kvnd erliden.
     Wie er leid ez die vil klare   der ez da mut vnd hertze
                                 kunde versniden.
5833 Vil kovme gein einem iare   moht siz vertriben.
     E daz die edel klare   die klag must von vnkraft lan
                                 beliben.
     Alsam daz rot den stahel vn isen izzet.
     Also tut leit dem hertzen   swo liebe rehter trewe
                                 niht vergizzet.

Jescute's fate is nearly identical to Sigune's. Just as both were helpless onlookers to fatal battles and fell unconscious in their misery, here both retreat from the world to mourn the deaths of their loved ones and soon die from their sadness.

Jescute is said to lament even more than Sigune, for she is guilty of 'wâre schulden'. Jescute's misery, however, is an expression of her 'rehte trewe' and her sincere repentance (5833-4).

Having subtly counterbalanced the two women at several points, Albrecht here joins them together on a symbolic plane. As representations of virtue they are now indistinguishable, having reached a sort of unity on a thematic level. Through repetition of motifs Albrecht has raised the closing of both their stories above the particulars of the *maere*.

Albrecht's mastery is most manifest in the crescendo of this last section with the necessary intensification of themes and allusions. Here one feels he is in his true element, in a genre with more similarity to the allegorical finesse of the *Roman de la Rose* than with the character-oriented narrative mode of Wolfram's works. He is bridging these two forms, and neither extricates himself fully from the structure of the one nor finds consistent expression in the other. Albrecht is a long-winded story-teller whose strengths appear most evident where he is forced to concentrate his narrative. High points such as the final scenes of Orilus and Jescute remain somewhat isolated, however, as the focus turns to other characters. For instance, Albrecht's reflections on Jescute are abruptly followed by the conclusion of Ekunat's story:

5836, 1 Ekvnat vil wunden   von im da het empfangen.

Such juxtapositions are anti-climactic, unsatisfying on a structural and narratival level. Yet, as we have seen, Albrecht's estimation of conclusions necessitated proper finishes for all concerned. The closing episodes demonstrate clearly the bifurcation of purpose in Albrecht's approach. On the one hand, explanations for individual actions are offered in specific cases, yet finally the behaviour of any given character is subordinated to external forces. The incentive comes from the frame itself. In the final scenes with Orilus and Jescute, motivation comes from the structural and thematic denouement which successfully closes up all obvious gaps and symbolically completes the last circle of narrative. In earlier episodes impetus came from a variety of momentary requirements of the plot. It seems clear that Albrecht's Jescûte is basically a shell, a court beauty with conventional attributes who manifests different personal characteristics in different scenes of the poem according to thematic necessity. Her piety springs no more than Orilus's from internal resources, or from a belated understanding of the leash's message. Jescute's withdrawal from the world is a final gesture of homage to both Orilus and Tschinotulander and like all her actions serves the overriding purpose of Albrecht's message.[74]

In the depiction of secondary characters, basic differences between Albrecht's and Wolfram's narrative techniques emerge with clarity. Wolfram's style is dramatic in that the action unfolds before the audience. A coherent perspective is provided as we view a series of events mainly through the protagonist's eyes, often sharing his ignorance. The hero is thus a sort of surrogate for the listeners who experience the narrated events through him. This technique establishes an empathetic relationship between character and audience. The secondary figures in *Parzival* are depicted with a refined psychological insight and maintain consistency as personalities within a single scene and throughout the poem. Through vivid gesture and dialogue they achieve a poignant reality, adding depth and richness to the world of Parzival's adventures. This impression is heightened by the repetition of narrative patterns and images which subtly enhances the unity of the tale. In addition the audience is challenged to active participation in the tale not only on the level of plot but on that of narrative artistry leavened with irony.

Albrecht's narration, in contrast, is generally undramatic and shows little attempt to engage the reader as a participant. An intellectual distance is maintained by frequent disruption of time and place, a tendency to summarise events rather than recount action, and discontinuity within the character depictions themselves. The reader is stimulated to exercise mind and memory by recognising allusions and subtle interconnections, but not to experience the tale emotionally or to identify with specific figures. Thus analogues and repeated patterns supplant personal characterisation in defining a scene or explaining an action.

Albrecht's secondary characters function primarily in two capacities: as catalysts to move the plot along and as recurrent theme-bearers within the structural network of the poem. Their importance as thematic elements becomes especially apparent in the latter part of the JT where motifs re-echo and merge into concluding emblems. The story of Orilus and Jescute is initially paralleled with that of Tschinotulander and Sigune in the competition of both couples for a single object. The pattern of contrasts and analogies continues until Jescute and Orilus are finally brought into the shadow of Tschinotulander and Sigune as though they were imperfect reflections of the latter.[75] Jescute's jealous tenacity alternates with generous sharing of the leash as Sigune's insistence on having it yields to her claiming its insignificance. The pattern of inconclusive battles, near resolutions, interrupted idylls, and final tragedies supports Albrecht's moralised structure, bringing the lives of these characters within a scheme of *lêre*. Albrecht's comment on Jescute's fate places her emblematically within a general message: the excessive joy brought by the leash must be counterbalanced by sorrow (5835). Albrecht's language itself reflects the essential pattern of opposites and balance.

3. PLOT MOTIVATION: THE GRAL AND THE 'BRACKENSEIL'

The stories of Parzival and Tschinotulander are built around each hero's quest for some elusive object - in one case the Gral, in the other the *brackenseil*. These motifs sustain the narrative focus, motivate the plot, and ultimately come to symbolise an essential purpose guiding the composition of each poem. The differences between the motifs and in their treatment - as objects and as objectives - further delineate the differences in ethos which separate the two works.

THE GRAL IN *PARZIVAL*

To examine the Gral motif in *Parzival* is to pursue the organic structure of Wolfram's poem, for the presentation of this theme is closely bound into the unfolding story of Parzival himself. Though not mentioned, the world of Munsalvaesche is already present in the opening books where Gral and courtly realms are joined in the union of Herzeloyde and Gahmuret, and this dual heritage passed on to the young Parzival. From his first glimpse of it in Book 5 the Gral realm becomes an explicit factor in Parzival's story, entwined into his consciousness and into the portrayal of his evolving character. As the Gral becomes an obsession for Parzival, it finally becomes inseparable from his identity. Though the Gral itself actually appears only twice in *Parzival*, the motif is developed through a number of episodes. First revealed as an object of mystery, the Gral grows as a concept to include a way of life and a system of ideals. It also changes as the objective of Parzival's quest as its ethos becomes increasingly central to his own goals. Similarly the audience is led to reinterpret its significance as the Gral changes from a magical *dinc* at the centre of an esoteric cult to the symbolic focus of a Christian ideal.

Within the story of Parzival, the Gral realm can be seen as the external manifestation of the hero's drive for self-realisation. His very nature compels him to be what he is. Thus, when he first hears of the chivalric world of Arthur's court he at once sets out to find it. There he proves himself a paragon of knightly virtue, attaining the heights of traditional courtly values, *êre, minne, prîs*. Parzival's destiny embraces another realm as well, though at first he is no more aware of it than as a boy he was aware of the world of chivalry. Just as with his earlier initiation, once he learns about the world of the Gral he cannot rest until he has found it. This is a more difficult process, and its stages – Parzival's gradual assimilation of the ideals of the Gral world – are outlined for the hero and for the audience through Wolfram's careful orchestration of the Gral motif.[1]

The Gral is not introduced to the audience or to Parzival until Book 5, after the young hero has mastered the chivalric arts. Here Parzival is made welcome at a mysterious castle where he witnesses a resplendent and fantastic ritual – the ceremony of the Gral. Just as the reader visualises the architecture of this strange place through Parzival's eyes, so too is the ceremony viewed from the hero's perspective, with each event described in order as it passes cinematically before him. No explanation is given to Parzival – in fact he is not told the name of the object nor of the place – and Wolfram restrains his narrative comment as well (see above, pp. 19ff.).

In this first episode the Gral appears as an object which can fulfil all worldly needs. The *dinc* is the centre of an enigmatic celebration strangely characterised by the paradox of great splendour and deep sorrow. The presentation of the Gral is the high point of the ceremony, and Wolfram devotes many lines to the foregoing procession without mentioning the Gral itself. Thus he builds up curiosity and dramatic tension over the significance of the spectacle as we share Parzival's wonderment and sympathise with his confusion. As the Gral is carried before Parzival, Wolfram's narrator names it for the audience:

235, 23   daz was ein dinc, daz hiez der Grâl,
                 erden wunsches überwal.

The events at Munsalvaesche have all converged on this
moment.[2] Wolfram has imbued his descriptive account of
riches with tense excitement, leaving his audience bewildered
yet transfixed along with Parzival. The Gral enters the story
at the same moment it enters the hero's life, and with the
same degree of mystery. Though the audience is told that
Parzival should have asked a question, the placement and brevity of the narrator's reference serve to heighten the aura of
magic rather than clarify the issue. He offers no comment at
the presentation of the lance or the Gral, but only with the
gift of the sword (240, 3-9). He will not be hurried in his
explanations and explicitly defends his method of story-
telling in the much-discussed bow metaphor (241). We, like
Parzival, must wait *sô des wirdet zît* before learning more
about the Gral. This image suggests Wolfram's awareness of
the dramatic potential in his narrative technique and his un-
willingness to lessen this through omniscient commentary.

The subtlety of Wolfram's skill is exemplified in his depiction of events on the morning following the ceremony. The
audience shares in Parzival's confusion at finding Munsalvaesche deserted, and despairs as the drawbridge clanks shut
behind him. The way to Munsalvaesche is now physically
impassable, and it will gradually become evident that it is
barred to Parzival on another level as well. As Parzival finds
himself alone outside the castle he does not realise that for
the next five years his life will be bound by a quest to return.
Wolfram alludes only vaguely to the sorrow which Parzival
will endure for having once seen the Gral and lost it (248,
6-13). Parzival's real adventures begin only now: 'alrêrst nu
âventiurt ez sich' (249, 4). In this first episode the object itself
has played a major role. The aura of magic is strongly suggestive of pagan rituals; it is as though Parzival has wandered into
an enchanted forest. Although he will intrude unknowingly
upon the Gral realm in Book 9, neither Munsalvaesche nor

the Gral itself will appear again in the foreground of action until near the end of the tale. Yet this realm has entered his life, and its significance will from now on grow increasingly more obvious to him and to Wolfram's audience.

The following scene takes the hero to a place physically and spiritually between the Gral and courtly worlds. Here the motif is elaborated and undergoes a subtle change. Parzival loses track of the Gral horses, but for the second time comes upon his cousin Sigune. In their first meeting (138, 9ff.) Sigune told Parzival his name and lineage, the lands and consequent responsibility he had inherited. Here too she imparts valuable information, with a brief account of the Gral family, Anfortas's sorrow, and finally the great significance of the question Parzival failed to ask. There is still an element of magic in her description of the Terre de Salvaesche, especially in her lengthy explanation of the sword (253, 24–254, 19), yet the overall emphasis in this scene has moved away from the Gral itself to focus on its context – the land and people of Munsalvaesche – and its powers:

254, 26   den wunsch ûf der erden
               hâstu volleclîche:
               niemen ist sô rîche,
               der gein dir koste mege hân,
               hâstu vrâge ir reht getân.

It is clear that Sigune only touches the surface of the Gral's mysteries, but the audience, like Parzival, is tantalised by the additional information. Sigune's outline of the Gral hierarchy at once clarifies and obscures, for in revealing only part of the truth, it hints at undisclosed complexities. She says nothing of her own or Parzival's place in the family tree, nor does the narrator clarify this for his audience. We must accept each piece of the puzzle as it falls to Parzival and be patient with the gradual emergence of the poet's design as we accompany Parzival on his dilatory progress towards enlightenment.

Sigune functions here as a catalyst, for it is she who sets

Parzival towards the conscious goal of rediscovering Munsalvaesche and the Gral through the information she imparts
and through the challenge of her angry denunciation.[3]
Although her explanations are by no means complete, she has
revealed much more than just the names of Terre de Salvaesche
and some of its inhabitants. She has provided a context for
the *groezlîch wunder* Parzival saw there as well as for the
forebodings of his dreams (251, 26; 245, 1ff.). For she assures
him that the potential gains have been lost forever. Parzival
now learns that, had he but asked a question, he would have
all he desired on earth. Sigune deems his silence to be a lack
of compassion and predicts that his failure will never be overcome but will shadow him the rest of his life:

255, 20   ir lebt, und sît an saelden tôt.

255, 26   ze Munsalvaesche an iu verswant
           êre und rîterlîcher prîs.

It is through conversation with Sigune that Parzival first
becomes aware of his failure at Munsalvaesche and the scope
of its consequences. This represents the first step in his understanding. The focus is on the unasked question, and it is this
he repents as he rides off. Neither Parzival nor the audience
can yet know the full extent of what has been lost, for the
Gral's blessings have been presented in worldly terms (also
254, 26f. quoted above, p. 112):

250, 25   diu ist erden wunsches rîche.

252, 5   wan swaz die lüfte hânt beslagen,
           dar ob muostu hoehe tragen:
           die dienet zam unde wilt,
           ze rîcheit ist dir wunsch gezilt.

Yet coupled with this image of earthly power are suggestions
of more abstract values, for Parzival has lost not only *êre* and
prîs but also *saelde*. Sigune presents the inhabitants of Munsalvaesche as perfect in virtue, fully deserving of the happiness
Parzival could have given them.

113

The mystery of the Gral realm has been enhanced by this episode while the Gral's relevance to Parzival's life has been partly revealed. As Parzival's cousin, Sigune embodies the promise of the hero's own dual nature, and through her Wolfram has linked the world of Munsalvaesche to Arthur's court geographically and thematically. The return to Terre de Salvaesche is thus established as a transcendant goal for the unhappy Parzival, even though Sigune insists that it cannot be found by searching for it. Munsalvaesche has become at once more tangible and more intangible.

As Parzival rides on, he grieves over his failure to question Anfortas. When the hero's feelings about the Gral are next mentioned, he is said to be preoccupied with two weighty burdens: longing for Condwiramurs, his wife, and sorrow for his failure at Munsalvaesche:

296, 5   sîne gedanke umben grâl
                unt der küngîn glîchiu mâl,
                iewederz was ein strengiu nôt:
                an im wac für der minnen lôt.

The narrator says that *minne* was the greater burden. This is understandable not only because of the emphasis in this passage on *minne*, but because of Parzival's still limited awareness of his fatal relationship to the Gral and the Gral kinship. Thus far, the world of Munsalvaesche has been a source of sorrow and failure for him. Before it can become his primary objective, the concept of the Gral must evolve and expand further in his awareness.

Cundrie's denunciation of Parzival at Arthur's court constitutes the next episode in the development of the Gral motif, although no specific insights into the nature of the Gral or Gral society are given.[4] This passage serves rather to illuminate the gravity of Parzival's failure at Munsalvaesche and to humiliate him in front of Arthur's court, thereby corroborating Sigune's prediction and reaffirming the necessity for his quest. The high drama of the scene is emphasised by the lengthy and powerfully visual description which accompanies Cundrie's arrival at court. Wolfram presents Cundrie to his audience just as Parzival and Arthur's court see her.[5] Her ghastly, unearthly appearance underscores the intensely bitter and damning force of her message, and the awesomeness of her figure as well as the content of her words augments the aura of supernatural power which surrounds the Gral. Her judgement rings forth with seemingly unredeemable damnation:

316,7   'gein der helle ir sît benant
ze himele vor der hôhsten hant:
als sît ir ûf der erden,
versinnent sich die werden.'

Cundrie's speech is the climax of all the events thus far related to the Gral.[6] With each episode the motif has grown in metaphorical dimension as well as in catalytic power within the plot. From complete ignorance of the Gral's existence, Parzival now perceives it as the driving force in his life. When he voices his own feelings in this scene, he admits that the search for the Gral has become uppermost in his mind:

329, 25   ine wil deheiner freude jehn,
ine müeze alrêrst den grâl gesehn,
diu wîle sî kurz oder lanc.
mich jaget des endes mîn gedanc:
dâ von gescheide ich nimmer
mînes lebens immer.

He does not comprehend the significance of this quest but feels shamed and begins to question the meaning of his failure (330, 1 ff.).

Cundrie's denunciation and the subsequent scenes serve to isolate Parzival from Arthur's court in several subtle ways. In a short episode following her departure, an unknown knight accuses Gawan of dishonourable deeds and challenges him to a duel in forty days' time. This most obviously establishes a parallel between Gawan and Parzival, and brings Gawan into the foreground of the action. Furthermore, the agitation of this concluding section detracts from the disturbing lack of curiosity on the part of the court about the Gral and Parzival's experiences at Munsalvaesche.[7] Wolfram's audience too is led away from Parzival by the narrator's focus; they, like Arthur's retinue, are given no opportunity to question. Parzival's actions themselves draw attention away from his plight, for instead of trying to cope with his own dilemma he is depicted selflessly aiding Clamide and learning more about Feirefiz from the heathen woman.[8] He seems to be acting quite alone, however, amidst great activity. It is as though he were already excluded – no one pays his plight much attention, no one can support him (331, 8-10), there is no specific goal towards which they can aid him. Gawan, on the other hand, responds immediately with action, and the other knights follow his example. Thus the contrast between Parzival and the Arthurian world is subtly extended.

Yet another important narrative element is added here as Gawan bids farewell to Parzival: 'dâ geb dir got gelücke zuo' (331, 27). Parzival responds with uncharacteristic violence:

332, 1   Der Wâleis sprach 'wê waz ist got?
           waer der gewaldec, sölhen spot
           het er uns pêden niht gegebn,
           kunde got mit kreften lebn.
           ich was im diens undertân,
           sît ich genâden mich versan.
           nu wil i'm dienst widersagn:
           hât er haz, den wil ich tragn.'

Religion has played only a minor role in the poem thus far. Parzival's understanding of it is apparently based on his mother's advice to him as a child (119, 18-30), her explanation elicited by a naïve entreaty remarkably similar to Parzival's words to Gawan: 'ôwê muoter, waz ist got?'[9] Now Parzival rejects the God who he feels has turned against him. He shuns

Christianity and, shunning Arthur's court as well, goes forth alone, determined to be self-reliant in overcoming whatever inadequacies he may possess. Thus Parzival rejects those aspects of the civilised world which he has come to know. He has excelled in the courtly realm almost instinctively, yet this has not prevented his failure. Religion, not a powerful force in his life thus far, seems to him similarly impotent. There is a felicitous paradox in Parzival's gesture of angry self-reliance, for here, at the moment when he first consciously sets out to find the Gral, he rejects that which is essential to its discovery: humility and faith in God. As he sets out so defiantly and alone, it is as if a chapter of his life has closed.[10] The Gral, still an unknown quantity, is the incentive which draws him towards a long period of lonely searching.

In these first three episodes concerning Parzival and the Gral (Munsalvaesche, Sigune, Cundrie) the concept of the Gral has been transformed from a kind of magical cornucopia to the symbol of a way of life shared by a select group of people. The Gral itself is mentioned only in passing by Sigune and Cundrie, yet its power as an image has continually increased. Just as Parzival cannot forget the Gral and the company he saw at Munsalvaesche, so too the audience is continually reminded of the Gral world as a separate yet present realm. Even in the following two books where Gawan and his adventures usurp the stage, the tale of Parzival and the object of his quest remain strong undercurrents. This is achieved by Wolfram's subtle paralleling of Gawan's and Parzival's adventures.[11] Gawan's sure course repeatedly crosses the track of a mysterious knight known only for his love of a lady named Condwiramurs and his urgent search for the Gral. Wolfram's skilfully interwoven glimpses of Parzival maintain a constant awareness of his struggles. Thus contrasted with Gawan's exciting and often amusing escapades, Parzival's steadfastness and solitariness are subtly emphasised. Likewise the gaps in this fragmented view of Parzival's adventures must be filled by imagination. His unseen exploits take on an epic scope and a randomness which could not be achieved through straightforward narration (witness the confusion that results in the JT from attempting to detail Tschinotulander's career). Though Parzival's search for the Gral is scarcely referred to in these books, Wolfram makes sure that it is not forgotten.

In Book 9 the narrator returns to Parzival and his relentless quest. This central book is the crux of the poem and of the Gral motif. Parzival, once more the main figure, is marked by a series of encounters: with Sigune, a Gral knight, a family of pilgrims, and Trevrizent. Each episode is narrated with remarkable freshness and poignancy as an independent vignette, while together they maintain suspense about the success of Parzival's search. Although the Gral motif is not explicitly present in all of the episodes, they form successive stages which prepare Parzival to achieve his goal. The theme which pervades is the importance of faith in God as essential for personal salvation as well as for achieving entry into the Gral kingdom.

The Gral theme is raised at once when the narrator interrogates Frou Aventiure about Parzival's attempts to reach Munsalvaesche. As Parzival's story is taken up again we find him riding through a wood where he comes upon a newly built hermitage. Inside he finds his cousin Sigune mourning her dead lover.

435, 10   der junge degen unervorht
                reit durch âventiur suochen:
                sîn wolte got dô ruochen.
                er vant ein klôsnaerinne,
                diu durch die gotes minne
                ir magetuom unt ir freude gap.

Several factors are striking about this encounter. First of all it is not by chance that Parzival happens upon Sigune for the third time. Rather, God seems to have guided him: 'sîn wolte go dô ruochen'. This recalls Parzival's first approach to the Gral castle when he let his reins fall in a similar fashion. Though the narrator made no specific reference to God's intervention at that point (224, 19–21), the scenes are clearly parallel. Secondly, the physical and spiritual proximity of the Gral realm is suggested by the fact that Cundrie arrives from Munsalvaesche each week with food for Sigune.[12] As before, Sigune inhabits a realm midway between the Gral and courtly worlds and represents a link between the two. When Parzival last met her she appeared as the symbolic guardian of the exit from Terre de Salvaesche and condemned him as he departed. His encounter with her now further suggests that Parzival has returned to the proximity of Munsalvaesche, and her kind encouragement holds a promise for his success. Thirdly, and most important for our present discussion, the tone of this scene is strongly devout. The episode begins with a reference to God's concern for Parzival, and Sigune's piety is stressed not only in her manner but in a direct statement by the narrator:

435, 25   ir leben was doch ein venje gar.

Parzival himself appears less impetuous and more mature as he explains his quest. His life is still governed by two forces, first his search for the Gral and then his love for Condwiramurs:

441, 11   nâch ir minne ich trûre vil;
            und mêr nâch dem hôhen zil,
            wie ich Munsalvaesche mege gesehn,
            und den grâl: daz ist noch ungeschehn.

As before, Parzival does not grasp the meaning of the punishment he is suffering, but his previous bitterness has turned into sorrowful resignation. The subtle echoes emphasise his determination. Sigune too serves to remind the audience of past events, and the contrast between her former bitterness and present compassion is striking. She tells us nothing more about the Gral, only that she is nourished by it. But, after enquiring about his search, she sends him in the direction Cundrie has taken with a wish that God may help him find

119

Munsalvaesche and his joy. With her encouragement and bless-
ing she is in fact recanting her earlier position that the Gral
cannot be found by searching for it:

442, 9   si sprach 'nu helfe dir des hant,
       dem aller kumber ist bekant;
       ob dir sô wol gelinge,
       daz dich ein slâ dar bringe,
       aldâ du Munsalvaesche sihst,
       dâ du mir dîner freuden gihst.'

Parzival's encounter with Sigune is imbued with the presence of God as no other episode in the poem has been. When
Parzival loses Cundrie's tracks the narrator pessimistically
remarks, 'sus wart aber der grâl verlorn' (442, 30). Yet it is
clear that Parzival is within the Gral forest, for in the following scene he is challenged by a *templeis* for trespassing on the
territory of Munsalvaesche (443, 6ff.). After winning this
rather comic battle by default, Parzival realises he must be
leaving the Gral kingdom, for no one else challenges him.
Given his objective it is of course somewhat inconsistent that
no attempt is made to follow the *templeis* (though he is
across a ravine!). In fact, this episode at first glance appears
to be a set-back in the hero's progress and of little conse-
quence in the emergence of the Gral motif. Yet, by inserting
this vignette (it has no counterpart in Chrétien's poem),
Wolfram has introduced a number of thematic elements which
greatly enrich his tale. First, this joust demonstrates that
Parzival is close to his goal, yet suggests once more that the
Gral cannot be achieved through *rehtiu manlîchiu wer* alone
(451, 19). Secondly, Parzival does prove himself the superior
warrior – or at least charger! – and as token of his victory
takes possession of his opponent's horse, a Gral horse, another
sign that he is nearing his objective. It is because of this horse
that Trevrizent later mistakes Parzival for Lähelin, who also
won a Gral horse by jousting with a *templeis* though he killed
his opponent. The ambiguities in the ironic parallels between

Lähelin and Parzival are crucial to the presentation of Parzival's
failures and to the precision of Book 9's thematic structure.[13]
Wolfram is careful to nudge his audience to attention by
directly comparing Lähelin and Parzival (445, 21ff.). Hence
this minor episode constitutes a further plateau in Wolfram's
treatment of the Gral motif.

Weeks pass in a few lines, and Parzival's isolation is emphasised by Wolfram's brief sketch:

446, 3   desn prüeve ich niht der wochen zal,
                über wie lanc sider Parzivâl
                reit durch âventiure als ê.
                eins morgens was ein dünner snê,
                iedoch sô dicke wol, gesnît,
                als der noch frost den liuten gît.
                ez was ûf einem grôzen walt.

A chill day brings Parzival's next encounter, this time with a
group of pilgrims. Neither Munsalvaesche nor the Gral is mentioned here, though the snow recalls Parzival's sorrow after
his first visit when it also snowed in Terre de Salvasche.[14]
Furthermore, this episode enhances the increasingly pious
atmosphere of Book 9 and is integrally linked to the portrayal
of Parzival's religious awakening. As a turning point for
Parzival it cannot be overlooked in a discussion of the Gral
motif, for the emphasis here on Christian faith and love provides the impetus which finally leads Parzival to Trevrizent
and the way back to the Gral.

Parzival's encounter with Sigune was strongly devout in
tone, and this scene emphasises religion still more, especially
the formal, traditional aspects of Christianity as opposed to
Sigune's more personal piety. This encounter spurs Parzival
on, and the vignette depicts his character and his inner suffering with remarkable poignancy. The simple love of these
people, the obvious warmth of their family relationship, and
the sensuous attraction of the girls' beauty all serve to emphasise Parzival's lonely struggle and inability to find a place for

himself. Furthermore, Parzival is faced with his own physical and spiritual disorientation. Not only is he wandering in an unknown wood, he has lost all track of time. He is unaware that it is Good Friday and that this day should have a meaning for him. Wolfram's audience is also temporally disoriented, uncertain of the time that has passed since Parzival rode away from Arthur's court in Book 6. The precise setting of the scene in the Christian calendar at once continues the pious mood of the Signune episode. In reminding Parzival of the meaning of the day, Kahensis stresses God's *triuwe* and man's sinfulness. That Parzival is now ready to take such a lesson to heart is symbolically indicated by his presence once more in a place not far from the Gral or from those who are links to that realm.

Kahensis's homily is very appropriate to Parzival's situation,[15] and its impact on the young hero is heightened because of the human context in which it is delivered. For it is on this level that Parzival most clearly responds. The Grey Knight and his family represent an ideal blend of Christian piety and human warmth made vividly appealing in contrast with the solitariness of Parzival in his chilly armour. They are maintained by their love of God, each other, and their fellow man. The invitation to share their food and fellowship is presented with a subtle emphasis which recalls the first Jeschute scene, for the focus turns to the daughters – warm, lovely, and feminine:[16]

449, 26   Parzivâl an in ersach,
            swie tiur von frost dâ was der sweiz,
            ir munde wârn rôt, dicke, heiz:
            die stuonden niht senlîche,
            des tages zîte gelîche.

Here again we seem to see through Parzival's eyes, and the suggestion is then made explicit, as in the Jeschute scene, by the narrator's comment (450, 1–8). Yet, as in his first encounter with feminine charms, Parzival does not react as we are led to expect. Here he is clearly aware of the girls' beauty

– he notices it at once (above) and again when he returns to them, when the appreciation is reciprocal:

451, 27   die juncfrowen im sâhen nâch;
                 gein den ouch im sîn herze jach
                 daz er si gerne saehe,
                 wand ir blic in schoene jaehe.

Parzival does not see them as an amorous challenge, as the narrator would suggest. Their loveliness is an inspiration to him, helping awaken in him a sense of the futility of his defiant independence and leading him to ponder God's *hilfe*. The pilgrims have provided temporal and physical orientation on more than one level, for through them Parzival is shown a world removed from that of chivalric exploits, a world whose value he recognises yet which he senses he is unprepared to join. His awareness of this incongruity is a sign of the progress he has made towards his goal.

Parzival's isolation is vividly demonstrated as he departs courteously and begins to consider his plight. He belongs to no order. The inappropriateness of his armour to the chill weather implies the inadequacy of the chivalric world to his present needs. Neither can he accept human compassion and love of others as a solution. He is blessed with many chivalric virtues – here the narrator names *manlîchiu zuht, kiusch unt erbarmungen*, and *triuwe*. Yet these alone have not been enough. Now his hatred for God begins to waver as his inborn *riuwe* rises in his heart:

451, 8   sich huop sîns herzen riuwe.
                 alrêrste er dô gedâhte,
                 wer al die werlt volbrâhte,
                 an sînen schepfaere,
                 wie gewaltec der waere.

This crucial realisation that God may help him, that perhaps he cannot achieve his goal alone, is a climactic turning point for the hero. The aura of these good and devout pilgrims draws Parzival back. Quickened again by the radiating warmth of the girls' beauty, he departs once more, much less politely, giving his horse its head for God to lead if he will. This deliberate act is as much a gesture of desperation as a challenge.[17] One feels the crisis of the moment strongly. Parzival realises he cannot carry on in the way he has for so long. He has rejected the comradeship of the pilgrims, and by retracing his steps he likewise rejects knightly self-reliance as an answer. His earlier encounters in Book 9 have led to this, first Sigune's attempt to direct him and then his aborted joust with the Gral knight. Each provided a link with his goal yet left him finally alone. In this third encounter the underlying theme at last becomes dominant: the importance of personal faith without which neither chivalric virtues nor human love can assist him.

Giving himself up to fate is thus an acknowledgement of a further possibility, symbolically an act of faith, met immediately by the intervention once more of the hand of God as Parzival's horse takes him to Fontane la Salvatsche, the home of the hermit Trevrizent. The compact narration leaves little doubt that Parzival is no longer wandering aimlessly and that the forthcoming encounter will be important:

452, 29   an dem ervert nu Parzivâl
            diu verholnen maere umben grâl.

The narrator generally functions as a vehicle for transmitting the story as it happens and rarely announces significant developments in this way. At this critical point in the plot, however, he interrupts in order to address his audience directly on the recension of the Gral story. Here Wolfram again defends his narrative technique against his critics, blaming the constraint of his source for the delay in clarifying the nature of the Gral: 'mich batez helen Kyôt' (453, 5).[18] The effect of the narrator's intervention is twofold: first, it gives credibility to the poet's information by documenting a source; secondly, the passage creates a distinct break

in the narrative thread, thereby serving as an emphatic introduction or prologue for the following events. Having established the reliability of his material, Wolfram returns to
Parzival's confrontation with Trevrizent. The poet has carefully set the stage for the most crucial episode in Parzival's
development as a character as well as the hero's and the
audience's understanding of the Gral's significance.

The narrative continues as Parzival approaches Trevrizent,
confesses his sinfulness, and asks for help. His first words to
Trevrizent are framed by a redundancy:

456, 25   mit grôzer zuht er vor im stuont.
            er tet im von den liuten kuont,
            die in dar wîsten,
            wie die sîn râten prîsten.

457, 4   'nu sagt mir wer iuch wîste her.'
            'hêr, ûf dem walt mir widergienc
            ein grâ man, der mich wol enpfienc:
            als tet sîn massenîe.
            der selbe valsches frîe
            hât mich zuo ziu her gesant.'

Parzival's double testimony emphasises the pilgrims' role
once more, yet it has further implications. This kind of repetition with variation is similar to the *laisses similaires* which
have been discussed by Ryding as a feature of rhetorical
amplification in chansons de geste.[19] Ryding's analysis of the
use of this device seems appropriate here: 'Furthermore, the
procedure tends to be used at points in the story that constitute lyric peaks, moments of moral beauty, rather than at
moments when the development of the plot has to be understood' (p. 78). Here the repetition frames Parzival's confession of sin (456, 29–30), indeed a moment of moral beauty
marking a turning point in his life. In addition, the repetition
of his exchange with Trevrizent makes the dramatic irony in
Parzival's words unmistakable: we have seen Parzival give
himself over to God's guidance and have witnessed his direct

progress to Trevrizent's cave. Clearly God has led him hence, but he himself is still not ready to acknowledge the full presence of God's hand in his fate. Yet at this very point he is acknowledging God, a crucial step towards a full understanding of his power.

The theme of divine intervention is continued in Parzival's initial refusal to relinquish his horse's reins (458, 20f.), for this recalls yet again how he was brought here – by giving the reins over to God. Thus when he does pass them to Trevrizent we must sense the symbolism of the gesture.[20] Aided by the pilgrims, Parzival began to recognise his need for help[21] and now, however hesitantly, he is able to accept the offered warmth of a fire and human compassion. From Trevrizent Parzival learns that more than four and a half years have been spent on his fruitless quest. Thus the hermit, like the pilgrims, helps Parzival to locate himself within a temporal scheme, an initial stage in the complex process of self-realisation to come. As before, the audience must absorb the information and adjust along with the hero. When Parzival expresses anger at God for having allowed him to suffer so much and confesses his rejection of Christianity (461, 1–26), Trevrizent responds at length, instructing Parzival on God's grace and his wrath. Thus an episode resonant with the piety of Trevrizent's manner and mode of living emphasises Christian teaching in the opening section. From here the discussion turns to the Gral which Parzival says is his greatest sorrow (467, 26f.). Trevrizent responds with a lengthy explanation of the Gral stone which he calls *lapsit exillis*. He discusses several aspects of the stone: its effect of prolonging youth, its life-sustaining qualities, and its means of calling people to its service. Each of these attributes augments the Gral's established aura of mystery and power. In addition, Trevrizent alludes twice to a direct connection between God and Gral. He tells of the appearance of a dove each Good Friday, bringing a wafer which refurbishes the Gral's power. This allusion to Christian ritual is striking, yet typical of Wolfram it remains unelucidated. Similarly no mention is made of the coincidence that this day is Good Friday. The hermit goes on to relate that in the early history of the Gral God sent the neutral angels to earth to guard it, and he has provided for its protection ever since:[22]

471, 26   des steines pfligt iemer sider
                 die got derzuo benande
                 und in sîn engel sande.

Whatever the ambiguities, a direct relationship between God and the Gral kinship is suggested, placing the world of Munsalvaesche in a different sphere from the rest of humanity, a distinctly Christian sphere.

All information about the Gral in this section has come through Trevrizent's own words in the course of direct dialogue; thus Wolfram's audience learns along with Parzival. From a magical *dinc* the Gral is emerging as a highly charged symbol of moral and Christian purity, growing always within the framework of active narrative. This pattern continues as Parzival boasts that he deserves to be called to the Gral, and Trevrizent counters this with a lecture on humility and moderation. The irony of both positions would not be lost on the audience. Likewise, as Parzival gradually learns the full extent of his lineage and his sins, the implications become clear to Wolfram's listeners as well. The web of the Gral world has been complicated and Parzival's paradoxical position clarified; he is at once closely bound to that world and firmly barred from it. As Trevrizent speaks (477–84), the audience must share Parzival's interest in the tale as well as the anxiety that has kept him from revealing his final sin: his failure to help Anfortas. Wolfram's narrative technique has maintained tension throughout this scene by leading the audience again to experience each revelation along with Parzival. As the complexities are revealed the suspense continues to mount over Parzival's remaining confession. When at last the truth is out, Trevrizent's response is remarkable for its wisdom and compassion. Even the hermit's initial expression of sorrow is expressed gently:

488, 21   der wirt sprach 'neve, waz sagestu nuo?
           wir sulen bêde samt zuo
           herzenlîcher klage grîfen.'

Although he accuses Parzival of not using his wits properly (26-7), he does not condemn or reject him but sustains him. This support is subtly expressed in his use of *neve* and his unbroken use of the familiar form of address.[23]

This is a moment of denouement for Parzival and for the plot, as the hero confronts all his past misdeeds and his true identity. Trevrizent does not allow the young knight to dwell on his agonising guilt, but with wisdom and humane insight urges him not to grieve overly or to falter but to trust in God's compassion. He quickly turns to the subject of the Gral and engages Parzival's attention with an explanation of the ceremony of the lance (489-93). Astrology and the occult figure strongly in his account, recalling the atmosphere of magic and mystery surrounding Parzival's original visit to Munsalvaesche. The hermit then describes the selection of the Gral company and something of their ethical code (493-5). Here his terminology is strongly Christian and God's closeness to the Gral realm is stressed. Parzival's remaining fourteen days with Trevrizent are not described in detail. The young knight, having abandoned all external values when he set off in defiance from Arthur's court, is guided by Trevrizent to a highly personal conception of Christianity.[24]

The aura of the Gral world is greatly amplified in Book 9. In spite of the details given about the Gral's origin and nature, the object itself remains secondary to its symbolic value, to the concept of the ideal Christian society which it serves. The expansion and intensification of the Gral motif establish in both Parzival's and the audience's minds an awareness of the higher level of existence towards which Parzival is striving. A close bond between Christianity and Munsalvaesche becomes manifest not only directly, as in God's guiding of Parzival's horse or in Trevrizent's speeches, but indirectly through the strong religious mood which pervades Parzival's main encounters. Physically and spiritually isolated from the courtly world, Fontane la Salvatsche establishes an island of Christian serenity in the centre of the poem. When Parzival leaves this place behind to continue his struggle, he is no longer completely alone.

Parzival is inspired with renewed determination by his stay with Trevrizent. As he rides off once more one is reminded of previous departures. At several points he has set off alone from what have been essential stages in his education.[25] In four of these his departure is preceded by some discussion of God, and there seems to be a definite hierarchy in this sequence. Herzeloyde's simple explanation of God accompanies Parzival as he leaves her for Arthur's court. That he interprets his relationship to God in chivalric terms of service is clear in his bitter rejection of God as he departs from Arthur's court. His concept of God has begun to alter as he rides off (twice!) from the Grey Knight and his family. Now finally, with Trevrizent's help, he comes to a new understanding of God, one not so distant from his mother's, but one he has had to struggle to achieve. He must continue his quest 'des willen unverzagt' (502, 28) in the only way of life he knows, but his understanding of his quest has changed. He has learned from Trevrizent to remain undaunted in courage and in faith, *an got niht verzagt* (489, 16). Whereas before he was trying to find the physical route back to Terre de Salvaesche, now his tireless striving is itself an expression of faith and personal patience, obedience to God's will. The Gral has become part of him.

For the next four books the adventures of Gawan once again occupy the foreground. Thus the central book is structurally framed and set apart from the surrounding narrative, just as Parzival's experiences in that book are isolated from events in the courtly world. The intensity of this central section is heightened by its isolation, and its spiritual content is emphasised by the contrast with the Gawan episodes during which Parzival's quest for the Gral, imbued with new meaning, continues again in the background. In Book 13 Parzival reappears in an episode which returns him temporarily to the courtly world and brings Gawan's adventures to a satisfactory conclusion. Wolfram's focus returns to Parzival's mission again at the close of Book 14 where, seeing the joy of those at Arthur's court, Parzival realises his own *freude* is not to be found there. His great love for Condwiramurs sustains him in his quest for the Gral; the two now seem inseparable forces in his life.

732, 19   sol ich nâch dem grâle ringen,
                 sô muoz mich immer twingen
                 ir kiuschlîcher umbevanc,
                 von der ich schiet, des ist ze lanc.

Parzival leaves the realm of the Round Table physically and emotionally behind him, realising it cannot be his world:

733, 17   gelücke müeze freude wern
                 die endehafter freude gern:
                 got gebe freude al disen scharn:
                 ich wil ûz disen freuden varn.

The transcendent ideals of the Gral realm have become his own and he can accept no less. This solitary departure culminates the series of leave-takings. Now he has achieved an unprecedented level of understanding and faithful resignation to God's will: 'got wil mîner freude niht' (733, 8), and his heart does not falter: 'wand ez nie zageheit gepflac' (734, 26).

In Book 15 when Parzival returns momentarily to Arthur's court in the company of his half-brother Feirefiz, it seems as though an earlier scene is about to be replayed. Feasting and celebration are interrupted by the arrival of Cundrie bearing the Gral emblem (778, 23), but this time her message is joyful – Parzival is to be Lord of the Gral. The high drama of this scene is intensified through a lengthy, detailed description of her appearance which Wolfram offers just as she rides up to Arthur's circle. As on the occasion of her first appearance, Wolfram's audience experiences wonder and shock at this exotic apparition along with Parzival and the court. Cundrie's speech makes clear the vast influence of the Gral realm over which Parzival will rule. She assures him he will want nothing there.[26] This recalls the original description of the Gral:

235, 23   daz was ein dinc, daz hiez der Grâl,
            erden wunsches überwal.

but goes far beyond the imagined scope of that first image. In the final lines of her speech Cundrie reflects on Parzival's conduct:

782, 29   'du hâst der sêle ruowe erstriten
            und des lîbes freude in sorge erbiten.'

Her words distinguish between the satisfaction of the soul and that of the body. She clearly implies that Parzival has already achieved the first (*der sêle ruowe*) – his personal peace with God – and is now ready for the second, which the Gral can offer him (*des lîbes freude*). Correspondingly, Parzival's search for the Gral has not been in essence geographical but spiritual, a Job-like testing of faith and fortitude. The distinction made here between *der sêle ruowe* and *des lîbes freude* is consistent with the depiction of the Gral's power throughout *Parzival*. We have watched the growing importance of personal faith in God as a prerequisite to Parzival's success and have seen the Gral motif extend outward to embrace the values of Christian piety. Yet it is also true that the Gral itself does not provide these values for Parzival. The spiritual forces associated with it come to it, not from it. As we have seen, when the specific powers of the Gral are detailed, they are worldly in character – the dispensation of food (238–9), Sigune's description of its temporal

power (252, 5-8), and even Trevrizent's elucidation of its
power to sustain life (469) or dispense the good things of the
earth (470). Thus while intimately associated with God, the
Gral does not give blessedness or joy (like the *brackenseil*)
but gives of the earth's bounty to those who already live in
the joy of God's love.

The various manifestations of the Gral motif are brought
to a culmination in Book 16 where Parzival returns to Munsalvaesche and asks the healing question. Here the Gral reappears in the narrative foreground with its magical aura
intact, while the power of God is manifest as the overriding
shaper of events. Reflections of Parzival's previous visit cast
light on both episodes. As Parzival and his companions ride
towards Munsalvaesche the scene changes to Anfortas, who is
kept alive by being taken to view the Gral every four days
(788, 23ff.). The magical, exotic quality of the first Gral
descriptions is again evoked through astrological and occult
references. That Anfortas must look upon the Gral to be
aided underscores its hermetic aspect. The lengthy description of Anfortas's lavishly ornamented bed recalls the impression of riches and luxury at the castle when Parzival first
visited there, creating an atmosphere redolent of exoticism
and the supernatural.[27]

Even as Parzival and Feirefiz approach the castle Wolfram
maintains tension by the near tragedy of Feirefiz's charging
the *templeise* who have come to meet him and his brother.
Here one recalls Parzival's overreaction to the jester on his
first visit. The two knights are received with joy and escorted
to the hall, scene of Parzival's initial failure which he can at
last make good. The posing of the question demonstrates
Parzival's changed awareness of the Gral's significance, as the
intimate compassion of his words reflects the depth of his
own real love and kinship.[28] The hero faces in the direction
of the Gral, genuflects three times, and asks the compassionate question. Thereupon Anfortas is healed – by God.

795, 30   der durch sant Silvestern einen stier

796, 1   Von tôde lebendec dan hiez gên,
                unt der Lazarum bat ûf stên,
                der selbe half daz Anfortas
                wart gesunt unt wol genas.

Although the mystery of the relationship between the Gral and God ʼor Christian dogma is not made clear, it is unquestionable that the hand of God has directly intervened. The implication of God's protection and guidance of Parzival has culminated in this act, at once healing Anfortas and fulfilling Parzival's destiny to become Lord of the Gral. Thus at Munsalvaesche Parzival's quest began and has ended.

Parzival has achieved his ultimate goal through faith and perseverance.[29] The Gral itself, the mysterious *dinc*, has appeared to his eyes only once, but its aura has grown steadily since that first vision, imbued with a Christian power unequalled by any relic or other holy object. The climactic moment stresses the religious, not the magical aspects of Gral ritual. Wolfram has consistently developed the motif throughout the poem, always aiming at this culmination.

The healing of Anfortas represents the completion of Parzival's quest, and the Gral, brought forth only for *hôchgezîte*, appears once more in the narrative at a joyful celebration which repeats the original ceremonial presentation of the Gral. Wolfram reminds us of the sadness surrounding Parzival's first visit and vividly contrasts the present scene as though it were a clarified reflection. As with Jeschute, Parzival has been granted a chance to redeem himself. In these final episodes he retraces his steps, now bringing the joy he was destined to impart.

The celebratory presentation of the Gral provides the motivation for Feirefiz's conversion, a miraculous tale recounted with generous humour and abounding with parallels to the saga of Parzival's redemption. Feirefiz cannot see the Gral as Parzival could not 'see' its significance. Feirefiz admits a desire to see it, though his wish is clearly secondary to his longing for Repanse's love.[30] Virtuous *minne* is thus the sustaining force behind his Christian salvation, as it was for Parzival. And, like his half-brother, Feirefiz mistakenly assumes he can achieve God's grace through knightly battle (814, 25–30), for neither can fully imagine what it is they seek – the visual properties or the essence of the Gral. They must first accept, then faith will reward them. For both Feirefiz and Parzival the Gral is made manifest only when each has made himself ready for it. First *der sêle ruowe*, then *des lîbes freude*. It is Christian faith that performs the miracle; the appearance of the Gral is the sign that Feirefiz has become a Christian, it is not itself the agent of his conversion.

In this final section of *Parzival* Wolfram terminates the many narrative threads carefully woven into his tale.[31] Condwiramurs is reunited with her husband (800–1); Trevrizent modifies his account of the neutral angels (798); Kardeiz is crowned king over Parzival's lands outside the Gral realm (803); Sigune is buried (804–5); and Feirefiz departs to spread Christianity in the east (820–3). The final summary of Loherangrin's adventures is like an epilogue, a reminder of the distance between the harmony of Terre de Salvaesche and the courtly realm's imperfection, as well as of the bonds joining the two worlds.

The Gral is the binding motif throughout Parzival's story. Though not overtly expressed in the first two books of the poem, it is symbolically present in Herzeloyde's genetic bequest to her son. Parzival has inherited ties to two worlds. His mother joins him to the Gral kinship and his father to the courtly world of chivalric prowess. Herzeloyde and Gahmuret thus represent the two realms in which Parzival slowly matures and which finally comingle in him.[32] The Gral motif openly enters Parzival's life as an external catalyst and gradually becomes an internalised drive toward the fulfilment of his heritage. This change occurs subtly as Wolfram unfolds the story before his audience, refraining from inter-

pretation and allowing the motif to emerge naturally in con-
junction with Parzival's experience. Though Parzival starts
out on a search for his mother, the Gral becomes instead the
object of his quest. This substitution is rich in symbolic overtones, for Herzeloyde represents Parzival's link to the Gral
family. His quest is therefore a continuation of the search for
his mother as well as an attempt to achieve the full expression of his own identity – his proper place. Furthermore,
Anfortas is Herzeloyde's brother, and Parzival's final relief of
his suffering can be seen symbolically as atonement for having
caused his mother's sorrowful death.

Parzival searches for an inscrutable object and for unknown
rewards. He is confused, yet he is driven to continue, to make
himself worthy of rediscovering the ideal realm of Munsalvaesche. He learns to repent and to await the time of his *heil*
(783, 15). The Gral motif evolves, just as Parzival himself
evolves. This motif is not an object which can be plucked out
of its context and examined like a geological specimen. It
exists through its effect on events in the poem. It exists in
the mind of the poet and the lives of his characters, from
which it is inseparable. Wolfram's gradual unfolding of this
motif may well have made his audience impatient, especially
those already familiar with the story through Chrétien's
romance. It is likely that criticism of his technique and doubts
about the authority of his sources were aired after the first
section of *Parzival* itself was made public (probably Books
3–6), where Wolfram introduces but fails to elucidate the
Gral.[33] Whether as a defensive reaction or a preventive mea-
sure, Wolfram defends his narrative technique at several points
in his tale, and specifically in relation to his handling of the
Gral motif. Twice he reassures us that his reticence is well-
founded, and in Book 9 he acts indirectly as his own literary
critic, not merely defending but analysing his method. However brief, this insight is invaluable in demonstrating Wolfram's
awareness of what we have found to be the essence of his

narrative technique. Preceding the long-awaited disclosure of the Gral's history, the narrator alludes to his impatient critics and attributes his restraint to the demands of his source, Kyot:

453, 1   Swer mich dervon ê frâgte
            unt drumbe mit mir bâgte,
            ob ichs im niht sagte,
            umprîs der dran bejagte.
            mich batez helen Kyôt,
            wand im diu âventiure gebôt
            daz es immer man gedaehte,
            ê ez d'âventiure braehte
            mit worten an der maere gruoz
            daz man dervon doch sprechen muoz.

The stylistic instructions related by the fictive Kyot[34] are in fact consistent with Wolfram's technique as revealed in his portrayal of character and setting. The superiority of Wolfram's method is corroborated by the highest authority, for it is Frou Aventiure herself who instructed Kyot on this manner of presentation: to speak of each element only when it achieves its natural place in the developing *maere*. Thus Wolfram's treatment of the Gral motif exemplifies that aspect of his narrative technique which he defends in his famous bow metaphor.[35] We have seen the Gral motif emerge through a series of controlled stages, carefully bound into the rich conceptual and formal structure of the poem. Consequently, even an audience already familiar with the plot will feel tension and suspense, be humoured and challenged and teased, and always led to experience events along with the drama of Parzival's life.

THE *BRACKENSEIL* IN THE JT

Wolfram leaves much about the Gral unexplained. Albrecht undertakes to remedy this by relating its early history in detail as well as giving a brief account of its destiny following the events of *Parzival*. This material does not constitute the bulk of the JT, however, but serves as a frame for the story of Tschinotulander and Sigune, more a prologue and epilogue.[36] In spite of Sigune's links to the Gral family, the world of Munt Salvasch is not integrated into the central plot.[37] Within the tale of Tschinotulander and Sigune, however, the motif of the *brackenseil* has a function similar to that of the Gral in Parzival's story. Tschinotulander's love for Sigune is quickly bound up with his quest for the leash. As the story follows Tschinotulander from the tender innocence of young love to the highest achievement of knightly skill and fame in both east and west, his responsibilities and animosities become more complicated, yet the leash remains symbolically the most important object of his quest and the reminder of his failure.

As discussed above, Wolfram provided the source for this motif in *Parzival* and in the second *Titurel* fragment. A brief look at the relevant part of *Titurel II* reveals four main sections: first the idyllic woodland scene interrupted by the baying of a hound and its capture by Schionatulander (132-6); second, a physical description of the hound and its leash (137-43); third, the background of this leash as revealed through the jewelled inscription which Sigune reads (144-53); and fourth, the hound's escape and Schionatulander's vow to retrieve it for his beloved.

Wolfram's short text abounds with detail, comprising a fascinating and powerful vignette. The handling of the leash motif differs greatly from that of the Gral in *Parzival*, primarily because the leash, though presumably destined to be the object of a great quest, remains a mundane, tangible object without the supernatural aura of the Gral. The leash is surrounded by mystery and seems almost magical in its rich beauty, yet it is kept entirely in the realm of the possible. This is accomplished in two ways: by the natural manner in which the hound is integrated into the plot and its appearance explained, and by the precise details given about the physical

appearance of the hound and leash. Wolfram's efforts to
concentrate a detailed description into a few stanzas are
especially apparent in these passages, and demonstrate the
remarkable flexibility he was able to achieve within the
confines of this stanza form.

As Sigune begins to read the text, further aspects of
Wolfram's narrative mode become apparent, especially his
gift for ironic complexity. Not only is the story she reads of
interest in itself, but also it relates the prior history of the
leash and prefigures Sigune's own fate. The hound's name,
Gardeviaz ('guard the paths'), is in itself a didactic element,
and is explained as such in the opening lines of the inscription
(144). Following this is the brief tale of Florie whose great
love for Ilinot ended in tragedy.

147   . . . Flôrîen,
      diu Ilinôte dem Britûn   ir herze, ir gedanc und ir lîp
                                        gap zâmîen,
      gar swaz si hete, wan bî ligende minne:
      si zôch in von kinde unz an   schiltlîche vart und kôs
                                        in vür alle gewinne.

The tender devotion between Sigune and Schionatulander is
like an echo of this love, and Sigune will shortly repeat
Florie's denial of *bî ligende minne*. Indeed, Sigune's demands
on her lover will lead to a tragic ending which is poignantly
presaged in the leash's account of Florie and Ilinot:

148, 1 der holte ouch nâch ir minne un –   der helme sîn
                                        ende . . .
148, 4 Flôrîe starp ouch der selben   tjost, doch ir lîp nie
                                        spers orte genâhte.

Thus when the hound escapes before Sigune has finished
reading, her emotional demand that Schionatulander retrieve
it is manifestly a fatal step towards her own misfortune. The

audience recognises not only the parallelism in the two plots but also knows the unhappy conclusion from Sigune's words in *Parzival*:

141, 16   'ein bracken seil gap im den pîn.
           in unser zweier dienste den tôt
           hât er bejagt, und jâmers nôt
           mir nâch sîner minne.
           ich hete kranke sinne,
           daz ich im niht minne gap.'

It seems clear that Wolfram is demonstrating Sigune's own contribution to her final tragedy. Her mistake does not constitute guilt in a Christian sense, but she is at fault for not controlling her emotions and for childishly demanding that her desires be fulfilled. Her action can be seen as an exaggeration of the female role in a courtly love relationship and thus a subtle criticism by the poet of the chivalric code of service.[38] It is also a poignant comment on the fragility of young love, its idealism, and its blindness to its own impermanence. The irony is further complicated in that, captivated by the tale on the leash, Sigune overlooks its moral, and in her fervour proceeds to re-enact the tragic story. She does not desire the leash for its own sake, for its richness and beauty, but for the story its jewels spell out. Yet the leash cannot be separated from the story, and it is the leash that Schionatulander must bring back to her. The subtlety and inherent ambiguity in this image are masterfully portrayed and left enticingly unresolved. For Wolfram's story ends here. The outcome is known, but the details are omitted. This short fragment presents a vivid, dramatic scene filled with exciting possibilities for the imagination. In spite of their obviously fragmentary nature, the stanzas form a satisfying unit, the scenes and images perhaps even more compelling because they are thus frozen, terminated at a moment of beauty and potential tragedy. Presumably Wolfram recognised this and no doubt felt that to extend the poem to epic length would be inappropriate. Albrecht, however, undaunted by either formal or thematic problems, expanded the *Titurel* fragments more than thirty-five-fold.

In spite of the essential differences between leash and Gral the two can be profitably compared as catalysts within the JT and *Parzival* respectively and as formal elements within each poem's thematic structure. The problem of maintaining the leash as a credible motivating force set Albrecht a number of tasks which we have seen Wolfram deal with in his treatment of the Gral. The object should stay vivid and tantalising for both hero and audience, remain inaccessible without losing importance, continue to be elusive in spite of revelations, in fact increase in significance. These points cannot be applied stringently, for the leash is essentially mundane in comparison with the Gral and is not the crux of the JT as the Gral is revealed to be in *Parzival*. Yet Albrecht endows it with a magical and moral essence that raises it to a symbolic plane quite different from that in *Titurel*. Though within the plot the leash fails to remain a credible force, in structural terms it, like the Gral, serves as a cohesive element.

Albrecht develops the motif gradually, at first following Wolfram's account. The initial appearance of the leash in the JT coincides with its appearance to Tschinotulander and Sigune in their forest idyll (1173ff.). This episode constitutes a near-verbatim transmission of the second *Titurel* fragment with minor changes in word-order to fit Albrecht's more intricate rhyme scheme, along with a few additional details about the leash and hound.[39] He then continues directly with the main subject of his poem, Tschinotulander's heroic quest to retrieve hound and leash.

The story of Tschinotulander falls into three main sections, and the leash serves to bind them together structurally and thematically. These narrative blocks depict Tschinotulander's progress towards what becomes a self-imposed goal: ideal Christian knighthood. Tschinotulander moves from the west to the east and then back again to the west, demonstrating his unique prowess. The leash recurs in each cycle of adven-

tures, established first as a powerful catalyst and gradually
losing its significance as a tangible goal while gaining in symbolic meaning. There is a certain similarity here to the development of the Gral from magical *dinc* to symbol, as there
is in the leash's ultimate superfluity as an external motivating
force for Tschinotulander.

The first narrative block of Tschinotulander's adventures
is of the greatest interest in an analysis of the leash motif, for
it is here that the leash is established and elaborated as a symbol. The geographical setting for this section is the west, initially the *walt* of Wolfram's *Titurel II*, then King Arthur's
court, and finally Floritschanze, the scene of Arthur's greatest
festival. Already one can distinguish a symbolic progression
reminiscent of *Parzival* as Tschinotulander emerges from the
isolated woodland idyll with Sigune to become accepted by
the Round Table and finally prove himself at Floritschanze
against all the greatest knights of the western world. Albrecht
continues Wolfram's fragment with Tschinotulander's preparations to undertake his quest for the leash. Meanwhile the
dog is apprehended by King Teanglis and then won from him
by Orilus (see above, pp. 70ff.). Initially the leash appears
to be coveted for its costly decoration alone, since Teanglis
and Orilus wage a mighty battle over it without reading or
presumably even noticing the inscription (1298–1305).

As we have seen, Albrecht's purpose is to interweave the
objectives and lives of his characters, keeping the tragic outcome, already known from *Parzival*, always in mind. Hence he
does not significantly enhance the description of hound and
leash given by Wolfram. In fact, though Albrecht has already
begun to weave a complex web around the coveted *brackenseil*, it is not mentioned in the Teanglis–Tschinotulander
scene by either the characters or the narrator. The narrative
point of view continues to switch from the hero to other
characters and then back. Having related the hound's initial
appearance to Tschinotulander and Sigune, the story follows
the dog to Teanglis, then drops the hound in favour of

Teanglis. The focus returns to Tschinotulander as he challenges and defeats several of Arthur's knights before rushing off in pursuit of a hound he believes to be Gardivias (1362-8). The narrator does not follow him, but relates the attitude of the Round Table company and Keie's supercilious comments about the young stranger's sudden exit (1364ff.). This section is enriched by unspoken parallels between Tschinotulander and Parzival.[40] The death of Arbidol introduces the second ground for strife with Orilus and Lehelin. Tschinotulander's departure then postpones the battle with Orilus, and tension is kept high by the suspension of so much potential action. The leash has become part of a complex of animosities which serve to heighten its importance. Yet it is still an object of mystery to the audience and to most of the characters.

When Tschinotulander returns to the Round Table and actually engages Orilus in battle for the first time (1397-1401), the crucial nature of the encounter is not lost on the reader who has been watching the threads become entwined. Orilus and Tschinotulander, on the other hand, are singularly unaware of the complexities of their situation. Orilus knows that this stranger who he thinks may be Ither killed his nephew. Tschinotulander knows neither the name nor the family of his opponent; and neither he nor Orilus knows of the other's connection with Gardivias and the leash. When the battle ends indecisively, only the narrator and his audience are aware of the implications. Ekunat von Berbester recognises his nephew Tschinotulander and halts the fighting, but still the characters are not aware of all the forces binding them together. Finally Tschinotulander tells his uncle of Sigune's demand for the leash, and Ekunat responds sympathetically (1422-8). Curiously he makes no mention of the hound or leash, though they originally belonged to him and we know he is eager to retrieve them for himself.[41] When Ekunat returns to Arthur's court to plead for Tschinotulander he still does not speak of Gardivias (1446-59). Only

as Orilus angrily takes his leave does Ekunat explain that
Gardivias had belonged to him (1466).

The three couples who are to vie for possession of the leash
have now been introduced into the story and are involved
with each other. Certain inconsistencies of motivation have
already arisen, which Albrecht attempts to ease. For instance,
the lack of curiosity at Arthur's court[42] is explained by the
fact that Jescute has kept the leash to herself (1468). We also
learn that Ekunat initially refrained from mentioning the
hound for fear of harming Clauditte's reputation (1469–72),
but decided for Sigune's sake to let the leash's existence be
known. The justification for Ekunat's previous silence seems
unsatisfactory as an attempt at psychological motivation of
character, the more so in that it is offered as belated justification. The motives given are unconnected with a portrayal
of Ekunat as an individual but are bound instead to this point
in the story where Albrecht may have sensed his audience
could expect an explanation. In fact, Ekunat's silence is
crucial to the ironic lack of recognition which drives the
characters to inexorable animosities. Now the story is further
complicated by involving all of Arthur's company in the
knowledge of the leash, while the tension is maintained. It is
such structural exigencies that take priority for Albrecht,
leaving Ekunat's expression of tender regard an isolated
gesture.

As the narrative continues so too does the pattern of
thematic complexity and haphazard motivation. We have seen
Jescute refuse to relinquish possession of the dog (above, p.
80), increasing the tension among the three couples. A major
plateau in the motif's development is finally reached, however, as Jescute reads the script aloud to the assembled court.
Albrecht does not reveal the contents of the inscription to
his audience at this point, but the effect of the reading is
described:

1505, 3 si liez di schrift vil uberlut da hŏren,
      di vor aller vreude   ungemŭte kund so wol zustŏren.

1506   Von worte hin zuworte   wart hie diu schrift
gehŏret.
    hie bi an dem orte   wart ir aller herz in vreud
enpŏret,
    als in di aventiure wart gekundet.
    ir gemŭt sich swingen   kunde aldar, da sich der
valk enzundet.

1507   Von edelkeit der steine   was disiu kraft der worte.
    als man der schrift ein cleine   vernam, ie gerner
man si furbaz horte.
    da mite was di schrift also geheret
    durch Ekunat, den fursten.   ir beider lop daz
wart do hoch gemeret,

1508   Ich mein, des von der wilde   und der magt
Clauditten.
    uf erde menschen bilde   in der ersten werld noch
in der dritten
    kom nie grŏzer liep in oren hŏre,
    dann an der strangen was geschriben,   und da zŭ
tugende lere, untugende stŏre.

The text, as would be expected, brings *lob* not shame to
Ekunat and Clauditte. More important, it brings joy to all
listeners. This comfort-giving power is more reminiscent of
the Gral's effect than of the inscription's original appeal for
Sigune. It is not yet clear how the impact is achieved, however, though Albrecht offers several hints. First, the *âventiure*
raises the spirits as it unfolds *von wort hin zuworte*, and the
schrift embodies this power (above and 1517). Yet Albrecht
also claims a component of magic in the jewels themselves
(1507, 1) which increases the mystery. Finally, we learn that
in addition to an incomparable love story, the text contains
a *tugende lêre*.

This short passage performs a triple role within the narrative structure of the JT. First, the reading of the inscription
functions as a *deus ex machina*, cancelling Orilus's bitterness

so that he and Jescute will remain at court for further confrontations with Tschinotulander. Secondly, the leash motif
has been granted new significance through the magic aura of
the jewels and the moral promise of the *tugende lêre*. Finally,
Albrecht's audience is tantalised by the incomplete information given them. They, like any listener, want to hear more:
'als man der schrift ein   cleine vernam, ie gerner man si furbaz horte'. Albrecht is not yet ready to reveal the inscription,
however, but will provide a more dramatic context for its
presentation.

A basic distinction between Albrecht's and Wolfram's
approach is already apparent in the audience's experience of
the narrative at this early stage in the motif's presentation.
Albrecht's characters are not surrogates for an audience whose
perceptions are thereby defined. Not only does Albrecht's
audience generally share in the narrator's omniscience and
thus appreciate the dramatic irony of many events in the
plot, but the opposite can likewise be true. Here the audience
is denied an experience shared by the characters. Albrecht's
audience is being told a different story than the characters
are experiencing. For Albrecht it is this, the audience's story,
that dictates the plot. The narration involving the leash illustrates the point well, for our response to and knowledge of it
are carefully controlled by the narrator. The programmatic
embellishment of the leash motif reflects Albrecht's didactic
bent as well as his concern for structural finesse. For him the
maere is in constant service to this overall purpose. While
subordinating characterisation or credible motivation of
action, however, he does not lose sight of his dependence on
the narrative matter. Yet the overriding principle is the unfolding of the leash motif, a compositional factor external to
the psychological realities within the plot. This approach
leads to what seem from a twentieth-century perspective disruptive lapses.[43] When not in the foreground, characters seem
to cease existing; Tschinotulander, for example, appears
forgotten by the narrator as well as by the court while we

145

observe Orilus's anger, the debate over ownership of the leash, and the reading of the inscription. Why does Jescute wait until this point to read the inscription? Why has there been no previous indication of its euphoric effect?

Albrecht's mode of narration makes great demands on his listeners, for they must remain attentive on several levels concurrently. The involved plot and changing point of view require an excellent memory.[44] Furthermore, Albrecht's linguistic expertise and rhetorical virtuosity demand a sophisticated and educated sensitivity quite separate from emotional involvement in the story. And both these levels must be viewed as supports for the central meaning of the poem, its moral lesson. Thus, by exercising memory, by familiarity with literary convention and intellectual appreciation of form, the audience itself provides a continuity which is absent in the story line. The message resides in the process of assimilating Albrecht's *lêre*.[45]

The evolution of the leash motif illuminates this principle. In the context of formal, structural elements the leash appears to have three general functions thus far in the poem. First, it is the object of Tschinotulander's quest and as such the prime motivator in the plot. Secondly, it is an object of contention, providing the focal point for the growing enmity between Tschinotulander, Orilus, and Ekunat. Thirdly, the leash, surrounded by an aura of magic and mystery, is a tantalising symbol of the hero's ultimate goal, as yet not clearly expressed.[46] Though varying in relative importance, each of these motives operates throughout the JT. The leash's material reality has not been elaborated, however, and this continues to fade as the spiritual significance of the inscription increases. The mention of a *tugende lêre* and the power of conferring joy are the first major steps in changing the emphasis from that of the *Titurel* fragments. In Albrecht's initial summary of the leash's influence one hears echoes again of the Gral's effect:

1517 Wan swer die schrift erhorte,   des herze wart gevriet
     vor leid, und sich enborte   sin gemŭte wol raste hoch
                                   gedriet.
     siecheit, wunden, dar zŭ ander smerzen
     wart im da von geringet,   so daz er sin vergaz gar an
                                 dem herzen.

The Gral relieves the body of suffering, and the leash likewise lessens pain by bringing joy to the heart. Yet the inscription's influence is of shorter duration. More important, its effect is on one's perceptions whereas the Gral actually affects the material world. The leash remains a covetable object, bound to the courtly mundane world. Yet by endowing it with mysterious powers Albrecht is separating its effect from the object and preparing us for the allegorical exegesis which is to come.

Albrecht surrounds the climax of the next public reading with an elaborate description of the great festival held at Floritschanze. This is the most resplendent festival ever held by Arthur (1649), and Albrecht's description strives to equal it in magnitude and elaborateness. Descriptions of jousts between warriors from all parts of the world fill hundreds of stanzas, until one must sympathise with Borchling's view of the 'unendliche Namenverzeichnisse, die den Leser mit schauderndem Entsetzen vor dieser Poesie erfüllen' (p. 43). Yet Albrecht is thus setting the *brackenseil* inscription like a jewel against the brilliant foil of courtly life.[47]

The narrator builds slowly to the public recitation. On the fifth day of festivities what should be a crucial turning point in the plot is reached when Sigune at last reads the entire inscription (1868-9). No explanation is given for how she came to have the leash. It must be assumed that Jescute voluntarily lent it to her. Sigune sates her desire by reading it through three times. Then it is read aloud to the entire court once more, when Albrecht's audience also hears it.

Sigune's reading of the inscription radically alters the leash's motivating power both as object of Tschinotulander's quest and as focus of contention between him and Orilus. Though Albrecht does not discard these two aspects, they retain their force mainly on a structural level, while within the story their reappearance is somewhat strained (see below). The symbolic impact of the *brackenseil* is greatly augmented at this juncture, however. Until now Albrecht has relied mainly on Wolfram's depiction of the leash, heightening the aura of mystery which surrounds it by showing its effect on characters within the plot. Although individual characters seem to have coveted it for its beauty, the leash's function within the narrative structure has gradually shifted to a more symbolic plane. The mystery of the inscription is paramount. Sigune's threefold reading of the text provides the crescendo leading to the disclosure of the contents. Arthur's court prepares for the presentation of the inscription as befits its importance. A learned scribe is summoned, and the people gather around to listen:

1871 Einen schriber wol geleret   man lesen hiez di strangen.
     nu moht diu schrift geheret   uber al von man zu
                                              manne niht gelangen.
     da von must man si von ring zu ringe
     lesen al den werden,   vrowen schar und herren
                                              sunderlinge.
1872 E daz man ane hube,   geboten wart ein stille,
     zuht luter, sunder trube: swer ein wort spraech
                                              dankes oder unwille
     dar under, daz den jar und tak verbaere
     aller vrowen gruzen   und in des kuniges hulde niht
                                              enwaere.
1873 Da mit so wart sich hebende   diu schrift an dem seile,
     gruz des ersten gebende   und dar nach ler gen aller
                                              menschen heile
     den, di si mit volge wolten halden.
     Clauditte was des wernde,   di kunde solcher tugend
                                              witze walden.

148

These stanzas are Wolframian in their sense of drama, for Albrecht's readers become part of the attentive audience along with Arthur's court, and the impact of the inscription is direct.

The inscription itself is divided into five sections which seem to follow a rather uneven progression from the courtly to the mystical. The entire text is a letter from Clauditte to Ekunat (the stanzas read originally by Sigune [*Titurel*, 144ff.; JT, 1191ff.] are not included here).[48] The first section (1874–82) consists of Clauditte's greeting to Ekunat filled with praise of his knightly and manly virtues. The second section (1884–93) begins moralising on the theme of *hŭte wol der verte* (i.e. 'Gardivias'), which occurs in the last line of each stanza throughout the remainder of the inscription. The advice here is generally concerned with honouring and serving God and clerics, and it encompasses chivalric tenets of honour, justice, and kindness to widows and orphans. The third section (1894–1900) is a series of moralising similes probably taken from bestiaries.[49] In each stanza a different human feature is compared with the same feature of an animal and then a moral is drawn. The content is still worldly while the presentation has shifted to a metaphorical plane. The virtues recommended here are again courtly – for instance a sense of shame, *zuht*, courage, generosity. The fourth section treats love, developing the theme from the plane of *ritterliche minne* (1901) to a more mystical discussion of love (1905–8), ending in an echo of Wolfram's *Parzival* regarding the need to honour women and priests:[50]

1910 Die vrowen sint uns bernde   zer werlt, zu got die
                                                               pfaffen.
     wer ist uns hoher wernde   deheiner seld ane got, der
                                                               da geschaffen
     si hat uns und uns in zallem heile?
     nu hŭte wol der verte,   so bistu hie und dort der
                                                               selden geile!

149

These stanzas alluding to *minne* in a religious context set
the tone for the remaining section which describes a crown of
twelve virtues. With the exception of *milt* the virtues here
listed differ from those in the bestiary section above.[51] The
open didacticism of this allegory is unambiguously Christian,
with references to Biblical figures and to the ultimate goal of
heavenly salvation (1925). The *brackenseil* inscription is then
rather awkwardly concluded by two stanzas discussing the
negative practices of *verligen* and *vervaren*.

These five sections constitute the message of the leash.
Instead of the moving stanzas originally read by Sigune we
find a eulogy to abstracted virtues. Helping build to this
climax is the constant repetition of *hüte wol der verte*, punc-
tuating and emphasising each stanza both rhythmically and
figuratively. Albrecht has thus fundamentally altered the
symbolic nature of the leash through moralising Christian
content. The story of Florie and Ilinot remains only a
memory, its ironies irrelevant in face of the inscription's
tugende lêre, its implications for the tale of Sigune and Tschinotulander overshadowed by the array of universal truths. No
longer does a tale of love transport a creature of innocence.
Now, a moralised vision of Christian perfection stands like a
complex revelation before the whole courtly world: 'ler gen
aller menschen heile' (1873, 2). Sigune's feelings upon reading the inscription are no longer important, since the leash
has become a symbol for her and Tschinotulander just as it
has for the others. These changes reflect the overall difference
in emphasis in Albrecht's poem where a didactic and intellectual tone has superceded the intimacy of Wolfram's fragments. The public presentation of the leash and its allegorical
content are both consistent with the tenor of the JT. One
must feel a twinge of regret, however, at the transformation
of Wolfram's tender and naïvely impetuous Sigune.

As the narrator describes the reaction of Arthur's court
the emphasis on *lêre* becomes paramount:

150

1928 Nu was do solcher maere   niht vil mit wiser lere.
güter pfaffheit laere   was diu werlt dannoch einvalt
                              in ere.
des gie di ler in zeherzen solcher wise,
sams an den stunden weren   geborn zu vreuden vruht
                              in paradise.
1929 Der hiute selten horte   wehe rede süze,
wol tusentvalt enporte   iz baz diu herz in hoher
                             vreuden grüze,
dann daz den oren wirt vertaegelichet.
sus wart von dirre lere   ir aller herz an vreuden hoch
                              gerichet.
1930 Alle vreude cleine   uber al uf Floritschanze
was wider der aleine,   swenne man in do las di lere
                              ganze.
die vreude der schrifte gie von der steine krefte,
dar uz di büchstab waren.   di liebtens mere dann von
                              meisterschefte.

The inscription's uplifting effect is described in terms one would apply to a sermon. The praise of moralising texts is doubly interesting in light of Sigune's original concern with finishing the *âventiure*, and as a comment on courtly romance in general. The critical view of common fare, 'daz den oren wirt vertaegelichet', is consistent with Albrecht's own moralising bent and his evaluation of the JT. Indeed, there are clear parallels between his comments on the inscription and his assessment elsewhere of the JT text. Both are models of *lêre* and lead to blessedness.[52]

6207 Nu prvfet alle werden   die wirde dises bvches.
Von devtscher zvnge vf erden   nie getiht wart so
                              werdes rvches.
Daz lip vnd sele so hoch gein wirde wiset.
Alle die ez horen lesen   oder schriben der sele müzze
                              werden geparadiset.

The JT is thus in some ways an epic version of the *bracken-seil* inscription – a love story combined with a *tugende lêre*. Albrecht smooths over earlier self-contradictions by explaining that the entire inscription must be read to achieve the effect of bliss.[53] This of course leaves much unexplained, but repeats the emphasis on wholeness which we have observed in Albrecht's own aesthetic. That his own listeners may not feel the full impact of the inscription is explained by several factors. First, Arthur's court was unused to such spectacular sermons – unlike Albrecht's audience! Secondly, the jewels themselves are said to contribute to the joyful effect (also 1507, above p. 144). It is left ambiguous, however, whether the *vreude* comes from the text, written in jewels, or from the magical qualities inherent in the stones themselves.[54] Clearly, although the *steinen krefte* augment the inscription's impact, it is the meaning conveyed by the words that embodies its power. The text of the leash represents an elaborate glorification of virtue, a complex formal pattern whose flourishes and repetitions support an essential canon of chivalric ideals which epitomises the ethical message of the JT. Through the reading of the inscription, the leash, though less mysterious, has achieved new moral power. Instead of being merely an object to be coveted, it has become a symbol of ideal Christian courtliness and a model of the power of language, both essential to the message of the JT.

This initial sequence of Tschinotulander's adventures (the festival continues for another 500 stanzas) has related his knightly superiority in the west as a Christian and chivalric ideal. The leash has been essential in motivating this entire section and has achieved its fullest expression as sought-after object and symbol. The inherent ambiguities in motivating potential cannot be erased, however. The most obvious problem is Sigune's changed attitude towards possessing the leash. She no longer insists but in fact argues the leash's irrelevance (1946).[55] Thus the responsibility for continued struggle becomes Tschinotulander's. He feels he has not yet fulfilled his promise of service (1932) and must not relent in his striving for *prîs*. Although Tschinotulander's interpretation of service seems exaggerated, Albrecht does not criticise his motives, only once briefly suggesting a connection with the tenets against *unmâze* on the *brackenseil*.[56] As Ragotzky has pointed out, Tschinotulander's exploits are an expression of his perfection. His continued fighting demonstrates the virtues of knighthood, indeed the courtly virtues of the *brackenseil* inscription, in a continuous succession of 'Bewährungssituationen' (p. 121). Like Gawan rather than Parzival, he is not working towards achieving these virtues, for he already possesses them. His endless victories demonstrate the virtues; each joust is confirmation of the ideals.

The theme of the leash will thus persist throughout the rest of Tschinotulander's adventures, reappearing at crucial junctures as a structural and symbolic link. Before disappearing from this initial section, however, the leash plummets anti-climactically from its symbolic heights as Orilus offers it as a bribe to Tschinotulander hoping to release Lehelin from his bond to fight in the east (above, p. 82). The leash's function as a pawn and the near resolution of conflict are recurrent motifs which serve to create tension in the plot and revitalise the leash as object of a quest. That Albrecht is striving to keep these aspects of the motif alive is evident in the narrator's woeful comments (i.e. 1940–1). His repeated forecasts of doom at the end of this episode remind the audience of the tragic outcome known from *Parzival*. To conform with Sigune's words there, the *brackenseil* must remain a potent impetus to tragedy. This explains Albrecht's need to reinvigorate it as the object of Tschinotulander's quest. The suddenness with which the symbolic potential of the inscription seems to disappear is surprising, however. All three couples react to the leash once more as a coveted object, with no mention of its spiritual aspect. The incongruities are difficult to overlook, yet Albrecht seems to expect his audience's acquiescence. He has developed the *brackenseil* motif

153

consistently, building to the climax of the reading at court. Its ownership is then again debated, it is tentatively offered in an attempt to allay the conflict, and it is finally re-established as object of strife and possession. This pattern is repeated in the remaining sections of the JT, creating a for-mal unity essential to Albrecht's ultimate statement.

If we look briefly at Tschinotulander's subsequent adven-tures we find the leash reappearing at important junctures. Throughout most of the first sequence describing the hero's campaign in the Orient (2574–4394), the leash's position as motivator is disregarded. Here Tschinotulander not only achieves his goal by avenging Gamuret[57] but spreads his own fame as a warrior throughout the east, achieving even loftier heights than his predecessor and mentor. Tschinotulander's great victories and Gamuret's funeral are followed by a rather anticlimactic vignette describing the western army's winter stay in Baldac. Here, at the end of this section, earlier motifs reappear, thematically and structurally linking the eastern adventures with the previous activities in the west, and lead-ing the plot gradually into the third and final section. Two themes – the anger of Orilus and Lehelin over the unavenged deaths of their nephews and the unresolved question of the leash's ownership – appear together. In addition the motif of bribery recurs, as the Baruch offers Lehelin mountains of gold if only he and his brother will end the hostilities with Tschinotulander and allow Signune to have the leash.[58]

The appearance of the leash at this point is unexpected. There has been no mention of it, even allusion to it, since Tschinotulander left Arthur's court (about 2,000 stanzas ago!), and at that time its intrinsic value and motivating power were ambiguous. This section has been primarily con-cerned with Tschinotulander avenging Gamuret; thus, sudden emphasis on the leash appears incongruous. Furthermore, the Baruch's offer is illogical since the leash is not Lehelin's to give away. Here again the explanation is to be found in the structural aspects of the poem. By inserting references to the

154

leash at this point, Albrecht preserves formal continuity: first in rejuvenating the motivating power of the leash; secondly through the repetition of thematic elements. The leash dispatched Tschinotulander on his first cycle of adventures which ended with Orilus's attempt to buy Lehelin's release from duty by giving the leash to Sigune. Now, at the end of a second cycle of adventures, the leash appears once more, symbolically signalling the end of the episode, relating this part to the whole, and foreshadowing once more the ultimate doom to come.

In the final section of events dealing with Tschinotulander's renewed adventures in the west, the leash reappears in its familiar guise as object of strife and potential pawn while the inscription is again ignored. Having avenged Gamuret, the prime motivation is now Tschinotulander's need to resecure Waleis and Norgals. The leash, however, is cursed by Orilus as the source of all woes (4419–20). Given the many other developments which have locked him into a fatal enmity with Tschinotulander, this laying of blame appears exaggerated. Not only is it incompatible with the spiritual and moral value of the leash, but it is a vast oversimplification. The narrator does not question Orilus's attitude, however, but seems to incorporate this ambiguity into his own portrayal of events. The leash's inherent joy-bringing power, useful in dispelling Orilus's anger in the earlier scene, would here be disruptive. Hence, in not alluding to these aspects of the leash, Albrecht turns his audience's attention from them as well. Instead he continues to employ the leash in its formal capacity as motivator and coveted object, rehearsing familiar patterns. Thus it is again used as a pawn in yet a third attempt to resolve the conflict. King Arthur attempts to bribe Jescute and Clauditte in order to secure the leash for Sigune (4431–5). The bargaining for and pursuit of the leash are carried out in a manner unfitting both its original role in the *Titurel* fragments and its symbolic significance in the JT. Once again Albrecht's intention is more visible if one concentrates on context.

Structurally Albrecht has conceived an artful plan. However, it is not surprising that the many complex patterns create some discord. The careful cyclical unity of themes and motifs is an external pattern, not motivated from within the plot's natural development but superimposed and thus sometimes incongruous, even with previous passages. Though the leash may have been given distinctive attributes at one time to fit the author's purpose, these do not remain integral to the object but are disregarded when no longer relevant.

In some ways the construction of the JT compares to the intricate patterns of an oriental carpet. Various themes and motifs are repeated continually; certain prescribed colours and patterns predominate (names and motifs), and the basic stitch is unchangeable (stanza). As in Albrecht's poem, a small section may contain all the colours and patterns of the whole, although not all the variations. This metaphor cannot be strictly extended, for, while in a carpet if one has the formula one can often construct the rest of the pattern from a small section, Albrecht's poem is not this precise or controlled. Yet a certain cohesiveness is achieved in this manner, if not perfect symmetry, and it seems justifiable to argue this sense of structure as Albrecht's basic formal mode. Thus Jescute's possessiveness should not be viewed as contradictory with her former generosity regarding the leash, but as the repetition of an earlier theme. Likewise, Tschinotulander's passionate avowals that he will win the leash only through battle (4435-6) should not be viewed simply as redundancies, nor as evidence of either myopic single-mindedness or self-denying hubris, but again as a well-known pattern adding to the richness of the whole.

Although this metaphor clarifies certain aspects of Albrecht's narrative technique which are remote and difficult for a twentieth-century audience, it of course cannot explain all of the poem's incongruities. For, as we have seen, one important motif which is not repeated is that of the leash's magical powers.[59] It is tempting to posit explanations based

156

on a psychological reading of the text. For example, the failure of all the characters to make use of the leash's power could be read as proof of their sinfulness, a blindness to the moral code emblazoned on it. Yet Albrecht does not offer such an interpretation. A reflection of the inscription's moral code, however, can be seen in the narrator's comments on Tschinotulander who is said to have only one vice, *unmâze*, which in his case seems paradoxically an excess of virtue.[60]

3568   Gamuret dem jungen   ist hie di aventiure
       zehohem lobe entsprungen,   also daz nie ritter so
                                    gehiure
       wart, den man gen aventiur kan mezzen,
       dann ot nur daz eine,   dar an beleip er leider sich
                                     vergezzen,
3569   So daz in niht genůgen   wolte rechter maze.
       daz kan noch schaden fůgen   und kunde do. iedoch
                                was er uf straze
       niht des nides noch der ubermůte:
       zeliebe der rechten pflege   twanc in unmaz ein teil
                              in rehter gůte.

In a sense Tschinotulander's immoderation itself lifts him above normal human vices. This aspect of Tschinotulander's portrayal befits his representation as embodiment of virtue and is thus part of the central didactic message of the poem. We have little sense of his response to the inscription as an individual character. Indeed, he seems more remote than ever, acting more as a personification. Tschinotulander is by now scarcely recognisable as the barefoot young fisherman who promised to seek the leash for his beloved's sake:

Titurel, 167   er sprach: 'sô wil ich gerne um   daz seil
                                      alsô werben.
       sol manz mit strîte erholn, dâ   muoz ich an
                              lîbe und an prîse verderben
       oder ich bringez wider dir ze handen.

wis genaedec, süeziu maget, und   ·halt niht
    mîn herze sô lange in dînen banden.'

Albrecht's Tschinotulander cannot escape his fate. Thus he
continues to strive valiantly, if needlessly, for the leash.

For several hundred stanzas there is no mention of the
leash. Then, during Tschinotulander's penultimate duel with
Orilus, it reappears as party to yet another attempted bribery
(above, p. 92). Jescute's disruption of the battle saves Orilus
from certain defeat while keeping the leash a force in the
story line. It is inconsequential that her action is mistakenly
unrealistic. As before, regardless of the individual's attitude
towards the leash, it continues to function as a motivator
either because of timing or because of misconceptions of
characters. By repeating the leitmotif of the leash as pawn, the
previous attempts to dissuade Tschinotulander from continued
battle are recalled, underscoring the irony we experience as he
seals his own tragic fate through his stubbornness.

The final appearance of the *brackenseil* as a pawn is highly
anticlimactic. Hoping to cancel the final duel, Jescute secretly
sends the leash to Sigune (4891–3) who reads it but seems
little elevated by its powers (4894–5). At last Sigune is in
possession of the leash, yet the occasion is empty of any
sense of fulfilment or joy. Structurally one can recognise this
moment as the culmination of a cycle and view it as a portent
of the tragic end so long prepared for. Within the plot, however, the leash has lost all potential for creating tension and
the motif appears sadly deflated.

The final plunge of the leash as a coveted object comes
when Tschinotulander and Sigune meet once again at Arthur's
court, just before the fatal confrontation with Orilus. Sigune
reads the inscription aloud to her beloved, yet – essential to
the plot – without effect. The sorrow of these two cannot be
mitigated; they seem to realise Tschinotulander's approaching
death, for they both prepare for it in different ways. Although
Tschinotulander will not allow Sigune to accompany him as
his **knecht**, **he agrees to ride with her** to the Gral where she

can do penance. As they are leaving, Ekunat asks that the leash be given back to him:

4991 Ekvnat was gerende   clauditten der vil wisen.
     Ob sie die wil enberende   wolte sin der strange daz
                                       sol ich prisen.
     Ev beiden hoch und wer sie tusent lande.
     Wert sie wirt din eigen   darvmbe ste min werdekeit
                                         zv pfande.
4992 Sigvne iach mit girde   daz sie ez gerne tete.

What an ignoble end for the glorious leash! It seems totally to have lost its aura of richness and joy-giving power, and has become irrelevant as a motivator. Ekunat's repossessing it is inconsistent with his former desire to gain it only by fighting; it is as though he too senses the end approaching and is resigned. At least he recognises the futility of holding on any longer to chivalric oaths. Each of these factors is important for the present denouement of the plot, however. Tschinotulander and Sigune are locked into their final pattern, and the portents of this seem reflected in their actions. Albrecht has brought his story full circle, returning the leash to its original owner, with the stage clearly set for Tschinotulander's destruction.

This concludes the active role of the leash in the JT. It appears just once more, 800 stanzas later, where it is destroyed. Albrecht would certainly not regard his poem as finished had he left anything like the leash unaccounted for. Therefore, as Ekunat wears it on his helmet during the retributive battle with Orilus it flashes and flames with spectacular fury as it is finally destroyed (5800ff.). The active motivating influence of the leash finishes with Tschinotulander's defeat. Having developed from a coveted object to a moralised Christian symbol and powerful catalyst, the leash shrinks to become a superficial balm, a soother of faint symptoms. Finally, it is diminished to a useless, unwanted bauble, passed from hand to hand as a burdensome nuisance.

From a structural point of view the role of the leash is more consistent. The *brackenseil* itself remains a catalyst in all three sections of Tschinotulander's adventures. The inscription too, though appearing only in the first sequence of adventures, reflects the moral ideals of the entire JT and can thus be seen as pervasive in a conceptual sense. Although the extensive delineation of the message on the leash appears to be a sort of dead end in terms of plot development, the jewelled inscription can be seen as a central emblem of the whole poem. Like a large decoration in the middle of a carpet, it is not repeated in its entirety anywhere else, yet each of its elements recurs repeatedly throughout. For its message 'hůte der verte', its emphasis on *minne, triuwe*, and *mâze*, and its strongly Christian didacticism are the basic threads from which the JT is woven. The poem is a vast demonstration of the virtues listed in the *brackenseil* code.

As an emblem the leash recalls Albrecht's Gral temple, for its rich beauty reflects its spiritual value. Furthermore, its moral essence is isolated from the ongoing plot in a way similar to the temple's solitariness. Both are tangible objects imbued with spiritual meaning; neither is successfully integrated into the plot but stands apart as a direct statement addressed to Albrecht's audience. Both can be seen as monuments to the power of art, the leash specifically as an image of language. For words – temporal bearers of spiritual truths – are shown as the essential links between two levels of reality. Their physical manifestation can be destroyed, as are the leash and its jewels, yet their meaning lives on. Likewise the JT moves its readers to enlightenment and stands as mediator between them and higher truths.

By maintaining the leash as a leitmotif, however arbitrary its appearance may sometimes seem, Albrecht has formally unified the vast tale of Tschinotulander and continually stressed his poem's ethical tenor and proclaimed worth. Within the plot it has remained, though artificially, a motivating force, echoing the Gral's role in *Parzival* in its perseverence as a structural element, as an elusive and continually tantalising goal, and as the representation of a Christian ideal. The logical inconsistencies in its integration are overshadowed by its formal and thematic significance.

The selection and treatment of dominant motifs betray many of the fundamental differences between the two authors' respective approaches to narrative. Whereas the leash physically eludes Tschinotulander through the abrupt and complex movements of the plot, the Gral is elusive for its conceptual intangibility as well. Whereas Tschinotulander seeks the reward of consummated love through performance as an ideal knight, Parzival seeks to complete the very essence of his own being. Though the leash's text offers a code of virtue, this is never integrated into Tschinotulander's consciousness of his quest. Parzival, however, must come to recognise and attain the virtues which the Gral represents before its realm becomes accessible to him. In this respect the leash retains an identity separate from its pursuer, whereas the Gral is bound up with the developing awareness of the hero who seeks it. On another level both Tschinotulander and the leash are static whereas Parzival grows as a character, just as the motif of the Gral evolves as the story progresses. Albrecht has contrived his tale with the omniscience of a puppeteer who never yields up his right to manipulate each object and character discretely. Wolfram, on the other hand, allows his story to develop as though through its own internal mechanisms, admitting of all the ambiguity which such a perspective entails.

Indeed, by his own testimony, Wolfram openly disavows the right to intrude upon the autonomous workings of his tale (above, pp. 135-6). Already in the prologue to *Parzival* he self-consciously establishes his position as a narrator bound to respect the integrity of the story he has inherited. The narrator's intrusions into the text take the form of personal observations, a marginal dialogue with Frou Aventiure, or rhetorical statements to his audience. But he seldom deigns to interpret or impose himself on the inviolate flow of the narrative. When the story meanders this is its will, its true path, which in the final analysis is direct because it follows the hero as he proceeds towards his goal by the most direct path he can discover:

805, 14   es ist niht krump alsô der boge,
             diz maere ist wâr unde sleht.

The story emerges consistently from Parzival's point of view. The poem as a whole retains its coherency.[61]

Albrecht, on the other hand, can be sensed continually behind the movement of his plot. His narrator does not leave his audience to grope for understanding along with his characters but is omnipresent as guide and interpreter. The leash motif, like the treatment of Jescute and Orilus, reflects Albrecht's overriding concern with structural patterns and his consequent neglect of credible motivation and consistent characterisation. Albrecht's orchestration of the *brackenseil* motif is not subtle but proudly explicit. We are perpetually aware of the literary craftsman hovering over his tale, filling gaps, offering judgements, interpretations, and belated explanations, nudging his players from one square to the next in composing his grand design.

4. THE ROLE OF THE NARRATOR

Wolfram von Eschenbach has long been recognised as a superb story-teller, but only recently have scholars begun to analyse the particulars of his narrative technique. This emphasis has resulted in a growing sensitivity to the role and function of Wolfram's narrator persona and led to an enthusiastic recognition of yet another dimension to the poet's artistry.[1] A tale implies a teller, and in the medieval period we can assume that the first-person narrator was conventionally identified with the author. Indeed, in a tradition of oral delivery the author was often the actual reciter of his own poetry. Surely the poet did identify to a certain extent with his narrating persona, but this does not rule out a separation of viewpoint. A poet sophisticated enough to put a self-conscious narrator into his text must necessarily have possessed an awareness of the distinction between his real self and that 'self' within his literary creation. The audience too would perceive this ambiguity and be delighted by the additional level of play. As Kane has pointed out in reference to Chaucer, the narrator is 'a function of the relation between the poet and his contemporary, immediate audience. More profoundly, the narrator would serve to focus that sustained challenge of poetry to define the relation between artistic reality and historical actuality which is a factor in its power of engagement.'[2]

It would be inappropriate to submit medieval romances too strenuously to literary critical categories developed for analysing narration in the novel. In any case such a study would go far beyond the bounds of the present one.[3] Of importance here are those aspects of narration in *Parzival* and the JT which distinguish the works both within their respective rhetorical traditions and from each other. Comparison of fundamental aspects of the narrating persona in each poem – the narrator's projection as an individual, his reliability, his attitude towards his sources, towards his subject and his audience, as well as his own evaluation of his function - reveals much about the concerns of each poet.

A growing self-consciousness in the narrator persona is characteristic of the high medieval period. That is, a narrator typically expresses awareness of himself as author of his text.[4] In Chrétien's *Perceval* the poet-narrator still remains generally unobtrusive in relating the tale, coming forward to name himself and his patrons and occasionally alluding to his role as narrator through formulaic expressions ('ce me samble') or rhetorical questions ('Et savez por cor?'). Aside from the prologue and infrequent short comments on the story, however, he does not impose a point of view through commentary or dramatic presence.[5]

In *Parzival* we find a further stage in the development of dramatised narration. Wolfram the author becomes highly visible as narrator of his poem. He appears to emerge as an autonomous personality whose individualised reponses are an essential part of the total work. As a self-conscious narrator he reflects not only on the content of his story but on the process of story-telling itself. Yet the narrator of *Parzival* is not always consistent or reliable. He is not wholly a dramatisation, another character in the plot, nor is he fully identical with Wolfram the poet. Wolfram sometimes speaks through him but also hides behind him, making use of the ironic potential in a separation of viewpoint.[6] The narrator's role as lively interlocutor is thus a crucial element in Wolfram's narrative technique and one that clearly distinguishes his poem from Chrétien's *Perceval*. Although Wolfram's narrator remains an observer, he does not maintain an impartial stance but reacts to the events he recounts on a very human and often ambiguous level. While intrinsically interesting as a 'character', he becomes an important factor in the audience's perception of the poem.

The role of the narrator

Though presenting himself as a personality identical with the author, Wolfram as narrator assumes numerous and often contradictory stances in *Parzival*. At times he bewails his helplessness, at other times assures us of his power:

734, 5   ich tuonz iu kunt mit rehter sage,
             wande ich in dem munde trage
             daz slôz dirre âventiure.

From the conventional position of omniscience a narrator can set scenes, describe the action and thoughts of his characters, look back or ahead, and indulge in marginal commentary. Yet Wolfram was in many respects not a free agent but, in good medieval tradition, followed a model, if not always to the satisfaction of his critics.[7] His shifting stance as narrator allows a glimpse of his awareness of the difficulties involved both in 'translating' Chrétien's *Perceval*, his major source, and in deviating from the text.

An obvious problem for Wolfram, and one that has incessantly troubled scholars, is the relationship between the Parzival and Gawan episodes.[8] When Chrétien turns from Perceval to Gavain he does so with a mere three-line introduction:

4813   Et mesire Gavains s'en va.
           Des aventures qu'il trova
           M'orrés conter molt longuement.

Wolfram's concern with this crucial juncture is readily apparent in the number of lines devoted to the transfer:

338, 1   Der nie gewarp nâch schanden,
             ein wîl zuo sînen handen
             sol nu dise âventiure hân
             der werde erkande Gâwân.
             diu prüevet manegen âne haz
             derneben oder für in baz
             dan des maeres hêrren Parzivâl.
             swer sînen friunt alle mâl
             mit worten an daz hoehste jagt,

der ist prîses anderhalp verzagt.
im waere der liute volge guot,
swer dicke lop mit wârheit tuot.
wan, swaz er sprichet oder sprach,
diu rede belîbet âne dach.
wer sol sinnes wort behalten,
es enwelln die wîsen walten?
valsch lügelîch ein maere,
daz waen ich baz noch waere
âne wirt ûf eime snê,
sô daz dem munde wurde wê,
derz ûz für wârheit breitet:
sô het in got bereitet
als guoter liute wünschen stêt,
den ir triwe zarbeite ergêt.
swem ist ze sölhen werken gâch,
dâ missewende hoeret nâch,
pfliht werder lîp an den gewin,
daz muoz in lêren kranker sin.
er mîdetz ê, kan er sich schemn:
den site sol er ze vogte nemn.

Chrétien's method of interweaving does not seem to have satisfied Wolfram, for he is clearly concerned with easing the transition between the two sections.[9] His justification for turning attention away from Parzival merges into an attack on those listeners who would not appreciate such a shift and on those dishonest poets who allow nothing to mar their heroes' pre-eminence. The vehemence of his self-defence stresses the importance of this juncture. The narrator commands his proper role of authority and responsibility in the arrangement of his *maere*.

This passage reveals several features of Wolfram the narrator. The most striking is the very personal nature of his involvement with the techniques of story-telling. He appears earnest and forthright. Yet one is struck by an elusive quality in the discussion. For all his loquacity, his abundant and vivid metaphors, the narrator's full intention is difficult to grasp. The concentration of reproachful thrusts creates an intensity of mood reminiscent of the prologue, and the content of his diatribe echoes his introductory stanzas: 'diu valsche erwirbet valschen prîs' (3, 7). The prologue motif of false women winning praise recurs in Wolfram's 'self-defence' at the end of Book 2. In both instances it has been interpreted as a disguised attack on the moral laxity of Gottfried's *Tristan*.[10] It does not seem far-fetched to view the modification of the motif here at the beginning of Book 7 as another disguised allusion to that rival poem. Through such protests Wolfram's narrator encourages appreciation of his own tactics while undermining those of his competitors and critics.

Certainly the literal level of the narrator's words does not seem to express the entirety of the poet's meaning. The ambiguity of the poet-narrator identity becomes apparent in the multiple levels on which the audience is being cajoled. In the transitional passage above, there are several aspects to the narrator's posture. He presents himself as a careful story-teller openly attentive to his narrative technique, a sensitive artist desiring his listeners' approval, a moralising preacher, and a vituperative critic of his rivals. The narrator gives the appearance of proceeding rationally through a series of indubitable statements: any poet who praises his favourite character to excess will not win praise himself; wise men accept sensible words; a false tale should not be countenanced. Yet his argument is a hotchpotch of not quite sequential assertions, his rhetorical question not clearly answered, and his tone unexpectedly subjective. He seems, in fact, to be playfully confounding us. Each statement appears acceptable in itself, and the listeners who are led through this maze by the expository tone of the narrator naturally commit themselves to this point of view. There is no choice for them but to identify with *die wîsen* and *guoten liute*. But what have they been led to advocate?

167

It is enlightening to turn to Gottfried here, for in his *Tristan* prologue where the discussion is also of praise,[11] he similarly manoeuvres his audience into accepting his story's tenets. Gottfried argues that praise should be freely given to a well-meaning poet (5–8), and that praise itself helps create that which is praiseworthy (21–4).[12] He decorously skirts the moral issue implicit in his subject matter and convinces his audience – through rhetorical argument (*insinuatio*) – to support him:

> 17   Tiur unde wert ist mir der man,
> der guot und übel betrahten kan,
> der mich und iegelichen man
> nach sinem werde erkennen kan.

Gottfried seems to be playing skilfully with different levels of meaning, arguing for good on an aesthetic level (good = bestowing of praise), and implying a moral level. Wolfram's comments can be seen as a response to this kind of manoeuvring, ironically presented in the same sort of elusive language. He implies that no matter how great a poet's skill, his creation will be discarded if it is seen to be untruthful. Indirectly he challenges his audience to adopt a position contrary to that suggested by Gottfried (for how can they not agree with the wise?), attacking those who do not seek and judge the moral implications of a tale's subject matter. The audience has been cleverly manipulated to accept the narrator's moral superiority and sense of *scham* in allowing another hero to share Parzival's limelight, to appreciate Wolfram's talent and his personal commitment to his narrative structure, and to feel themselves lacking in both aesthetic appreciation and moral judgement if they do not avow the superiority of his poem over those with just a single hero. It is tempting, though unnecessary, to see Wolfram's attack on lack of poetic integrity as a barb specifically shaped for Gottfried. In any case the ideal audience, which Wolfram must have encountered at times, would recognise these complex manoeuvrings and delight in the challenges thus offered.

Clearly this passage expresses matters beyond Wolfram's attention to the flow of his narrative, yet his concern with transitions is sincere. Equal care is taken at a later juncture between the tales of the two protagonists, and here the narrator appears in different guise as he attempts to clarify the structure of his source. In Book 9 the return of the story from Gawan to Parzival is facilitated by a discussion between the narrator and Frou Aventiure (433, 1 – 434, 10). Here Wolfram expresses curiosity about the young hero who has scarcely been seen in the last two books (see above, pp. 117f.). Clearly the narrator is playing a role different from that at the beginning of Book 7. He summarises Parzival's previous adventures and asks eager questions, at once standing in for the audience and their interests while reviving their curiosity and involvement with Parzival. That the story is returning to its true hero is touchingly depicted as Frou Aventiure bids entrance to Wolfram's heart in order to tell him (and us) the further adventures of *der gehiure*.[13] These verses also serve to reinforce the time continuum between the Gawan and Parzival sections. In Chrétien's poem there is no comparable bridge between the sections, but only a five-line passage:

6212   Ne d'aus ne del doel que il font
        Rien plus a dire ne me plaist.
        De monseignor Gavain se taist
        Ichi li contes a estal,
        Si commenche de Percheval.

Wolfram's additions evidence the self-conscious care with which he composed the tale. However, the image that emerges of Wolfram as narrator is not consistent in the two transitional passages. In the earlier case (Book 7) he was didactic, subtly and deliberately elusive, and defiantly proud of his narrative skill. He appeared in full control of his tale's progress. Here in Book 9 he is sweet and submissive, exchanging puns with the 'mistress of the tale', and seemingly ignorant of what will happen and what has happened in Parzival's life. If the narrator is viewed as identical with Wolfram the poet,

169

the inconsistencies are glaring. If he is viewed instead as a device, his contradictory roles become comprehensible. In both passages the narrator has expressed a concern with the composition and development of the story. The effectiveness of the tale on the audience is the foremost objective. It seems apparent that on a structural level Wolfram viewed his model as inadequate and at times downright mystifying. He felt the need to clarify it and occasionally expand on it, though not fundamentally to alter it. In fact he followed his source carefully, adopting the alternation of Parzival and Gawan stories as well as the device of withholding information from his audience – a pattern well-suited to Wolfram's purpose, if necessitating comment.[14] Wolfram's minor alterations in these traditional patterns, as in the Jeschute episodes for example, are indicative of his continual emphasis on the dramatic potential of his story. The narrator enhances this aspect as he mediates between poet and audience. His function is subtle control of the audience's involvement in the tale – luring them to acceptance or inspiring them to question.

Wolfram's respect for the integrity of his model cannot be gauged in the narrator's numerous references to the 'truth' of his story, most of which are spurious and in defence of the specifics of his account.[15] The majority of these are formulaic and cite the *âventiure* or *maere* as a source, supplemented by a few longer discussions of the narrator's reliability (i.e. 15, 8–13; 53, 26–8; 123, 13–17; 827, 1–14). An interesting aspect of these assertions is their often aggressive tone. The narrator challenges his audience to accept his word: 'swerz niht geloubt, der sündet' (435, 1).[16] He is establishing more than credibility with his listeners. He seems to be asking not merely for passive acceptance but active participation:[17]

59, 26   ine sagez iu niht nâch wâne:
               Gebiet ir, sô ist ez wâr.

The most extreme example of this kind of inversion occurs during the description of the Gral's dispensation of food during the ceremony at Munsalvaesche:[18]

238, 8   man sagte mir, diz sag ouch ich
                      ûf iwer ieslîches eit,
                      daz vorem grâle waere bereit
                      (sol ich des iemen triegen,
                      sô müezt ir mit mir liegen)
                      swâ nâch jener bôt die hant,
                      daz er al bereite vant.

Wolfram has exchanged the customary roles of narrator and audience, forcing the listeners to take the oath of verity. The high degree of self-consciousness in such manipulation of formulae reflects Wolfram's awareness of the ironic potential in the narrator's role.[19]

There are several aspects of this kind of ironical play which are important for understanding the narrative technique in *Parzival*. First, the success of such a surprising reversal depends on the sophistication and attention of the audience. As with his humorous twist of the conventional image of Arthur (281, 14–22) or his humble bowing before Frou Aventiure, the narrator is deliberately teasing his audience, toying with their expectations and challenging them intellectually to appreciate his manoeuvres as a story-teller. In addition to the irony of the role reversal, a further complexity is achieved by breaking in at this specific point of the Gral ceremony. The narrator has engaged the listeners' emotions and curiosity as they accompany the bewildered hero. The action seems almost to be taking place before them and their companion, the narrator ('seht', 233, 12 and 'âvoy nu siht man' 235, 8). Then, at a high point in the stream of miraculous delights, when the wondrous bounty of the Gral stretches imagination to the limit, the audience is unexpectedly called upon to testify. By choosing this point to elicit an assertion of truth, the narrator emphasises the significance of the Gral's power. In addition, he subtly reinforces the audience's sense of participation in the scene and their interaction with him as a separate figure. Wolfram is also relieving himself of some responsibility here, and as we have seen, this aspect of the Gral's power is not the essential one for him. By referring ironically to the *Tischleindeckdich* aspect of the Gral's powers he is showing that this is not the major factor; the audience can believe it if they wish.

An audience witnessing an oral recitation of Wolfram's *Parzival* is necessarily aware of the narrator as a dynamic, if enigmatic, presence. As seen in previous chapters, he does not impose himself constantly and often seems to disappear as the characters command the foreground. When he does intervene, it is frequently to draw attention to himself as poet-narrator, which he does through subtle reminders of his presence, occasional comments on the story's form, and repeated remarks about the process of narration.[20] These references to method, whether they be statements, challenges, or appeals for sympathy, serve to awaken an aesthetic appreciation in his listeners. Thus he serves to modulate the audience's intellectual and emotional involvement. His tale is presented as true, with the characters and motivations, as in real life, complex and often indecipherable. Throughout, the narrator continues to juggle the idea of his control over the tale with the notion of its having control over him.[21] For long periods the characters alone will carry the action, engaging the listeners' emotions in a dramatic account. The narrator's interruptions call the audience's attention to his technical feats as raconteur and lead them to confront the ethical and spiritual questions raised by the tale. Here again he generally offers encouragement but no direct guidance.

From his omniscient perspective, however, a narrator is in a position to be a guide, to make moral judgements and explicate his story for the benefit of his listeners. Yet Wolfram does not avail himself of his vantage point to offer such aid. As narrator he is typically non-committal in evaluating his tale, in fact he is far from candid in expressing his attitude towards central issues such as the relative merits of the female sex, *minne*, and even Parzival's guilt.

Let us look first at Wolfram's comments on women and *minne*. Presenting himself as an uneducated and impoverished knight, Wolfram often compares his meagre existence with the splendour in his tale or views the poverty of his own amorous successes in light of situations met by his characters.[22] These contrasts enhance the world of his tale at the narrator's expense. On one level such passages reinforce the ironic detachment evident in some of the narrator's comments on truth. He seems often to be playing with literary convention.

554,4   bî mir ich selten schouwe
            daz mir âbents oder fruo
            sölch âventiure slîche zuo.

Here the imagery recalls the amorous formulae of the dawn song, an allusion enriching in its tantalising humour. These passages also contrast the idealised world of the Arthurian realm with the prosaic existence of the narrator and, consequently, of those who must be content with his literary account of it. What is more, the narrator repeatedly insists on the distinction. Thus the realities he and his audience share are brought into focus alongside those of Parzival.

Wolfram also uses this kind of humorous intrusion to interrupt a dramatic scene, startling us with his apparent detachment. An excellent example occurs in the provocative description of Parzival's first meeting with Jeschute.[23] Having led us into the tent along with Parzival and displayed this 'wunsches âventiur' to our curious eyes, without warning Wolfram the narrator pipes up:

130, 14   ich waen mich iemen küssens wene
            an ein sus wol gelobten munt:
            daz ist mir selten worden kunt.

In the midst of a captivating scene the narrator breaks his dramatic thread for a moment to bemoan his lot, then returns to his description. We catch Wolfram's twinkling eye in this passage, as he – both poet and narrator – delights in the irony at the expense of his hero and his audience. In such an instance he is purposefully misleading, for his personal comment reinforces the misconception he has carefully seduced his audience into accepting: namely, that they perceive the scene as Parzival does. Such interruptions attest to Wolfram's consciousness of technique and the good humour with which he uses the narrator persona to influence the audience. One is enticed by the mode of story-telling and by the narrator's role into vicarious involvement with the story, only to be jolted by the recognition of the gulf between one's own reactions and those of Parzival. This playfulness was surely not lost on a sophisticated audience who could appreciate the levels of humour and laugh at both Parzival's naïveté and their own gullibility, gaining insight into the hero's behaviour and their own. The process of recognition sharpens attentiveness to the skilful dodges of the narrator persona as well as to the realisation, essential to an understanding of *Parzival*, that things are not always what they seem, and that a good listener must remain alert.

In addition to such personal observations, the narrator often makes general objective pronouncements on the customs and morals of his time. Nearly all of his remarks are concerned with *minne* and the problems she creates, with special emphasis on the negative traits of the female sex. Although it is in exactly this realm that the narrator has portrayed his own comical lack of success, he assures us that he bears no grudges:

334, 8   swaz in dâ wart ze teile,
                daz haben âne mînen haz:
                ich pin doch frouwen lônes laz.

In spite of the levity of such comments, in other cases there is a seriously negative tone in the narrator's utterances on love. These instances go beyond the topos of unhappy love or the motif of *liebe unde leit*. Although the matter of the

174

Parzival story contains many instances of joyful love, Wolfram's commentary stresses the negative aspects, accusing Frou Minne of *untriuwe* and treachery, most notably in the lengthy diatribe in Book 6, i.e.:

291, 19	frou minne, ir pflegt untriuwen
	mit alten siten niuwen.
291, 26	(iwer site kan sich hellen).
292, 4	iwer werc sint hâlscharlîcher vâr.

This address to Frou Minne interrupts the account of the succession of knights who attack Parzival as he stands transfixed by the drops of blood on the snow. Structurally the narrator's words function to heighten suspense over the hero's potential humiliation (291, 5-8) and invoke sympathy for his pain. The image of *minne* throughout this contradictory passage is generally negative. Love is depicted as an excruciating burden (292, 17),[24] and Gawan too reflects on the agony of love's rule (301, 22ff.). Yet the narrator weakens his own charges by suggesting that his vindictiveness stems from personal hardship in love adventures (292, 5-11). Furthermore, Wolfram's spiteful remarks are addressed here to a personification of love and seem restricted to a critique of the mundane manifestations of her authority: the power to influence man to perform irrationally. The struggle is given allegorical significance by the intercession of Frou Witze (295, 8). The narrator further complicates the issue by blaming Parzival's *triuwe* for robbing him of *witzen* (296, 1-4). In Chrétien's poem there is no corresponding attack on love. On the contrary, Perceval is made joyful by the remembrance of his love (4206ff.). Both he and Gavain regret that his happiness was interrupted by rude challenges (4442ff.).[25]

What can be made of the contrast between Wolfram's attitude as narrator and the supreme value of love as depicted within the story? The irony of this distinction was surely apparent to an audience familiar with the esteemed position of *werde minne* in Parzival's history.[26] However the contradictions are to be resolved, Wolfram the narrator grants Frou

Minne only negative characteristics in this passage. His taunting sarcasm goes beyond convention and consequently becomes a comment on that convention. By exalting the power of a personified Frou Minne, the narrator is simultaneously rendering her in a mundane form. Elsewhere too, while speaking of love's power, he demotes it from a mystical to a comically quotidian level:[27]

593, 14   ist diu nieswurz in der nasn
               draete unde strenge,
               durch sîn herze enge
               kom alsus diu herzogîn,
               durch sîniu ougen oben în.
               gein minne helfelôs ein man,
               ôwê daz ist hêr Gâwân.

Such incisive metaphors seem to toy with the chivalric tradition. The narrator's commentary stands in nearly paradoxical relation to the subject matter of the text where true love is depicted with great sensitivity. Indeed, Parzival's steadfast love for Condwiramurs reflects his inborn *triuwe*, and as such is both inspiration towards and promise of his ultimate success (see Chapter 4, n. 25). The tension between these opposing views is repeatedly apparent as the sprightly narrator pokes at the edifice of courtly *minne* from constantly shifting angles. In the case of Parzival, Wolfram is careful to keep the barbed remarks aimed at an abstract Frou Minne and not at his hero's specific condition. Gawan, however, is not left untouched by the humour. Yet, except for the dubious episode of Antikone,[28] the characters themselves exhibit no irreverence in their pursuit of love.

The paradoxical contrast seems to extend to the narrator's outspoken attitude towards women in general and the depiction of femal characters in the poem. As we have seen, virtuous women are Wolfram's most sensitive and inspired character portrayals, yet as narrator he repeatedly depreciates the female sex, including the personified Frou Minne. In

speaking of women Wolfram most often refers to his own
period, mocking the superficial display of feminine modesty
and virtue which according to him sometimes disguises in-
sincere motives. Many of his remarks in this context áre imbued with a spirit of fun, yet they are definitely barbed and
carry at least an undertone of serious criticism:[29]

515, 4   kampfbaeriu lide treit
          ein wîp die man vindent sô:
          diu waer vil lîhte eins schimpfes vrô.

A similar battle metaphor is used in describing the young
women of Arthur's court:

217, 13   und manec juncfrouwe stolz,
          daz niht wan tjoste was ir bolz:
          ir friwent si gein dem vînde schôz.

It is tempting to see an ironic comment on the tradition of
courtly love in this kind of figurative language.[30] The image
of love as a war, and the female sex as especially eager for the
fray, appears several times, and in Book 12 the narrator
directly accuses Frou Minne of foul play:

584, 26   dâ tuot frou minne ir zürnen schîn
          an dem der prîs hât bejagt.
          werlîch und unverzagt
          hât sin iedoch funden.
          gein dem siechen wunden
585, 1   solte si gewalts verdriezen.

Undeniably there is humour in the blend of love and battle,
yet, in the light of Wolfram's apparent censure of knightly
violence, the imagery appears to carry latent criticism of the
conventional practice of love as well.

The dangerous wiles and duplicity of women are among
Wolfram's repeated concerns in his role as narrator. Women
are seen as the instigators of man's weakness and in fact as
the source of all human perversity:

518, 25   diu wîp tâten et als wîp:
                etslîcher riet ir broeder lîp
                daz si diu werc volbrâhte,
                des ir herzen gir gedâhte.
                sus wart verkêrt diu mennischeit:
                daz was iedoch Adâme leit,
519, 1   Doch engezwîvelt nie sîn wille.

Malcreatiure's ugliness is due to woman as well:

520, 1   Von wîbes gir ein underscheit
                in schiet von der mennescheit.

Of course the maligning of women was a favourite topic in the Christian Middle Ages, fond as it was of the implications of original sin and the notion of Eve as the root of evil.[31] Yet Wolfram does not seem to be speaking only of abstract virtue and vice but of the reality he sees around him. How does his view relate to the image of woman represented in the matter of the tale? How can the narrator's pose help us interpret the message of the poem? There is a clear conflict between the virtuous women who are the heroines of *Parzival* – Herzeloyde, Condwiramurs, Sigune[32] – and the evils mocked by the narrator. The difference seems to reside in the inborn nature of each character. These women are not merely idealisations of abstract concepts but are represented as individuals. Each in her own way goes beyond the bounds of chivalric convention: Herzeloyde in her denial of courtly life; Sigune in her piety and devotion; Condwiramurs, the most conventional, in her youthful naïveté and undemanding view of love; all three in their extraordinary *triuwe*. The closest Wolfram comes to including any one of these women within a negative view of love is in the *Titurel* fragments where he laments the youthful love of Sigune and Schionatulander:

48 ouwê des, si sint noch   ze tump ze solher angest.
    wan swâ minne in der jugende   begriffen wirt, diu wert
                                         aller langest.

> ob daz alter minnen sich geloubet,
> dannoch diu jugent wont minne   bant, minne ist krefte
>   unberoubet.

There is no sense of condemnation towards the young lovers in Wolfram's words, only regret that *minne* came too early. The view of *minne* is different as well. The narrator does not taunt a profane Frou Minne here but expresses sorrow for the naïveté which will bind Sigune and Schionatulander too soon in the conventions of love.[33] Innocent adherence to rules is depicted with sensitivity and warmth in *Parzival* (Obilot, for example). Yet it seems part of the poem's message, transmitted through the narrator's contrasting view, that conventional behaviour is not enough. The women in the worlds of Arthur's court and the Gral are paragons because of their internal strength and character, not because of their external appearance or adherence to patterns.

The conflict between Wolfram's disparagement of women in his narrator's commentary and their representation in his *maere* is intentionally ambiguous. The discrepancy between the ideal and the real is thus continually thrust at the audience, forcing them to be aware of the difficulty in achieving perfection, and not allowing them to be content with the appearance of success. His remarks on inconstancy – including the barbs aimed at Isolde and Lunete – reinforce the idea that getting away with it does not make it right.[34]

Wolfram's most irreverent comments on love occur in the Gawan books. Even in the lighter and more playful atmosphere of these sections some of his observations are shockingly disrespectful towards the institution of courtly love:

> 601, 17   er solts et hân gediuhet nider,
>   als dicke ist geschehen sider
>   maneger clâren frouwen.

It is also in the Gawan books that Wolfram as narrator speaks

179

critically of the composers of love lyrics:

587, 7   maneger hât von minnen sanc,
                 den nie diu minne alsô getwanc.

In such statements as these (also 588, 1-6), in his ambiguous attitude towards women and love, in the veiled criticisms of the moral content of rival tales, and in his pride in himself as a man of action rather than letters, Wolfram commands a place both for himself and for his tale apart from the tradition of Minnesang and courtly romance.[35] By calling into question the traditional values of courtly love and the idealisation of the *hohe vrouwe*, he is forcing his audience to take a stand, to become conscious of their cultural roles and to learn to look behind the conventional practices for human value. The narrator's engaging commentary maintains the audience's awareness of the logistics of the story as form, leading them to appreciate his artistry on two levels. And his enigmatic treatment of the concept of chivalric love stimulates contemplation on the basic values of social conventions, involving the audience as literary critics on yet another level. The role of the narrator accustoms them to ask for more than entertainment from a tale and to approach its ethical stance from different points of view. Further, both within the tale and in their own experience, they are led not to accept convention and superficial success in place of deeper values. This is surely didacticism of a most unusual sort, for the lesson is not clearly stated but must be discovered. The artful shifting of the narrator's posture renders a summary of his view almost impossible. Yet, following the 'self-defence', he offers a concise, sober statement which may serve as well as any independent attempt at a synthesis:

116, 5   Ez machet trûric mir den lîp,
                 daz alsô mangiu heizet wîp.
                 ir stimme sint gelîche hel:
                 genuoge sint gein valsche snel,
                 etslîche valsches laere:

sus teilent sich diu maere.
daz die gelîche sint genamt,
des hât mîn herze sich geschamt.
wîpheit, dîn ordenlîcher site,
dem vert und fuor ie triwe mite.

This short passage seems to express Wolfram's view as a poet, a combination of the narrator's scepticism and the inherent idealism of the female characterisations.[36] The role of the narrator serves a didactic purpose in causing the listeners to judge their own society against the norms of the romance, yet this didacticism is generally covert. For Wolfram as narrator seldom pronounces but continues to elude his audience, enticing them to a crossroads and then leaving the decision to them. He demands from his listeners what Mohr has called 'schöpferische Mitarbeit', thus ensuring the richness of their experience.[37]

The narrator's often irreverent commentary on the standards of his own time seems all the more conspicuous given his reluctance to pass judgement on the actions of characters within the story. We have already heard his conviction that praise should be given only when it is deserved (above, pp. 167f.). Looking closely we find that he generally obeys this rule; in fact, he is even reticent in praising the deserving behaviour of his heroes and heroines.[38] At two points he indulges in lengthy apologies and rationalisations in defence of characters: once in his charming explanation of Condwiramur's coming to Parzival's bed (192, 1-20); and again in a lengthy defence of Keie (296, 13 - 297, 15).[39] Both are humorous additions which reveal the ironic stance of the narrator. Once more, Wolfram invites the audience to consider these characters as real, to question and analyse their motives rather than accept the word of the *âventiure* or the traditional implications of courtly literary standards.

Complementary to his reticence with praise, the narrator rarely ventures overtly negative judgements about his characters either, and then only on relatively minor issues.[40] In

withholding criticism he follows a conventional pattern
expressed concisely by Keie in Hartmann's *Iwein*:[41]

2493   ich prîs in swâ er rehte tuot,
         und verswîge sîn laster: daz ist guot.

Wolfram's narrator alludes to his own positive approach.
Describing Cundrie's terrifying appearance he apologises for
having to speak of a woman in such negative terms:

313, 26   mîn zuht durch wârheit missefuor,
            daz ich sus muoz von frouwen sagen:
            kein andriu darf ez von mir klagen.

His meaning is ambiguous. He claims never to have described
a woman so negatively, a justified assertion. But if it is excep-
tional that *wârheit* compel him to go against *zuht*, this implies
that he is not normally altogether forthright in speaking of
women – a back-handed compliment at best. Furthermore,
as we have seen, Wolfram's narrator speaks poorly of women
throughout his poem, and his depiction of Antikonie is at
best equivocal. He is again playing a role, ironically teasing
his listeners, warning them to listen carefully in order to
appreciate his subtlety.

   As narrator Wolfram can clearly exert a profound influence
on his audience's reception of the tale through indirect means.
This form of narrative guidance is especially crucial in the
realm of the poem's ethical code where little direct commentary is offered. In seeking to define the moral implications of Parzival's behaviour, for instance, one is struck by
the narrator's reserve, especially at three crucial junctures:
Parzival's slaying of Ither, his failure at the Gral castle, and
his turning away from God.[42] Any one instance would seem
to warrant comment as a crucial stage in the hero's development and thus within the overall scheme of the tale. In addition, each episode can be viewed as relevant to the audience's
grasp of important ethical and spiritual questions: the limits
of *zuht*, the moral justification of knightly combat, and the

role of Christianity. What is to be made of the narrator's reticence? He expresses sorrow at Ither's unnecessary death, pities the young Parzival for neglecting the question at Munsalvaesche (240, 3-9), and makes no comment as Parzïval denounces God (332-3). In fact, the question of Parzival's guilt or innocence provides a useful arena for studying Wolfram's subtle development of a moral position regarding his characters through narrative suggestion and narrative silence and through the 'hidden' commentary contained in the use of adjectives, adverbs, and word choice in general.

The recurrence of a crucial motif, the hero's *tumpheit*, reveals the persuasive manner in which Wolfram uses the narrator persona. Although the question of Parzival's guilt has engaged scholars for decades,[43] there has been little attention paid to the narrator's function in presenting the relevant passages. Similarly, many pages have been devoted to analysing the use of the word *tump* in *Parzival*, most extensively by Heinz Rupp and Alois Haas, but no one has focused on the significant role of the narrator in the use of this term.[44] Emphasis on *tumpheit* is of course consistent with the slow progress towards wisdom of *dirre toersche Wâleis*,[45] yet the nature of the pattern that emerges indicates a conscious structure and illuminates the subtle intricacy of Wolfram's narrative technique, particularly in his use of the distinction between poet and narrator.

In Middle High German the word *tump* generally meant foolish in the sense of simple-minded and inexperienced.[46] It is applied to Parzival in Books 3 and 9 with revealing changes of meaning. In Book 3 the word or its derivatives occur fifteen times, and the context unquestionably implies the meaning of foolishness stemming from immaturity and lack of experience.[47] Although the narrator predictably refrains from any overt discussion of Parzival's state, he fills his account with references to the young hero's *tumpheit*. Parzival's foolishness is mentioned by other characters as he passes **through his first experiences with the world outside his** mother's protection: the knights, Jeschute, Ither, and Gurnemanz. The narrator, however, utters by far the majority of these judgements (25 out of 32), and their pattern does not seem random.[48] Furthermore, throughout Book 3 it is the narrator alone who uses the word *tump*.

This section opens with a glimpse of Parzival's youth depicting him as compassionate and sensitive to nature's beauty (117ff.). His total lack of familiarity with the 'civilised' world is reflected in his interaction with the knights, and here he is first called *toersch* and *tump* (four times). His innocence is then given external form as his mother dresses him in fool's clothes.[49] In this section there are three references to his simplicity, two of these by the narrator. Again the word *tump* is used once to describe the young hero's state, the negative connotation lightened by a positive adjective, 'Der knappe tump unde wert' (126, 19).

The description of Parzival's encounter with Jeschute contains five references to his lack of experience, three by the narrator, and again one reference to *tumpheit* (139, 14). Notably Jeschute is the last character in Book 3 to refer to Parzival as a fool (*tor*, 133, 16); the remaining examples are all the narrator's. The Sigune episode contains only one reference to Parzival's simple-mindedness (*toersch*, 138, 9), but his naïve goodness and selflessness are demonstrated in his behaviour (139, 9ff.). The narrator reminds us of Parzival's *tumpheit* through epithets framing the episode with the fisherman, though the hero's actions are not specifically judged (142, 13 and 144, 11).

The section preceding Parzival's first confrontation with Ither is of extreme importance here. Though it does not contain any words connoting foolishness, it creates a powerful visual image of Parzival's naïve youthfulness and innocence through an affectionately humorous description (144, 17–145, 5). We are reminded of the lad's lack of education (in specific contrast with Tristan) and told that his ignorance of *kurtôsiê* is merely proof that he is *ungevarn* (analagous to his *tumpheit*). At Arthur's court Parzival continues to demonstrate his naïveté in his *unbetwungen* chatter and ingenuous behaviour. Thus, without openly imposing his own presence or opinion, the narrator continues to point out Parzival's simplicity while linking this with his beauty (which is a sign of his goodness)[50] and his excellent breeding:

149, 25   der wol geborne knappe
                hielt gagernde als ein trappe.

Such paradoxical images stress exactly the special blend of virtue and folly in Parzival's *tumpheit*.

The progressively concentrated sequence of images depicting Parzival's naïveté demonstrates how carefully the case has been presented. We have been shown a person of innocence and untutored good nature, and subtly but insistently reminded of his simple-minded foolishness throughout the episodes of Book 3. As we continue into the Ither episode the effectiveness of this methodical scheme becomes apparent; the way has been prepared for our acceptance of Parzival's slaying of his cousin. The poet has presented various points of view on Parzival's foolishness thus far, but with the Ither episode it is the narrator who bombards us with reminders, referring specifically to Parzival's *tumpheit* eleven times. He refrains from further commentary, however. Although the slaying of Ither is a deed of momentous significance within the ethical system of the poem,[51] Wolfram's narrator ignores the concept of sin altogether (as does Gurnemanz later, 170, 4). Rather he grieves for Ither because of the unheroic manner of his death (159, 5-12),[52] and relates the mourning of Arthur's court (155, 12-18; 159, 20-160, 30). His own opinion is given only in the passing references to Parzival's *tumpheit*:

156, 21   entwâpent wart der tôte man
                aldâ vor Nantes ûf dem plân,
                und an den lebenden geleget,
                den dannoch grôziu tumpheit reget.

185

161, 4   sîn harnasch im verlôs den lîp:
           dar umbe was sîn endes wer
           des tumben Parzivâles ger.
           sît dô er sich paz versan,
           ungerne het erz dô getân.

These do not seem to be terribly convincing excuses for a
deed of such gravity, and one wonders how the narrator would
defend himself at this point against his own criticism of poets
who mislead their public.[53]

The deed is certainly grave, in fact it is central to the moral
questions raised in both *Parzival* and *Willehalm*. As Mohr has
shown, the death of Ither has significance not only as Parzival's
sin against his cousin but reflects Wolfram's concern for the
problematic status of the chivalric code, a system perpetu-
ating Cain's original sin against the brotherhood of man.[54]
Given the crucial nature of the issues, the narrator's reticence
seems all the more remarkable. Yet his stance is in fact consistent if considered in light of Wolfram's narrative technique
throughout the poem. The narrator persona encourages the
audience to judge and influences their decision. Although he
does not commit himself in the form of moral judgement, his
repeated allusions to *tumpheit* serve to mitigate the impact of
Parzival's deed. Yet the narrator's very insistence on soften-
ing the implications betrays the gravity of the issue for
Wolfram the poet. The audience's sympathy, carefully enticed by near subliminal suggestion, thus embraces the lad
who commits fratricide and *rêroup*. Parzival's innocence is
not enough to excuse him, and the audience will come to
understand this along with the hero, yet the natural inclina-
tion to read Parzival's action as sinful has been subverted.
The audience cannot accept it as Arthur's court does – judging
it an unfortunate but not blameworthy occurrence – for its
gravity has been made clear. At the same time the references
to Parzival's *tumpheit* stress his innocence, so that his inad-
vertent sin against *triuwe* is less a personal failure than it is
an expression of his, and mankind's, sinful state.[55]

The ironic distance between the poet Wolfram and his narrator persona is apparent in this careful depiction of Parzival's deeds as unintentional folly. For the poet this point in Parzival's development warranted extreme care in presentation, so that its gravity would be realised without the hero's basic innocence being impugned. The pattern in the use of the term *tumpheit* thus supports the interpretation of Ither's killing as indicative not just of Parzival's individual error but of a basic failing in the chivalric order, itself reflecting a general human failing. Parzival does not repeat such a mistake, nor does Wolfram's narrator mention the hero's *tumpheit* again except in twice asserting it has been overcome (179, 23 and 188, 17) and once near the end of the poem when he recalls the Ither episode (744, 14–18).[56] This position reflects the view of the Arthurian realm which accepts Parzival as a mature knight, wise in the ways of chivalry. Parzival becomes a paragon of the chivalric order, and Wolfram's narrator does not venture beyond that code to judge him. The ironic discrepancy between the poet's knowledge and the narrator's limited viewpoint is maintained.

It is consistent with the narrator's wordly perspective on his hero that he does not judge subsequent occurrences within the Gral realm. He does not condemn Parzival's failure at Munsalvaesche but merely expresses sorrow that Gurnemanz's advice was followed with such painful results (239, 8–17 and 240, 3–9) – perhaps a further hint that codes should be taken as advice and not law. Of those who do censure the hero, only the squire who raises the drawbridge alludes to Parzival's stupidity: 'ir sît ein gans' (247, 27). Sigune and Cundrie condemn him utterly for want of *triuwe*; neither mentions his *tumpheit*.[57] However, in a passage which seems to express Parzival's own thoughts, the narrator indulges in a rare interpretive generalisation and provides a clue to the real significance of the hero's predicament. These few lines can be seen to form a bridge to the events of Book 9 when Parzival returns to the narrative foreground:

319, 4   was half in küenes herzen rât
           unt wâriu zuht bî manheit?
           und dennoch mêr im was bereit
           scham ob allen sînen siten.
           den rehten valsch het er vermiten:
           wan scham gît prîs ze lône
           und ist doch der sêle krône.
           scham ist ob siten ein güebet uop.

The importance of *scham* was Gurnemanz's first lesson (170, 16ff.), and here the assurance is given that this virtue will still support Parzival where his knightly skills cannot.[58] The narrative flow does not pause with this thought but returns to the action, yet these few words illustrate Parzival's next five years of lonely struggle. Although he perseveres in his *küenes herzen rât* and his *zuht bî manheit*, it is not these but his sense of shame, his ultimate humility, which leads him to repent and be forgiven. Thus Wolfram suggests that Parzival's salvation cannot come alone from the knightly skills which he possesses in abundance, but from a personal quality which goes beyond chivalric ideals towards Christian standards of humility. As Gurnemanz said:

170, 15   . . 'lâts iuch gezemn.
           ir sult niemer iuch verschemn.
           verschamter lîp, waz touc der mêr?
           der wont in der mûze rêr,
           dâ im werdekeit entrîset
           unde in gein der helle wîset.'

A sense of shame does not contradict chivalric codes, but must as a personal virtue go beyond them.

A further level in the meaning and application of *tump* occurs in the Trevrizent episode. As shown above, Book 9 is carefully orchestrated in a slow crescendo ending with Parzival's experience at Fontane la Salvatsche. Wolfram as narrator remains very much in the background, letting the dialogue and action tell the story. Yet the recurrence of the word *tump* in relation to Parzival makes this episode significant for the present discussion, and the narrator's reticence reveals yet another aspect of Wolfram's utilisation of this persona. Here the narrator's comments on Parzival are restricted to positive epithets such as 'der gehiure' (433, 8), 'kiusche vrävel man' (437, 12), and 'der degen' (435, 3 and 10). This position is consistent with his former evaluation of Parzival's achievements and with the fact that God is again guiding the hero (435, 12). The narrator's judgement agrees with appearances on the worldly level. Yet Parzival's foolishness is referred to directly and indirectly several times in this Book,[59] always by Trevrizent or Parzival himself. Since the discussion with Trevrizent leads Parzival to confront his past misdeeds, it is not surprising that the hero's previous *tumpheit* is discussed. Yet a new perspective is added in that the term is applied not just to the killing and despoilment but also to his silence at Munsalvaesche which was not judged to be *tump* before this and which, according to the narrator, occurred after Parzival had become wise. Even more intriguing is Trevrizent's use of *tump* in relation to Parzival's present state. He speaks twice of the young knight's foolishness in denying God (461, 28-30 and 463, 3) and calls him *tump* for his determination to find the Gral (468, 11). In each of these statements Trevrizent condemns the pride which attemps to do without God or acts in defiance of him. The hermit becomes more explicit in response to Parzival's challenge that God should recognise his skill as a knight:

472, 13   'ir müest aldâ vor hôchvart
            mit senften willen sîn bewart.
            iuch verleit lîht iwer jugent
            daz ir der kiusche braechet tugent.
            hôchvart ie seic unde viel.'

Trevrizent warns against excessive pride, citing the case of Anfortas, a great knight whose pride nonetheless undid him. The potentially negative influence of worldly love is affirmed once more in Trevrizent's words:

478, 30   'Amor was sîn keîe.
479, 1   Der ruoft ist zer dêmuot
           iedoch niht volleclîchen guot.'

Trevrizent speaks of the *tumpheit* of an unknown man who failed to aid Anfortas. As Rupp has shown, the term has reached a new level of meaning.[60] Trevrizent is not excusing a young, inexperienced lad from unintentional errors, but is in fact condemning a person for *tumpheit* as though this quality itself were sinful:

473, 17   ich ensol niemen schelten:
           doch muoz er sünde engelten.

The piety of Trevrizent and the sanctified atmosphere of Fontane la Salvatsche support the interpretation of his words as connoting a spiritual state of unenlightenment. He is not equating *tumpheit* and *hochvart* but is discussing them as similar elements in a value system quite different from that of the courtly world of Book 3 – and of Wolfram the narrator.

As Parzival struggles to come to terms with his sins he himself calls his failure at Munsalvaesche *tumpheit*:[61]

488, 14   'ir sult mit râtes triuwe
           klagen mîne tumpheit.

In Trevrizent's response the resonant chord of a spiritual-worldly dichotomy is struck again. He speaks of the uselessness of Parzival's five senses, implying not the presence of evil in Parzival but the lack of spiritual awareness which would have allowed his inborn *triuwe* to prevail, to dominate any external code he might be following (488, 26-9). The development of this profound theme is intricately wound into the fibre of conversation between these two characters. Trevrizent's remarks recall the narrator's words in Book 6 (see above p. 188), as the repetition of *tump* recalls his commentary in Book 3. Thus interconnections are formed on a thematic level as well as on the level of *sensus historicus*. Yet the dramatic intensity of the exchange between Parzival and Trevrizent remains undiminished. Their words seem independent of the process of narration; the scene seems to occur naturally before our eyes.

Wolfram's narrator is so reticent in this scene that he seems almost to vanish. He has presented himself as worldly and unlettered, not presuming to trespass on Trevrizent's discussion. It is consistent with his previous stance that he remain outside any talk of Christianity and the Gral, making no comments, explaining nothing – generally acting as if he were not there. Yet his rare shifts to the foreground in Book 9 are important from a structural point of view. He emerges from near invisibility to engage in lengthy commentaries only twice: in the opening discussion with Frou Aventiure (see above, pp. 169f.) and in recounting the story's transmission through Kyot (see above, pp. 135f.). Both are explicitly concerned with narrative technique. He also asserts himself in two shorter comic interludes: first joking at Parzival's meeting with the Gral knight and then commenting on the meagre fare at Fontane la Salvatsche (487, 1-12). In none of these instances does the narrator interpret or preach. He maintains a distance from the events he relates, though in each case his 'role' is different. With Frou Aventiure he is a humble transmitter, as ignorant of the story as his listeners, whereas in discussing Kyot he takes reponsibility for his tale (Frou Aventiure now tells Kyot, not Wolfram, how to proceed. Wolfram has withheld information at Kyot's request.) His comments when Parzival meets the Gral knight (445, 2-3, 10-12, 21-6) are restricted to a few rhetorical questions and humorous quips. Although in the last instance the narrator's sudden disruption of the Trevrizent episode at first seems discordant and even sacrilegious, if viewed formally and not symbolically it fits a pattern similar to his other intrusions. Wolfram asserts himself as narrator during a pause in the discussion between Parzival and Trevrizent. Following the lengthy discourse on the Gral and its history, and just as we expect a confession from Parzival, Trevrizent suggests a reprieve for food and exercise. This *retardierendes Moment* breaks the intensity of the experience yet maintains suspense, while in the pause Parzival 'sucht nach Kräutern und Worten'.[62] Wolfram thus keeps our interest, incites our laughter, and partly breaks the spell of the drama to stir the listeners' consciousness of themselves as observers.[63]

Clearly the narrator in *Parzival* does not lead his listeners by the hand or preach an ethical system, but suggests and stimulates personal involvement in the matter of the tale and in the telling of it. The narrator persona does not represent a consistent point of view or personality, but fluctuates enticingly, forcing the audience to confront the issues. In certain cases the narrator subtly influences the listeners' standards of judgement, at other times he makes no comment at all on the significance of events in his story; here his silence is itself an influence.[64] Sometimes he contrasts the world of the tale with his own or with that of the audience, sometimes he seduces them into misreading a scene. Wolfram's narrator is an animated 'character' who appears on the sidelines of *Parzival*. His comments and reactions are generally of a personal and even emotional nature, and thus, though often elusive, he never becomes tedious or pedantic. His influence on his audience is often covert, his stance contradictory. It is clear that he is not always a forthright representative of Wolfram the poet, and his elusiveness adds a delightful dimension to the effectiveness of *Parzival*.

The ethical questions raised in Wolfram's *Parzival* remain bound to a human element. They are not presented as dogma or abstraction but are entwined with human frailty through the actions and words of characters and of the narrator. There is certainly didactic intent in this format, but of a sort that eloquently appeals to a listening audience. The necessary physical presence of a narrator in a tradition of oral recitation serves as a buffer between the audience and the 'reality' of the tale, enclosing the action in a 'frame of commentary'.[65] The role of the narrator in *Parzival* serves both to intensify the dramatic illusion by carefully modulating the interweaving of commentary and dialogue and to stimulate and engage the listeners' intellectual appreciation at all levels of the poem.

The prologue to *Parzival* offers a condensed sample of Wolfram's roles as narrator, for here he appears both proud and humble, here he introduces the central themes of his story without explaining how they apply, here he is both lucid and mystifying, both ingenuous and evasive. How many of his statements are intentionally ironic has yet to be agreed upon, though much effort has been devoted to the problem.[66] It seems clear that the 'Wolfram' of the prologue is candid in his portrayal of at least one aspect of the poet Wolfram's nature: his sense of play.

In the prologue the term *tump* appears. The narrator mockingly applies it to any unsympathetic critics who fail to understand the meaning of his words.[67] He implies that those who see only the surface, not the essence of things, are *tumbe liute*. The denunciation of those seeking easy answers becomes a defence of his own narrative technique, ironically intensified through the complex and elusive language itself.

1, 20   zin anderhalp ame glase
             geleichet, und des blinden troum.
             die gebent antlützes roum,
             doch mac mit staete niht gesîn
             dirre trüebe lîhte schîn:
             er machet kurze fröude alwâr.

The narrator of *Parzival* plays a pivotal role in one's apprehension of the poem. He is a function of Wolfram's relation to his audience and serves to effect a balance between content and form, between emotional and intellectual response. What would this narrator have had to say about his reincarnation as the 'Wolfram' of Albrecht's *Jüngerer Titurel*?

193

ALBRECHT AS NARRATOR

The narrator of Albrecht's *Jüngerer Titurel* is carefully
modelled on his counterpart in *Parzival*. He uses similar rhetorical techniques, continues the subject matter, and claims
the name and biographical identity of his forerunner.[68] This
fiction implies a necessary distinction between the narrator
and the poet quite different from that in *Parzival*, a distinction which exists on the very surface of the work. In analysing the narrator's role in the JT, however, we find that within
the structure and philosophy of the poem the distinction
between poet and narrator vanishes. The narrator becomes a
direct spokesman for the intentions and ideals of the poet.

The prologue to the JT offers an obvious starting point,
for here Albrecht's narrator openly declares his intent to
transform the narrative technique of *Parzival*. The prologue
opens with a devotional section loosely modelled on the introductory stanzas in *Willehalm*. Then the narrator turns
attention to his critics:

18 Wirt ieman sund uf ladende,   der sol den zwivel hazzen.
   vor allen sunden schadende   ist der zwivel allen toufes
                                              nazzen.
   den zwivel han ich vor ein teil verbȯret.
   wie er nach helle verwet,   an Parzifal man daz von erste
                                              hȯret.
19 Di traegen (man da merket)   und witze di tunkel
                                              sehende
   mich zihent, ich hab verterket   ein pfat, vil wit daz lig
                                              der diet unspehende,
   da zů hab ich in schif und bruk enpfȯret,
   straz unde pfat verirret,   immer al ir verte ungerůret.
20 Hie wil ich nicht me sumen   der selben sache kunde,
   gar all ir straze rumen.   ir irreganc der wer mir lichte
                                              sunde.
   ich wil die krumb an allen orten slichten,

194

wan sumeliche jehende   sint, ich kunne iz selbe nicht
                           verrichten.
21 Wie Parzifal an hebende   si, des habet hie merke,
    mit tugende lere gebende.   dar zů geb uns der hȯhst
                           mit siner sterke,
    daz wir gevolgen aller gůten lere,
    daz wir gebenediet   noch mit got haben zeswen halp di
                           chere!

By taking credit for *Parzival* the narrator identifies himself with the poet Wolfram von Eschenbach. He further establishes this connection through the repetition of *zwîvel*, an allusion to the opening line of Wolfram's poem which is repeated almost verbatim in Albrecht's stanza 22 (see below, p. 197). The preceding homiletic stanzas provide an unambiguously Christian context for his summary of the moral lesson of the *Parzival* prologue: a warning against *zwîvel*, despair of God.[69]

In the following three stanzas Albrecht's narrator describes his literary procedure. Using a format borrowed from *Parzival* and *Willehalm* he responds to critical positions which judged *Parzival* too difficult and obscure. Like Wolfram's narrator, he begins by mocking his critics (19), yet he then accepts their judgement and admits that the obscurity of the text might be rightfully labelled a *sunde* (20). How unlike the wily Wolfram of *Parzival* who counters criticism with criticism, challenging his audience to raise themselves to his standards. Albrecht's narrator adopts a conciliatory mode. By clarifying passages from the *Parzival* prologue he intends to transform Wolfram's elusive hare into an easy prey:

50 Die fluge dirre spelle   fůr den tumben lůten
    fur oren gar zu snelle.   durch daz můz ich hie
                           worticlich bedůten,
    iz lat sich sanfter danne hasen vahen,
    ich mein, di sint erschellet: an sůche bracken mac
                           man iz ergahen.

The images used in stanzas 19 and 20 indicate the differences in Albrecht's conception of a narrator's function. He has become a guide, a leader who clears paths and provides needed bridges. Here we are given a clear statement of the intended changes in the narrator's role: rather than serving to stimulate and entice he will serve to conduct and explain. This is judged the narrator's proper duty, and he deserves blame if he fails to carry it out:

51 Ein glas mit zin vergozzen   und blinden troum, di
                                                                                    triegent.
    hat ieman des verdrozzen,   so wundert mich nicht, ob
                                                                                    di gen mir kriegent.

This reincarnated 'Wolfram' asserts his ability to present his tale directly and without ambiguity. He speaks with candour and authority about his role, vowing not only to make the story of *Parzival* clear but to elucidate the virtuous lessons of its prologue.

Further distinctions between Albrecht's 'Wolfram' and his model can be deduced from these statements on method. First, the high degree of self-consciousness in Albrecht's narrator becomes a theme in itself which exerts a constant influence on our perception of the poem. The Wolfram of *Parzival* seems consistently aware of himself as a figure relating an entertaining story directly to an audience, and his observations as a poet concerned with technique are subsumed within the first role. In the JT, however, Albrecht's narrator first expresses his continual absorption in style and in the process of composition, whereas his references to a listening public seem formulaic appendages. Already a more literary orientation is apparent. A second distinction can be seen in the narrator's stylistic goals: the mannered conceptions of 'geblümte kunst'. This attitude is in harmony with the poet's values as demonstrated in other aspects of his narrative technique where form itself conveys meaning. To a significant extent Albrecht's 'improvement' on *Parzival* is conceived in terms of structure and is manifested in thematic patterns and ornate language. A third quality differentiates Albrecht's narrator from his precursor: overt didacticism. The purpose behind his clarification is to broadcast successfully what he considers to be the *lêre* of *Parzival* (21).

Albrecht's narrator is candid about his goals and his methods. He illustrates this in an interpretation of the *Parzival* prologue that follows the remarks on narrative technique. Having cited complaints that the meaning of *Parzival* was not made clear, the narrator proceeds with an interpretative format very like the medieval practice of biblical exegesis.[70] He juxtaposes each section of textual material with its proclaimed significance, thus making sure the *lêre* is clarified.

22 Ist zwivel nachgebure   dem herzen icht di lenge,
daz mûz der sele sure   werden ewiclich in jamers
strenge.
herze, hab di staet an dem gedingen,
war minne, rechten gelouben,   so mac der sel an
saelicheit gelingen.

23 Gesmaehet und gezieret   ist ubel bi der gûte.
ob sich alsus parrieret   ein lip mit sunden clein oder
uber vlûte
und got darumbe doch in vorcht bechennet.
ich hoff siner erbermde,   so wirt di smaeh mit zierde
gar zetrennet.

24 Unverzagt an dem mûte   sol maenlich herze werben.
durch ubel sol daz gûte   maenlich herze nimmer lan
verderben,
daz sin aglaster varwe sich vereine
und werd uber al di blanke   und ob di blenke sich aber
dann entreine.

25 Dannoch si der geile   vor allem zwivel sunder,
swie er uf beidem teile   stet, des himels und der helle
hin under.
unstaeter mût dem zwivel wirt gesellet.
di selben sint geverwet   vinster var und ewiclich
gehellet.

26 So habent sich di blanken   mit varwe nach der sunne,
    di staeten mit gedanken.   di varwe git ein ursprinc aller
                                                brunne,
    der menschlich art alsus clarificieret,
    daz er von trûber aschen   der engel schar gelich sich
                                                kondiwieret.

Far from Wolfram's complex and challenging 'vliegende bîspel', Albrecht's stanzas are delivered by a sermonising narrator who arranges the images into an orderly system. The vocabulary comes from the *Parzival* text, but both the content and tone are distinctly Albrecht's. The sober narrator speaks with a voice of reason and moderation. In a homiletic appeal he includes himself with his listeners, emphasising his humility before God while pointing out the pious virtue of the JT's message. The wit and elusiveness of Wolfram's narrator have been tempered by solemnity and conviction of moral purpose, and the long lines of the stanza-form help establish this new mood.[71] Albrecht's exegesis of the *Parzival* prologue does not deal with Wolfram's introductory verses as a unit but gives each element an interpretation within a philosophical system established by the JT narrator. This 'wortilich bedûten' (50, 2) establishes a moral order of rights and wrongs, accented by Wolfram's white and black imagery to help illustrate the polarities of salvation and damnation.[72]

In a later section of the *Parzival* prologue Wolfram's narrator also addresses himself to the question of *lêre* raised by the audience (see above, p. 13, n. 22):

2, 5   ouch erkante ich nie sô wîsen man,
          ern möhte gerne künde hân,
          welher stiure disiu maere gernt
          und waz si guoter lêre wernt.

His reponse is couched in elusive metaphors and riddles, with the image of his sprightly *maere* dodging just ahead of the listeners and enticing them to pursuit (2, 9–22). In the JT this same passage has been adapted in a way that epitomises

Albrecht's approach. The evasive Wolfram has been transformed into a paternalistic figure who does not tease but asks humbly for acknowledgement of his tale's value, always emphasising the importance of his role as transmitter:

59 Ob sinnericher stiure   dise maer iht walten?
   si tůnt sich niemant tiure,   si nennent sich den jungen
                               zů den alten.
   und mugen sich die tumben dar gesellen!
   durch sinneriche lere   mův ich di wilden maer hie zam
                                 gestellen.
60 Und han doch nicht erkennet   man so rechte wisen,
   wirt im zu recht ernennet   ditze maer, ich waen, iz mův
                                 in prisen
   an witze kraft, iz si vil oder cleine.
   des bin ich ungerůmet,   wan iz hört an di aventůr
                                 gemeine.

The narrator no longer challengingly ridicules *tumbe liute* but offers them guidance.[73] Albrecht intends to make the surface reflect the essence.

The question skirted in *Parzival* is thus answered by Albrecht's narrator: 'durch sinneriche lere   mův ich di wilden maer hie zam gestellen.' This line expresses a critical judgement of Wolfram's obscurities and alludes to the opening of *Parzival* Book 9: 'Ez naeht nu wilden maeren' (503, 1), as well as to Gottfried's epithet for Wolfram: 'vindaere wilder maere'.[74] There is little doubt that Albrecht's audience was familiar with both *Parzival* and *Tristan* and would appreciate a play on the poets' rivalry.[75] The insertion of the reference at this point, however, raises further implications. Was Albrecht conscious of a veiled attack on Gottfried in the corresponding section of *Parzival*? Wolfram's discussion of human - especially female - vices is intriguing as a disparagement of contemporary behaviour and conventional standards of judgement. That it was also intended to criticise the dubious morals of certain literary heroines seems easily credible.

Interestingly, Albrecht omits these passages entirely. His narrator speaks of women at various points in the text, but not with Wolfram's censure.[76] Furthermore, throughout the lengthy JT neither Gottfried nor his poem is mentioned specifically.[77] One suspects that if Albrecht had been aware of the supposed intensity of the controversy, there would have been more explicit allusion to it. It appears that Albrecht and thus perhaps his audience as well were unconscious of any hidden polemic in these verses, that the choice of image was an allusion to the *Tristan* passage alone.[78] Though the JT fails to corroborate the idea of a Wolfram–Gottfried rivalry, this does not deny the feud. As we have seen, those facets of Wolfram's poetry which Albrecht so keenly appreciated were far removed from the subtle manoeuvring of the narrator persona. It was Wolfram's linguistic artistry and the Christian moral content of his tale that moved Albrecht, and it was these that Albrecht emulated. Wolfram's irony and playfulness, traits we now find appealing, were not those valued by Albrecht nor, we can assume, by his audience. Thus it need not be surprising that concealed jabs at Gottfried were not mentioned, perhaps not noticed.

Certainly such subtle means of persuasion were not adopted by Albrecht whose narrator is indubitably forthright in his pronouncements. Far from coaxing or teasing his audience, Albrecht's narrator is explicit in claiming virtuous teaching to be the ultimate justification of his work. Further, he implies that awareness of the edifying power of poetry requires the responsible poet to create a model of virtue. In describing his own method the narrator indicates some basic elements of Albrecht's narrative technique:

65 Dirre aventûre kere,   si si krump oder slihte,
     daz ist nicht wan ein lere.   darumb sol ich si wisen uf
                                                                    di rihte.
     hie vor ist si mit tugenden an gevenget,
     ir houbet, ir brust, ir siten,   ir fûze die sint mit tugenden
                                                                    gar gemenget.

The narrator expresses his control over the story; here his authoritative leadership extends to the *âventiure* as well as to the reader: he will tame and guide the *âventiure* as he will enlighten and guide the reader.[79] He speaks metaphorically about his method of composition: in order to fulfil its potential as great teaching the story is entwined with *tugenden*. On the first level this means that not only has the poem begun with virtue (stanzas 9–15), but virtue will be mixed throughout. By personifying the figure of *âventiure*, however, the narrator creates a symbol even more appropriate to Albrecht's method. The image of Frou Aventiure being arrayed in *tugende* is an apt portrayal of the poet's goals and befits his conception of poetry as a structure, as something visually perceived (see above pp. 13ff.). Further, the *tugende lêre* in the JT is a kind of raiment, not so much integral to the characters and action as it is something applied through the narrator's commentary.[80]

From the outset, the narrator of the JT expresses concern with the impact of his work as a philosophical and ethical exemplar. He also establishes himself as a model of erudition, an authority on religious, moral, and scholarly lore. The prologue illustrates this tendency in lengthy symbolical or allegorical digressions and concentrations of learned references. Though here the narrator restricts himself to Christian imagery, in later sections he betrays his knowledge of natural science, history, and other profane subject matter.[81] There is an implicit self-confidence in this learning which conflicts with the echoes of Wolfram's humility formulae. In a context of prolific erudition the 'Wolfram' of the JT is hardly convincing as an unlettered knight:[82]

68 Almehtic got der krefte,   di nie wart ubersterket,
   kunstlos, an meisterschefte   bin ich der schrifte, iedoch
                                   min sin wol merket:
   din kraft fur aller krefte wunder zeichet,
   di nie wart uber hŏhet   noch mit tiefe nieman
                                   underreichet.

The tone is pious and humble. Although Albrecht's narrator is not claiming illiteracy, from our point of view there is an ironic discrepancy between his refined scholarly method and humble assessment of his skill. In fact, he seems to exude self-confidence about relating the tale, and an amplified echo of Wolfram's humility formulae again expresses this while emphasising the narrator's meekness in the face of God and mortality:[83]

85 Iedoch swie wir ersterben,   doch můz wir leben immer,
    da nach als wir hie werben.   solche maere kund ich vol
                                 enden nimmer.
    ein ander werk han ich hie under handen:
    ob ich selb niunde were,   ich vorcht, iz wurde uns allen
                                 ser enblanden.

From our contemporary perspective there are in fact several aspects of Albrecht's prologue which seem ironic. The narrator has taken what was originally a subtle challenge to an impatient audience and transformed it into a mollification, thus reversing its effect. Further, an intentionally obscure and evasive passage now provides the basis for a discussion of the need for clarity, and this discussion is itself complex from a linguistic point of view. Finally, the 'explanation' of the *Parzival* prologue in the JT substantiates the aesthetic and moral philosophy of the latter poem while generally ignoring the first.

In spite of careful paraphrasing, repeated images, and the use of similar rhetorical devices, the narrator of the JT is distinguished in many respects from his counterpart in *Parzival*. Many of the differences are already evident in comparing the two prologues. Albrecht's narrator is highly conscious of himself as author and interpreter, and his copious remarks on the process of narration far exceed Wolfram's in both quantity and straightforwardness. The tone of the JT is solemnly didactic, a mode reinforced by exegetical style, learnedness, and dogmatic piety. Such a programmatic overlay onto the

subject matter of a chivalric romance is bound to result in
something quite unlike the engaging and dramatic tale of
Parzival. As we have seen, the effect of Wolfram's narrative
technique is to involve the listener both intellectually and
emotionally. As narrator Wolfram does not claim transcendent value for his tale nor stress its didactic merits, but rather
concentrates on the entertaining power of its narrative content:

3, 28   nu hoert dirre âventiure site.
           diu lât iuch wizzen beide
           von liebe und von leide:
4, 1   fröud und angest vert tâ bî.

In the *Willehalm* prologue as well Wolfram proclaims the
werdekeit of his tale, still stressing the value of the narrative
contents (5, 4ff.). For Albrecht's narrator, however, the
maere is something to be smoothed out; it is subsidiary to the
lêre which it exemplifies: 'Dirre aventûre kere . . . ist nicht
wan ein lere.' He does not speak of entertainment, does not
promise joyful and painful experiences, but is concerned with
teachings leading to spiritual enlightenment (which should,
like the *brackenseil* inscription, bring its own kind of joy).
The great popularity of his poem indicates that these values
were an accurate gauge of contemporary taste in literature.

Turning to the body of the poem we can study the narrator's execution of his intentions stated in the prologue. The
initial section, which relates the story of Titurel, serves as a
useful basis for illustrating the suitability of Albrecht's narrative technique to the close interweaving of story and interpretation. 'Wolfram' the narrator remains a faithful exponent
of the poem's ideological structure, playing a consistently
overt role.

89, 3 ich sol mich nu da mit in arbeit binden,
        wie Titurel der werde   wart geborn von richen
                                    kuniges kinden.

The narrator begins Titurel's genealogy as far back as Troy

and develops a complete history of the Gral kinship.[84]
Through reference to his *arbeit* in relating the tale he draws
sympathetic attention to himself and his task.[85] In a significant sense he becomes omnipresent. As he relates the Gral
family history his influence is always perceptible, not merely
through formulaic expressions (e.g. *ich waene*), or the fact
that he is the main agent for relaying information, but in his
tendency to summarise constantly and analyse from a point
of view specifically his own. There is seldom any sense here
of an anonymous transmitter, for even in reporting factual
material his concern with the implications of his story leads
him to interpretation. He often plays with the idea of his
own discursiveness, urging himself to keep up the pace:

107 Darumb ich doch volprisen   niht vor kan alle wurzen,
      noch all ir samen risen.   ich mǔz dem stam die zwie
                                    und este kurzen.
      Titurison, ein wurzel manger tugende,
      git mir so vil zu prisen,   daz ich bedorfte wisheit unde
                                         jugende.

In this passage Albrecht's narrator interrupts the genealogy of
praiseworthy men to point out humbly the necessity for
moderation in such accounts. This conventional device allows
for a pause which Albrecht uses to elaborate on the images of
wurzel, stam, and *prîs,* a digression continuing through the
following stanza after which he returns to the genealogy.[86]
It is indicative of Albrecht's narrator that there is very little
sense of directly addressing an audience, even in such a passage. In *Parzival,* Wolfram's narrator continually reflects
awareness of his audience's presence. When he feels himself
wandering too much he apologises (see *Parzival* 232, 5-8;
642, 10-13; 643, 1 - 644, 11). He says he will skip the details
for the sake of the audience and the tale (699, 27 - 700, 8;
809, 15-24). Albrecht's narrator, on the other hand, begs
Frou Aventiure not to include details for *his* sake (2290,
etc.). In spite of formulaic references to his listeners,[87] the

narrator of the JT seems isolated from his public, absorbed in the struggle to organise his material. The sense of drama characteristic of *Parzival* is lacking even in the narrator's exclamations in the JT. 'Der red hie si ein ende!' (112, 1) is in fact an example of self-reflection, the narrator turning in on himself and his material. A similar instance occurs in a later passage where, elaborating on the nature of *minne* and *unminne* in the midst of a tournament description, Albrecht's narrator dramatises his audience's impatience with his digressions:[88]

2143, 3 'se, waz sol in turnei dise predige?
      wir gen nach kurzewile.   her Wolfram saget, daz
                              truren von uns ledige!'

Wolfram alludes to his audience's impatience with his method of telling the tale (453, 1ff. and 734, 1–4) but never to impatience with his moralising. In any case Albrecht's narrator ignores the pleas, using the discontent as an illustration of his point (2144). Such interruptions seem more to exemplify the poet's process of composition, a reflective, personal one. His manoeuvring is in the realm of ideas, his interjections formal observations of his own rather than responses to an actual or even readily imagined listening audience. This introverted quality renders the JT more appropriate to reflective reading or solemn recitation than to the dramatic performance one can envision for *Parzival*.

Continuing the account of Titurel's ancestors, the narrator tells of their struggles to bring Christianity to the heathens and Jews (114–35) and of the long-suffering faith of Titurel's parents (136–65). He remains at a certain distance from the events of his tale, relating them in generalised concepts and moralisations. Specific actions are rarely described, so the discussion stays on an abstract level. Thus Titurison's tourneys are depicted as reflections of ideal concepts:

138 Zeturney was er varnde   der jungen diet zu lere.

> wan swer daz unrecht sparnde   ist, der weiz wol
> ritterliche ere.
> zu scherm der werld der ritter wart gesetzet,
> daz witwen unde weisen   unrechts gewalts beliben
> ungeletzet.

This kind of conclusive statement does not allow for dissenting opinion. The moral system established in the prologue is based on the need for and the existence of ideal forms, and the narrator is far from facetious in expressing his belief in such values. He is aware of mankind's failing – after all, the whole Gral realm must finally be transported to the east because of corruption in the west – yet he appears convinced of the perfection of chivalrous ideals. There is no indication that he shares Wolfram's doubts about the codes of chivalry themselves, but only regrets their imperfect execution.[89] What is the effect of this kind of narration on a reader or listener? Its appeal is primarily to the intellect and not to the emotions. The audience is not led to participate in action or to make independent judgements. Indeed, one cannot identify with abstractions. Rather, a credo is offered for which the story provides examples.

The concept of chivalry as the expression of a Christian ideal forms the basis of Albrecht's *Weltanschauung*. Each of his main heroes – Titurel, Tschinotulander, and Parzival – strives towards perfection as a knight, a goal equally valid in both the Arthurian and Gral realms.[90] In fact the ideal concept of Christian chivalry overrides the distinctions between the world of Munt Salvasch and Arthur's court, so the two appear nearly equal as remote visions of perfection. Glimpses of contemporary reality provide a contrast, for Albrecht's narrator does not present a totally whitewashed view of his world, though his remarks are limited and sometimes oblique. In his discussions of knighthood we find allusions to a discrepancy between the ideal and the real. Here the narrator praises tournaments as an art, and jousting without mortal blows its highest form of expression:

140 Recht schůl an ritters kunste   ist turney sunder vare,
    ob haz und liebe gunste   da werbent niht. wan ot durch
                                   kunst vurware,
    so wer ein turnei sunder all vluste
    des grŏsten, daz ich meine.   daz průfent wol di wisen
                                   under bruste.

These lines offer a glimpse of the unpleasant realities of knightly conduct – even mock battles were often bloody and genuine warfare violent. The narrator's sentiments reflect a Christian code and seem to admit the social realities of his time. He does not refrain, however, from an aesthetic appreciation of warfare (neither does Jeschute, see above, p. 77). The visual impact of a field filled with armed knights is described with delight:

1988 Der niwen schilte blicke   und der zimier wunder
                                   waehe,
    netze, kloben, stricke,   ich wen, ie man uf erde so
                                   vil gesehe,
    da mit diu herzen vreude kunnen vahen.
    swer da niht vreuden růchte,   der wolt ouch vreude
                                     nimmer me genahen.

Bloody encounters are admired as well. The narrator exults over the Christian victories against the heathen, and in the midst of describing slaughter on both sides he exclaims joyfully:[91]

917 Da was ein striten schone.   swer gern in strite waere,
    der hete da vreuden done   gehŏrt. mich dunket striten
                                   wunderbaere,
    wan strit vil mangem herzen vreude stŏret,
    und so ie grŏzer striten,   so manz ie gerner singen,
                                     sagen hŏret.

Suck lack of remorse is not at all unusual in medieval poetry – in *Willehalm* only the heroes' deaths are lamented – and defence of the Holy Church was a venerable expression of

207

piety.[92] Indeed, Tschinotulander kills more than once, and
not just heathens. The gusto of Albrecht's narrator seems also
a response to the formal aspect of battle, its visual and audi-
tory splendour a manifestation of the chivalric ideal. Lengthy
battle descriptions fill the JT, reflecting the complexity and
vastness of heroic combat, and allowing Albrecht an endless
supply of material for elaborate variations. Like the Gral
temple, the battles are described as astonishing achievements
which the reader or listener cannot comprehend or visualise
on any scale of common experience. The narrator implies
that the description itself becomes *wunderbar*, and its capacity to move an audience increases with its scale. Furthermore, the importance of literature as inspiration towards
chivalric ideals is repeatedly stressed:[93]

2958 Swer ritterlich geverte   sol ritterlichen triben
      in schimpf und ouch in herte,   der sol daz nimmer
                                              gerne lan beliben,
      ern hǒre da von lesen, sagen, singen.
      daz git im kunst und ellen   noch mere dann mit
                                              toren gampel ringen.
2959 Sprechen und gebaren   mit hovschen siten riche,
      des sol man gerne varen,   daz man zu hove kunne
                                              hoveliche
      werben gen den herren und den vrowen.
      erdaht durch tugende schulde   wart diutscher bǔch
                                              mit triwen unverhowen.

The 'Wolfram' of the JT proudly includes his poem among
those paragons of chivalric virtue, *diutscher bǔch* – a clear
contrast with Wolfram's emphatic claims in *Parzival*.[94]
Albrecht's narrator conceives of his poem as a model of
literary didacticism. In the Christian knight he recognises a
unification of worldly and spiritual perfection, and it is this
abstraction which he portrays. As his interest in individual
characters is concentrated on their abstracted significance as
exemplars, so too is he interested in battles not as specific
events but for their symbolic potential.

Further manifestation of this perspective is found in the narrator's domination of the story through first-person reporting. The sparing use of direct dialogue is a significant divergence from Wolfram's technique and in the JT complements the narrator's role of fitting the action he describes into an abstract framework. Returning to the tale of Titurel's early education we find the first occurrence of quotation in the angel's message at Titurel's birth which outlines his growth into ideal Christian knighthood (162–4). The introduction of direct speech marks a slackening in the narrative pace, formally signalling the advent of a main character. The use of quotation also emphasises the sanctification implied by such an annunciation, further affirming the perfection of the hero.[95] The function of this passage is thus formal and symbolic; there is no exchange of dialogue and the scene is not presented in visual terms. It is significant in establishing the idealised nature of Titurel.

In this manner the boundaries between matter and commentary are often indistinct in the JT. The account of Titurel's youth is continually blended with metaphorical generalisation and moralising digression. His physical perfection – a reflection of his soul's beauty – is pictured in striking images:

175, 4 ein meien zit der ougen   was dirre knab, die sinen
                                                 blick erholten.

176, 1 Von got erkouft mit golde   was dirre saeldenbaere,
        ein stam der blůmen tolde.   und het er vluge, ich
                                           wene, er engel were.

The metaphors are clearly borrowed from Wolfram's description of Sigune in *Titurel*:

32, 2 er kôs si vür des meien   blic, swer si sach, bî
                                            tounazzen bluomen:
        ûz ir herzen blüete saelde und êre.
        lât ir lîp in lobes jâr vol –   wahsen, ich sol ir lobes
                                            sagen mêre.

A further allusion to Wolfram's poetry can be seen in Titurel's almost supernatural beauty, recalling Parzival's near-perfection:[96]

> 123, 16 nie mannes varwe baz geriet
> vor im sît Adâmes zît.

In both of Wolfram's passages the physical descriptions are part of consistently developing characterisations and seem to capture essential aspects of each personality which are further manifested through action and dialogue. In the JT passage the description remains abstracted, part of an ideal vision for which the narrator personally vouches. After the concept of Titurel's *wirde* is elaborated on a spiritual level, the discussion returns to his youth and early penchant toward the *vita activa*:

> 184, 3 an der gramatik wart er schier vol varnde.
> sin wille stûnt gen ritterschaft,   kunst der bûche
> wold er sin nu sparnde.
> 185   Manheit von ritterschefte   was er gerne lesende,
> dazû, waz hoher krefte   di minne hat.

The paucity of direct dialogue naturally befits this kind of narration. Throughout the JT the narrator shows restraint in granting the characters a voice, and when dialogue occurs it most often functions as a formal element, delineating structural sections or elaborating points made by the narrator. When they do speak, Albrecht's characters seldom seem to engage in actual conversation but discourse for the benefit of the reader. Indeed, in many instances of direct quotation in the JT one character speaks and the narrator summarises the response. In the initial 300 stanzas of Albrecht's poem there are only eight occurrences of direct quotation, and in only three of these cases is there any exchange among the characters.[97]

Titurel is thus shaped into a flawless knight through a series of symbolic confrontations with the essential and interdependent aspects of Christian chivalry: love of God, knightly skills, and honour towards women.[98] As a character he remains more an abstraction than a personality with an individual history. He is a presentation-piece of the JT value system.[99] It is indicative of the narrator's high regard for the merits of literary didacticism that the inspirational power of literature plays such a crucial role in Titurel's education.[100] Similarly it is reading, not action, which introduces Titurel to the conventions of courtly life. In spite of stating Titurel's rejection of formal education (184) – thus providing a further link with Wolfram's *Parzival* – the young hero's training is founded on an intellectual base quite in contrast with the empirical method enjoyed by Parzival. It is also distinct from Schionatulander's painful learning about *minne* which Wolfram recounts in *Titurel*, emphasising the need for practice:

86, 3 minne in lêrte an staeten vreuden siechen.
swâ kint lernent ûf stên an   stüelen, diu müezen dar
zem êrsten kriechen.

In the JT Titurel's training is of great significance and this is emphasised by the number of stanzas Albrecht devotes to it (184–97), and through the use of direct dialogue – the only example in the Titurel section of a sustained conversation, in this case a discussion between Titurel and his *meister*. The passage illustrates nicely the use of dialogue in the JT: even when characters engage each other in conversation, their words are primarily an elaboration of the ideological system established by the narrator. Dialogues are important not as 'realistic' dramatisations but as a means of explication.

190 Er vragt den jungen maere,   wer im von minne sagete?
'Ovidium puellere   las ich von ir, daz mir nicht
behagete.
si ist vil licht ein schrat, ein geist von helle.
ich han iedoch di merke,   der lûte ist vil ir vriunt, ir
gůt geselle.'

191 Der meister im do lere   gap von ir under scheiden
     und jach: 'ir sult nicht mere   di minne iu lazen vor der
                                    werlde leiden.
     minne mûz man haben zallen dingen,
     zallen sachen minne,'   sprach der meister, 'iedoch
                                   sunderlingen

192 Ob allen dingen minnet   got vor uz aleine
     und sit also besinnet,   daz ir iuch vor allen sunden
                                          reine
     durch sin minn, die sûzen, halten wellet,
     als ůch der engel kunte.   da mit sit ir der engel schar
                                       gesellet.

193 Daz wer vil ungeschehende,   wolt ir di minne miden.
     got wirt nieman an sehende,   wan die gen im di waren
                                    minne riden
     kunnen so, daz man daz ubel laze
     durch sin ware minne   und sich gen allen gûten dingen
                                     saze.'

194 'Got was mir ie benennet   wert vor allen dingen,
     mir aber unerkennet,   alle dinc zu minnen
                                   sunderlingen.
     und hat sich minne so zu got gesellet,
     so will ich si niht hazzen   und wil si minnen, sint si
                                   got gevellet.

195 Si mocht ouch anders cleine   sulche kraft erziugen,
     daz si di werlt aleine   uber striten kan mit ir urliugen
     und da zů, swaz vliuget unde vliuzet.' –
     'nein, herre,' sprach der meister,   'wie mich al sulcher
                                   rede von iuch verdrůzet!

196 Man heizet einez minne,   daz wol unminne hieze.
     daz pfendet saelden sinne   und hazzet got mit
                                   starkem wider drieze.
     di selben minne heizet uns got miden.
     swer si dar uber minnet,   der mûz darumbe sin
                                   gerichte liden.'

The unmistakable similarity of Titurel's naïve questioning with Parzival's queries about God and knighthood illustrates the analogy between the two heroes. The subject matter and naïveté also link this episode with the questions of Signune and Schionatulander in Wolfram's *Titurel* ('minne, ist daz ein er? . . .' 64ff.) and with the 'Minnegespräch'-tradition as seen in Veldeke's *Eneit*, for example. Further, Titurel's intellectual capacity and moral purity are manifested in his attitude towards the profanation of love: Ovid's works were not included among the elect 'diutscher bůch', a not so subtle reminder that the JT *is* included.

Titurel's natural antipathy for non-chivalric views of love further echoes the narrator's value system. Similarly, the instructor's lessons provide a sort of sermon within a sermon, for the attitude is again that of the narrator, and the *meister* thus speaks to Albrecht's audience as well as to his pupil, teaching them too the Christian view of worldly and spiritual love. The clear subordination of earthly love, even if ideally courtly, to *wâriu minne* reflects the essential credo of the poem.[101] The advice is not the expression of an individual personality as, for instance, that given Parzival by Herzeloyde or Gurnemanz, but an impersonalised generalisation. Nor is it limited by the point of view of the character giving it; thus it does not need to be overcome and reworked in order to merge into the hero's personal system. It is not something he and the audience must go beyond, as are the many lessons offered to Parzival. Similarly, Titurel's confrontation with wordly *minne* is not portrayed as an emotional experience. Instead he is presented with the concepts and adopts them as his own. His understanding is at once complete; ideal *minne* is now added to his virtues.

Thus by careful selection Albrecht emphasises those principles and attitudes essential to his narrator's *tugende lêre*. In *Parzival* the vignettes of the hero's youthful simplicity stand alone as memorable scenes. Their symbolic significance is expressed in terms of action and personality, and these levels blend together in the listener's memory into the illusion of a 'real' character.[102] In the JT a different effect is achieved through the intermediary presence of a narrator. Seeing through the narrator's eyes and with the benefit of his omniscient vantage point, the reader is led to accept the poem's value system without question. The characters appear as figures in a morality play, while the significance of their actions is not left to grow in each listener's mind but is offered within the work itself. The narrator speaks with authority for the norms of his ethical code and thus functions as a trustworthy companion in interpreting the secular level of his tale as an expression of its sublime significance.

This is demonstrated further in the next hurdle Titurel faces in his education. From *minne* the narrator turns to the physical challenge of knighthood: 'Nu heten sich gemenget ot aber do di heiden' (198, 1). The hero's first campaign against the heathens is related in generalised terms; the Christian knights eagerly vanquish the enemy (201–5), and the most concrete description is that of the slaughtered Saracens (206). There is no mention of Titurel being instructed in battle techniques and no description of his actual performance. We are simply told that he acquitted himself flawlessly:

203 Si [the heathens] můsten im entwichen   und siner
                                         claren jugende.
    swa si hurticlichen   durch gedrange brachen, da was
                                          mugende
    wol di cristenheit hin nach zu varne.
    di da night wolden sterben,   die heiden heten vliehen
                                          nicht zesparne.

This episode in Titurel's development is not given a specific geographical or historical context, for like the lessons on *minne* it represents a symbolic stage of growth in the timeless period of Titurel's youth. Instead, the narrator eulogises

Titurel's divinely virtuous beauty and *vroude* (207–17), defending his own extravagant praise in a discussion of Titurel's humility (218). This is followed by a general attack on arrogance (219–20) in strong language that seems surprisingly bitter and might well be aimed at specific contemporaries of Albrecht. However, the imagery is reminiscent of Wolfram's commentary in *Parzival* and *Titurel*, re-emphasising the continuity between these poems and the JT.[103] Furthermore, in spite of the caustic humour of the metaphors, the narrator's homiletic mode maintains an impersonal distance.

Through commentary and symbolic digression the figure of the hero is shaped into the representation of an ideal. The *tugende* themselves form a compound image that comes to represent Titurel. The remaining aspect of Titurel's chivalric education, his conduct towards women, is similarly discussed on an abstract level (221ff.), which rapidly becomes a general analysis of *êre* in relationships between the sexes. Albrecht's narrator places blame on the male sex for darkening the brightness of chastity – imagery established in the prologue – and adds a strong defence of women:

231 Nu git man vil den vrowen   di schuld an der unstaete.
    immer unverhowen   wer al ir pris, swa man so maenlich
                  taete,
    daz wibes ere nach vluste nieman gernde
    waer, und ob si gerten,   daz si di man menliche wern
                  entwernde
232 Danne ot mit staet aleine   und daran staete beliben.
    so wurde ouch nimmer cleine   saelde und ere an
                  mannen und an wiben.
    nu hat unere so witen sich gepflichtet
    zesunden und zu schanden,   daz saeld und ere vil
                  nahen sint vernichtet.
233 Und doch vor gotes ougen   sint si in hohem werde.
    swer nu sunder lougen   der eren hoch an vrowen sus
                  begerde,

daz si vil werdicliche weren lebende
nach gotes ordenunge,   dem wer ouch got vil saelicheit noch gebende.

As in his evaluation of tournaments, the narrator allows a glimpse of contemporary social conditions. His advice is worldly and specific, cautioning men not to give in to base desires but to raise their minds to the acquisition of *saelde* and *êre* (235–7). The association between honourably serving God and women reflects Trevrizent's advice to Parzival and is consistent with the idealised relationships depicted in both poems.[104] There is no echo here, however, of the ambiguous attitude of Wolfram's narrator towards the female sex; if anything the narrator of the JT denounces such a position as he next engages Frou Aventiure in a discussion of female virtue and chivalric duty (240ff.).[105] The value system of the narrator is a consistent reflection of the tale he tells; the narrator persona and the poet are ideologically one. The counterbalance of Wolfram's narrator has been replaced by a unified viewpoint in which abstractions apply to both matter and contemporary reality alike. The didacticism is pervasive and straightforward.

The narrator is never really 'invisible' in this kind of presentation. His power if not his presence is continually perceptible as he organises and motivates the story's progression. He seems to control the basic structure of the plot, and the direct statements of characters are used to ornament or reinforce this underlying *lêre*. His account is rarely dramatised to involve the audience emotionally. Nor does the narrator himself seek to develop the strongly personal appeal of Wolfram in *Parzival*. True to his promise in the prologue, he serves as guide and interpreter. In spite of numerous formulaic expressions of involvement with his story (*ôwê* etc.) he seems to remain aloof, looking on from a certain distance.

In *Parzival* the narrator often becomes emotionally caught up in the action as though he were a bystander, and on such occasions he spontaneously addresses his characters.[106] This device is used in the JT, but with an indicative twist. Instead of addressing those present in the scene being described, Albrecht's narrator often rhetorically addresses absent characters. For instance, when he foresees danger for Tschinotulander he addresses Sigune who is thousands of miles away: 'Owe des, Sigune,   du maht nu vurhten wol des Anschevines' (4227, 2). This change is consistent with the narrator's role as moraliser and explicator in the JT. His interventions do not serve to enhance his own dramatic presence or the immediacy of the action taking place. Rather they serve to point out relationships, to foreshadow or otherwise tie events together in a significant and cogent fashion, and to emphasise his omniscient grasp of the material.

In relating the story of Titurel, Albrecht's narrator is faithful to the programme outlined in his prologue and in the *Verfasserfragment*. He interprets the actions of his characters from a consistent moral perspective. While continuing to emulate the 'Wolfram' of *Parzival*, however, he chooses a very different mode, adapting the stylistic and rhetorical mannerisms of his model to serve a new conceptual framework. One particularly revealing transformation of a Wolframian motif is Albrecht's portrayal of Frou Aventiure who in *Parzival* is called upon at the beginning of Book 9 to recapitulate the adventures of the absent hero (see above pp. 169ff.). In the JT the narrator frequently engages this personification in discussion,[107] asking that she explain her intentions. Their conversations predictably serve to elaborate the story's meaning and range over topics such as the nature of *minne* and *unminne*, womanly virtue, and the Gral (4015–29; 240–6; 607–11). Albrecht's Frou Aventiure is devoutly pious in keeping with the general propriety of the JT. No longer merely the confident source of information she was in Book 9 of *Parzival*, Frou Aventiure has extended her responsibilities to the telling and interpretation of her tale. She is the self-conscious muse of a self-conscious narrator!

The rhetorical device of an animated muse allows Albrecht's

'Wolfram' to alter his normally straightforward narrative mode
while further reinforcing his own goals. Albrecht plays up the
ambiguity of this situation by having his narrator repeatedly
call upon Frou Aventiure to justify her narrative technique.[108] The narrator's aggressive tone often recalls Wolfram's
attitude towards Frou Minne in *Parzival*, but Albrecht's muse
defends herself – occasionally with some vehemence. That
her explanations are consistent reflections of Albrecht's own
narrative technique, even including the use of similar metaphors,[109] adds a touch of ironic play to these passages:

667 'Ich var di rechten strazen,   di da di werden minnent,
    di sich der rechten mazen   gen stetikeit an selden wol
                                         versinnent.
    du tůst mir, sam ich stelen well und rouben.
    waz dann, var ich gen strite?   der schade get uf
                                         heidenschaft di touben.'

Only once does Frou Aventiure appear, as she does in
Parzival, at a transitional point in the JT story. Preceding the
tale of Tschinotulander's journey to the east, the narrator
poses a series of rhetorical questions about future events, a
format clearly modelled on *Parzival* 433. He does not address
Frou Aventiure directly here but complains of the burdensome chore of writing (!) this story under her relentless demands
(see also 3205). The leitmotifs of *kunst* and *sin* are woven
into an expression of humble determination:

2523 Wolt uns di aventiure   nu hovelichen mieten
    mit solcher vreuden stiure,   daz wir uns werdikeit
                                         da mohten nieten,
    so můst ich herze, můt und sin arbeiten.
    swie iz darumb gestande,   iz můz doch sin, ich wilz
                                         zu liehte breiten,
2524 Ob mich got bi libe   let und ouch bi krefte,
    so daz man furbaz schribe   die aventiur mit solcher
                                         meisterschefte,

der mich sin mit kunste kan bewisen.
ich ahte niht der wultzen,   ob iz di hoch gemůten
                                    wellen prisen.

Albrecht clearly enjoyed this kind of rhetorical play and also found discussions with Frou Aventiure a useful device. His narrator's interviews with her provide an alternate method of exegesis, allowing for variations in viewpoint which serve to reinforce Albrecht's message. Furthermore, though seeming to show the narrator in a subordinate role, the confrontations with Frou Aventiure increase our awareness of the poet-narrator's omnipresence and of his achievement. The ironical relationship between the narrator's dependence on the *âventiure* and the *âventiure*'s dependence on him is maintained, and the interplay of the two themes continues to accentuate the story as something told, something requiring a transmitter and interpreter.

The drama of Wolfram's poetry readily engulfs its audience or reader in the fanciful world of the story. The figure of the narrator serves to intensify one's perception by enlarging the scope of identification and involvement with the poem. His lively and often humorous commentary renders the exotic worlds of Arthur's court and Munsalvaesche intelligible through quotidian metaphors and analogies to his own experience. He further stimulates an intellectual appreciation of narrative technique through his comments on poetic composition, his playful twists of convention, and veiled criticisms of contemporary poetry. The listeners are enticed into speculation and find themselves juxtaposing their own reality with that of the poem. The narrator sets forth questions and provocations, but keeps the answers to himself. The lessons of Wolfram's *Parzival* are entwined into the very fibre of the poem. Provoking the commitment needed to understand the *âventiure meine* is itself an essential part of Wolfram's didactic purpose and the appeal of his art. In his role as narrator he challenges us to make that effort.

219

Though adopting many of Wolfram's mannerisms, the narrator of the JT is another creature altogether. He shapes Albrecht's lengthy poem into a cohesive unit, forging a continuous plot out of fragmentary narrative elements and elucidating each detail within the symbolic system of his *tugende lêre*. On the level of the *maere* he is omnipresent; on the level of interpretation he is omniscient. His omniscience requires that he remain more an abstract presence than an animate personality, and his occasional Wolframian quirks do not disrupt this function. The majority of his interjections are exegetical and homiletic, reinforcing the sense of distance between the audience's realm of experience and that of the tale. Albrecht recognised in Wolfram's *Parzival* and *Titurel* a moral philosophy and spiritual attitude which he fully accepted, and he made his narrator 'Wolfram' the spokesman for that philosophy.

CONCLUSION

The task Albrecht set himself was formidable: to complete the stories of Schionatulander and Sigune and of the Gral in the style and spirit of Wolfram. He succeeded to a remarkable degree, mastering the elegant *Titurel*-stanza while crystallising what he felt to be the message of Wolfram's life-work. Albrecht's pride in this achievement can be measured by his remarks in the JT and in the *Verfasserfragment*, and his work's success by its sustained popularity. Albrecht's interpretation of Wolfram clearly satisfied the imagination of succeeding generations who esteemed his poem and did not question the validity of his Wolfram-persona. Through the later Middle Ages the JT was taken as a model, its emphasis on *lêre*, its idealised vision of chivalry, and its *geblǔmete rede* presaging significant developments in German literary history.[1] When it was rediscovered in the Romantic era the JT was once again hailed as a masterpiece. It was not so much the formal achievement which compelled the Romantic imagination as the unprecedented episodic richness and the all-encompassing Christian vision.[2] In Tieck's words, 'das Ganze ist wunderbare, abentheuerliche Rittergeschichte, Liebe und Religion in der zartesten Mischung'.[3] *Parzival* seemed paltry by comparison.[4]

In spite of the long success of his masquerade, Albrecht's narrative technique must be understood as fundamentally different from Wolfram's. In granting the formal elements of poetry a significance independent of the *maere*, Albrecht engaged form itself to bear an unusually important part of the meaning. This can be seen in the individual stanza and in large thematic patterns, in the depiction of specific action and in the portrayal of characters. Figures and motifs familiar to us from courtly romance, particularly from *Parzival*, find their place within this framework, yet it is the frame that prevails, the patterning and the narrator's interpretation of it

221

that convey meaning. Albrecht's modifications of traditional elements are similarly significant. Like *Parzival*, the JT tells of an epic quest for an elusive object, but there is no crisis in the hero's progress, no doubt of his Christian faith, no faltering in his resolve. Tschinotulander struggles against fate, as mankind must struggle, and though he is finally unsuccessful in this temporal crusade, it is made clear that his tenacity and faith will be rewarded. Tschinotulander and the other figures in Albrecht's tale are emblematic constructs; like the Gral temple they are models of virtue on a scale appropriately grand to populate the monumental landscape of the JT. The narrator too partakes of a similar irreproachability, extraordinary in his erudition, moral conviction, and apparent humility.

Given that the heroes and heroines of Albrecht's tale are embodiments of virtue, it is fitting that their stories be told in a poetic language which itself strives to achieve an ideal level of artistry. The priority given to formal refinement is evident in all facets of the JT – in the stanza where formal precision constrains the flexibility of the *Titurel*-stanza; in the subject matter where thematic patterns impose continuity on characterisation and internal motivation; in images of static perfection like the Gral temple and the *brackenseil*; and in the poem's overall structure where the interlocking themes can be seen supporting Albrecht's vision of his work as a model of *lêre*, a monument to Christian virtue, and a celebration of rhetorical elegance.

In Wolfram's poetry compositional organisation and thematic development play an important role, for they are integrally linked to the *maere* and work subtly on our sensibilities. As we have seen, Wolfram seldom offers interpretations in the form of commentary, but covertly induces the audience to active speculation and judgement. The poet Wolfram von Eschenbach remains elusive in that his statement is the poem itself – he, like the Gral or Parzival, is understood only within the context of his creation. Albrecht, though eluding us biographically, is much more candid as a commentator. In spite

222

of his masquerade as Wolfram, a personal value system is evident in the structure of his poem and the moralising commentary of his narrator. For Albrecht *wort* and *sin* are not the means through which the *âventiure meine* is transmitted, they are themselves the *meine*, to which the characters and the plot give service.

In Wolfram's *Parzival* the matter evolves dramatically, engaging our empathetic response to the characters' lives. The audience is also drawn in and challenged on aesthetic and moral levels. Here too the experience touches our sensibility. There is a consistent tone of intimacy between the narrator and his audience which lends *Parzival* the immediacy of a recitation and indicates that Wolfram composed with this in mind.

The JT challenges its audience on other levels. On the one hand it is a reformist's creation directed towards moral enlightenment. It is offered as a resource of exempla, both moral and aesthetic. Rather than moving us by the vitality of its narrative, it is moving in its awesomeness and challenging in its sophistication. For a full appreciation of the JT depends on mastering its difficult language, on a sound knowledge of Albrecht's literary heritage, and on an appreciation of his poetic facility. It is hard to imagine a comprehensible oral delivery of the JT. This would require an audience blessed with astounding memory and infinite patience. These same qualities, though on a lesser scale, are required even of the private reader, who is free to pause, look back, or skip ahead. The drama and intimacy of Wolfram's narrative technique have been replaced by homiletic discourse, engaging the audience not as participants but as initiates.

Albrecht's literary context was already distanced from Wolfram's and it should not be surprising that in his hands traditional elements took on such a new cast. It is likewise consistent with Albrecht's perspective as a follower that in reformulating Wolfram's work he systematised it. Albrecht recognised in Wolfram a true poetic language, moral authority, and scope of vision which he emulated. In ordering

Wolfram's imagination, Albrecht may well have made it more accessible to his public. The world which Wolfram represented for Albrecht seems suspended in a legendary past far more distant than the few generations between the two poets. Perceiving the values embodied in Wolfram's poetry to be threatened and indeed vanishing from the world in which he lived, Albrecht was bound to uphold and enshrine them in his own work.

LIST OF ABBREVIATIONS FOR JOURNALS FREQUENTLY CITED

Beiträge	*Beiträge zur Geschichte der deutschen Sprache und Literatur*
DU	*Der Deutschunterricht*
DVjs	*Deutsche vierteljahrsschrift für Literaturwissenschaft und Geistesgeschichte*
GLL	*German Life and Letters*
GQ	*German Quarterly*
GR	*Germanic Review*
GRM	*Germanisch–romanische Monatsschrift*
JEGP	*The Journal of English and Germanic Philology*
MLN	*Modern Language Notes*
MLR	*The Modern Language Review*
PMLA	*Publications of the Modern Language Association of America*
WW	*Wirkendes Wort*
ZfdA	*Zeitschrift für deutsches Altertum und deutsche Literatur*
ZfdPh	*Zeitschrift für deutsche Philologie*

NOTES

INTRODUCTION

1 Hedda Ragotzky, *Studien zur Wolfram-Rezeption* (Stuttgart, 1971), analyses the reception of Wolfram in the thirteenth century, including a chapter on Albrecht (pp. 93-149). The early reception of several MHG works is discussed by Peter J. Becker, *Handschriften und Früdrucke mittelhochdeutscher Epen* (Wiesbaden, 1977).

2 Ragotzky, p. 148.

3 Recorded in 1462 by Jakob Püterich von Reichertshausen. Earlier Hugo von Montfort referred to it as 'aller tütsch ein bluom'. In 1491 it was recommended in a will as the 'gotlichste Lere, die man in dutschen Boichern finden magh, want da alle Doegent vnd Ere innesteit, wie die Fursten vnd Hern sich haben vnd regeren sullen'. References taken from the introduction to Wolf's edition of the JT text: *Albrechts von Scharfenberg Jüngerer Titurel*, Werner Wolf, ed., vol. 1 (Berlin, 1955), p. x. For further examples of early praise of the JT see Werner Fechter, *Das Publikum der mittelhochdeutschen Dichtung* (1935; rpt. Darmstadt, 1972).

4 Karl Lachmann, *Kleinere Schriften* (1876; rpt. Berlin, 1969), p. 353.

5 Conrad Borchling, *Der Jüngere Titurel und sein Verhältnis zu Wolfram von Eschenbach* (Göttingen, 1897).

6 See articles by R. William Leckie, '"Bestia de funde": Natural science and the "Jüngerer Titurel"', *ZfdA*, 96 (1967), pp. 263-77; '"Gamaniol, der Vogel": Natural science and the "Jüngerer Titurel" II', *ZfdA*, 98 (1969), pp. 133-44; 'Albrecht von Scharfenberg and the "Historia de Preliis Alexandri Magni"', *ZfdA*, 99 (1970), pp. 120-39. Also Kurt Nyholm, *Studien zum sogenannten Geblümten Stil* (Abo, 1971).

7 Erich Petzet, 'Über das Heidelberger Bruchstück des Jüngeren Titurel', *Sitzungsberichte der Münchener Akademie der Wissenschaften* (1903), pp. 308-11; Werner Wolf, 'Zu den Hinweisstrophen auf die Wolframfragmente in der kleinen Heidelberger Handschrift des Jüngeren Titurel', *ZfdA*, 82 (1948-50), pp. 256-64; Werner Wolf, 'Wer war der Dichter des Jüngeren Titurel', *ZfdA*, 84 (1952-3), p. 309. In Wolf's edition of the text the stanzas are located between 499 and 500 (A-F) and between 1172 and 1173

(A). Walter Röll, *Studien zu Text und Überlieferung des sogenannten Jüngeren Titurel* (Heidelberg, 1964), pp. 129–30 accepts the
first stanzas but believes the last one to be by an early fourteenth-
century redactor.

8 Wolf, 'Wer war der Dichter', pp. 317–19. Also see Wolf, 'Nochmals
zum "Ehrenhof" im Jüngeren Titurel', *ZfdA*, 85 (1954-5), pp.
311–13.

9 Kurt Nyholm, *Albrechts von Scharfenberg 'Merlin'* (Abo, 1967);
Hans-Georg Maak, 'Zu Füetrers "Fraw Eren Hof" und der Frage
nach dem Verfasser des Jüngeren Titurel', *ZfdPh*, 87 (1968), pp.
42–6.

10 This occurs in the 'Hinweisstrophe' inserted between stanzas 1172
and 1173, however, which is not universally accepted as by Albrecht
(see n. 7 above).

11 Ragotzky, pp. 149ff., compares the passage from Berthold with the
JT text and reviews the various arguments.

12 The history of this fragment is bizarre. First it was reported as
missing from the Heidelberg library since 1819 (*Wolfram von
Eschenbach*, ed. Karl Lachmann, Berlin, 1833, p. xxxi). In 1835
Sulpiz Boisserée published it from notes he had made in 1817
('Über die Beschreibung des Tempels des heiligen Grales', *Abhandlungen der philos.-philolog. Classe der könig. bayer. Ak. der Wiss.*,
I, 1835, pp. 384-92). Then it reappeared around 1900 and was
published by Petzet. Although the rediscovered fragment differs
considerably from Boisserée's description of it, this is generally
ascribed to Boisserée's carelessness and the poem accepted as
genuine. For details see Petzet, pp. 287–92. See the introduction to
Wolf's edition, pp. xxv–xxviii for a summary of Petzet's view,
which Wolf accepts, and pp. cvif. for a discussion of the fragment
(Wolf's ms. no. 57). Wolf published Petzet's version with a few
orthographic changes in *Albrecht von Scharfenberg. Der Jüngere
Titurel* (Bern, 1952), pp. 78-80, and more recently a version with
normalised spelling in 'Zur Verskunst der Jüngeren Titurelstrophe',
Festschrift für F. R. Schröder (Heidelberg, 1959), pp. 167-9.

13 Petzet, pp. 301-18. Klaus Zatloukal, 'India – ein idealer Staat im
"Jüngeren Titurel"', in *Strukturen und Interpretationen* (Vienna,
1974), pp. 408-10, n. 24, argues that the *Verfasserfragment* may
have been written as early as 1269.

14 Helmut de Boor, 'Drei Fürsten im mittleren Deutschland', *Beiträge*
(Tüb.), 95 (1973), pp. 238-57. De Boor's thesis also helps explain
Albrecht's impersonation of Wolfram.

15 See the introduction to Wolf's edition, pp. cviif.

16 Röll's findings are questioned in a review by Kurt Nyholm, *Beiträge* (Tüb.), 87 (1965), pp. 442–60.

17 'Drei Fürsten'.

18 See the introduction to Wolf's edition for full details about each manuscript.

19 K. A. Hahn, ed., *Der Jüngere Titurel* (Quedlinburg and Leipzig, 1842).

20 As for its accuracy, I tend to agree with F. P. Pickering: 'It seems that there are only two alternatives for the editors of medieval works transmitted in a number of manuscripts; either a critical edition which will be "wrong", or a more or less diplomatic edition of two or three manuscripts (parallel texts) which will "not be an edition at all".' From *Literature and Art in the Middle Ages* (London, 1970), p. 147, n. 1. Wolf has combined the best of both approaches by offering a careful edition, alternate readings, and the complete text of ms. X (the oldest representative of group II). Wolf is praised for this format by Joachim Bumke in a recent review of a new *Willehalm* edition, *Euphorion*, 64 (1970), p. 431.

21 In the introduction to his edition Wolf includes an annotated survey of scholarship on the JT until 1954. More recent literature is listed by D. Huschenbett, 'Albrecht, Dichter des "Jüngeren Titurel"', *Verfasserlexikon*, I, 1977, cols. 172–3.

22 Hanspeter Brode, Untersuchung zum Sprach- und Werkstil des 'Jüngeren Titurel' von Albrecht von Scharfenberg (Freiburg i. B., 1966).

23 See also the review of Ragotzky's book by D. Huschenbett, *Anzeiger*, 87 (1976), pp. 114–22, especially pp. 118–22 on Albrecht. Huschenbett's own book on Albrecht, *Albrechts 'Jüngerer Titurel'. Zu Stil und Komposition* (Munich, 1979), appeared after the present study was completed.

24 From his introduction to 'Approaches to medieval romance', *Yale French Studies*, 51 (1976), p. 3. A. C. Spearing, *Criticism and Medieval Poetry* (London, 1972), pp. 1–7, speaks of the recent application of modern literary criticism to medieval works and the resulting benefits.

CHAPTER 1

1 Uwe Pörksen, *Der Erzähler im mittelhochdeutschen Epos* (Berlin, 1971), chapter 2; Bruno Boesch, *Die Kunstanschauung in der mittelhochdeutschen Dichtung* (1936; rpt. Hildesheim and New York: Olms, 1976), pp. 75–80; Günther Schweikle, ed., *Dichter über Dichter in mittelhochdeutscher Literatur* (Tübingen, 1970).

2 Both Rudolf von Ems and Konrad von Würzburg discussed the art of poetry and the question of artistic inspiration from a more abstract perspective. See Heinz Rupp, 'Rudolf von Ems und Konrad von Würzburg', *DU*, 17 (1965), pp. 5-17.

3 Wolf's edition follows the majority of manuscripts in presenting stanza 85 as the end of the prologue and 86 as the beginning of the tale itself (ms. D, for instance, includes a title at this juncture: 'Hie hebt sich an das lied und auenteur von thytureles vorden'). Yet stanzas 86 and 87 seem in fact to constitute the end of the prologue, repeating the poet's intentions and reminding us again of his responsiveness to audience demands.

Quotes from the JT through stanza 4394 will be taken from Wolf's edition; subsequent stanzas will be quoted from Hahn's publication.

4 The reference to *edeler diet* is reminiscent of Gottfried, as are other aspects of Albrecht's prologue.

5 Requests for known material are recorded elsewhere, but Albrecht's authoritative manner is unusual. Boesch, *Kunstanschauung*, pp. 110-12.

6 Ragotzky, pp. 103 and 137ff. argues that Albrecht intended his mask to be seen through, and that his audience recognised his deception and enjoyed it. There is no way of convincingly demonstrating this, however.

7 Scholars have consistently referred to the Venetian temple as St Mark's, though Albrecht does not name it.

8 Quoted from Wolf's edition in 'Zur Verskunst'. All quotations from the dedication fragment will be taken from this normalised edition. Surely the answer to the question in the last line is 'yes'. It is not clear to me why Wolf has inserted a question mark.

9 In MHG *tihten* and *getiht* are often synonyms for *bauen* and *Gebäude* as well, and the poet's function as 'creator' paralleled with that of the *Weltschöpfer*. See C. Stephen Jaeger, 'Der Schöpfer der Welt und das Schöpfungswerk als Prologmotiv in der mhd. Dichtung', *ZfdA*, 107 (1978), esp. p. 14.

10 For a discussion of the problems literary critics face in evaluating 'post-classical' works see Hugo Kuhn, *Minnesangs Wende*, 2nd edn (Tübingen, 1967), pp. 1-2, 176-9, 192-6; and Wolfgang Stammler, 'Ideenwandel in Sprache und Literatur des deutschen Mittelalters', *DVjs*, 2 (1924), esp. p. 755.

11 Though the question of quality is seldom raised, a concern with proper endings is a traditional motif in medieval German poetry. Boesch, *Kunstanschauung*, pp. 108-12; Carl J. Lofmark, 'Wolfram's source references in "Parzival"', *MLR*, 67 (1972),

p. 820. Wolfram himself was critical of the ending of his source (*Parzival* 827, 1–18), though it is likely that his remarks extend to other aspects of Chrétien's poem as well. See Jean Fourquet, *Wolfram d'Eschenbach et le 'Conte del Graal'*, 2nd edn (Paris, 1966), p. 171.

12 Albrecht concentrates the closing section of his tale into relatively few stanzas: Parzival's last visit with Sigune, her death and burial (5773–90); Ekunat's final defeat of Orilus (5792–829); the fates of Jescute, Ekunat, Kaylet and other minor characters are related (5830–67) – most of them retreat into lives of religious asceticism. These precede the discussion of conclusions which is followed by Lohengrin's tale (5918–63) and the subsequent history of the Gral (it is transported to the East and the lands of Prester John). We also learn about the nature of the Gral: it is a precious stone shaped into a dish, the plate of the Last Supper ('mandat', 6166–74). Finally Titurel dies (6184–5).

In attempting to clear up Wolfram's obscurities Albrecht occasionally does the opposite. For instance, in describing the Gral as the *mandat* or in assigning the early care of the Gral on earth to angels, Christ, and then Joseph of Arimathaea (6172–6), he contradicts Wolfram and his own earlier testimony. The weight put on Parzival's responsibility in his mother's death also stands out as an anomaly (6203) since little attention was paid it before. These changes suggest French sources for this section (Borchling, p. 105). On the other hand Albrecht does tie up several loose ends, including the Gral sword, which is given to Ekunat and thus ultimately avenges Tschinotulander (5722–60). He also explains Sigune's presence in the linden tree (5107–11). Leckie, 'Albrecht', p. 132, notes that Albrecht used information in source blocks in the later sections of the JT and conjectures that he used this format as an expedient (pp. 138–9). Wolf disagrees ('Wer war der Dichter', pp. 341–2). He believes the last section was written over a longer period. Both agree Albrecht finished out of a sense of duty.

C. S. Lewis speaks of the characteristic medieval will to organise and codify. His remarks seem especially appropriate to Albrecht: 'There was nothing which medieval people liked better, or did better, than sorting out and tidying up. Of all our modern inventions I suspect that they would most have admired the card index.' *The Discarded Image* (Cambridge, 1964), p. 10.

13 This accords with Petzet's view, see above p. 3.

14 For a more detailed comparison of Wolfram's and Albrecht's stanza structure see Borchling, pp. 111–19; Wolf's introduction to his edition, pp. cix–cxix and his article 'Zur Verskunst'; and Brode,

pp. 12-21. On Wolfram's *Titurel*-stanza see Ludwig Wolff, 'Wolframs Schionatulander und Sigune', in *Studien zur deutschen Philologie des Mittelalters* (Heidelberg, 1950), pp. 126-30. Both Wolff and Margaret F. Richey ('The "Titurel" of Wolfram von Eschenbach: structure and character', *MLR*, 56 (1961), pp. 180f.) stress the emotive qualities of Wolfram's stanza, its capacity for elegiac, tragic expression, yet disagree on its suitability for a lengthy poem. Richey believes Wolfram purposely wrote only these two short sections, recognising the limitations of his stanza (p. 191). Wolff feels that although only one further section was intended, the stanza's freedom is well-suited to a longer narrative poem (p. 128). The difficulties in determining the exact form of Wolfram's original *Titurel*-stanza and the JT's relation to it are discussed by Bumke in two articles on the manuscript tradition: 'Zur Überlieferung von Wolframs Titurel', *ZfdA*, 100 (1971), pp. 390–431; and 'Titurel-überlieferung und Titurelforschung', *ZfdA*, 102 (1973), pp. 147–88. Similar conclusions are reached by Wolfgang Mohr, 'Zur Textgeschichte von Wolframs "Titurel"', in *Wolfram-Studien*, IV, ed. W. Schröder (Berlin, 1977), pp. 123-51, who believes the *Titurel* fragments represent work in progress, and that Wolfram himself was still experimenting with the stanza form. Albrecht's efforts thus continue those of Wolfram (mss. H and M show yet further reworkings). Though it seems impossible to define the exact genre of the *Titurel* (Bumke refers to this problem as 'hoffnungslos', *Die Wolfram von Eschenbach Forschung seit 1945* (Munich, 1970), p. 339), it does seem that it – and the JT – were sung. On the *Titurel*/ JT melody see Karl Bertau and Rudolf Stephan, 'Zum sanglichen Vortrag mhd. strophischen Epen', *ZfdA*, 87 (1956-7), pp. 253-70; and Volker Mertens, 'Zu Text und Melodie der Titurelstrophe *Iamer ist mir entsprungen*', in *Wolfram-Studien*, I, ed. W. Schröder (Berlin, 1970), pp. 219-39.

15 Borchling counts only 370 masculine endings at the caesura in line 4, i.e. less than 6%. Wolf ('Zur Verskunst') argues that Albrecht gradually refined his form, moving away from the use of *stumpf* endings, though Wolf's material is not conclusive (Bumke, *Wolfram-Forschung*, p. 42).

16 Ever since Lachmann denounced the JT in 1829 (*Kleinere Schriften*, p. 353), scholarly opinion has geen generally negative. E.g. see Gustav Ehrismann, *Geschichte der deutschen Literatur bis zum Ausgang des Mittelalters*, part IIii (Munich, 1935), pp. 71-4; and Boesch, *Deutsche Literaturgeschichte in Grundzügen* (Bern, 1946; English edn, *German Literature. A Critical Survey*. London: Methuen, 1971), p. 75, who calls the JT 'confused, obscure and

generally unrewarding'. Even Wolf expresses serious aesthetic reservations (see esp. 'Der Jüngere Titurel, "das Haubt ob teutschen Puechen"', *Wirkendes Wort*, 6 (1955-6), pp. 2 and 6). Though the increasing appreciation for *Epigonen* and elaborate style over the last two decades has brought a revaluation of the JT, it is only very recently that the complexities of Albrecht's language have been penetrated and properly assessed. See Peter Kern, 'Der Kommentar zu "Parzival" 1,13f. im Prolog des "Jüngeren Titurel"', in *Studien zur deutschen Literatur und Sprache des Mittelalters*, ed. Besch et al. (Berlin, 1974), pp. 185-99.

17 Brode, pp. 62-8, gives some examples of unclear passages.

18 For a detailed description of word-plays and other mannerist elements in Albrecht's style see Brode, pp. 35-56. Similar word-plays are found in Wolfram's works, but Albrecht uses them much more extensively. On Wolfram's puns see Otto Springer, 'Playing on words: a stylistic note on Wolfram's *Titurel*', *Research Studies*, 32 (1964), pp. 106-24; and 'Etymologisches Spiel in Wolframs Parzival', *Beiträge* (Tüb.), 87 (1965), pp. 166-81.

19 Mohr, 'Fiktive und reale Darbietungszeit in Erzählung und Drama', *Volksüberlieferung*, ed. Harkort et al. (Göttingen, 1968), pp. 525-6, discusses the popularity of works like the JT which in spite of their vast scale were known well, in some cases partly by heart!

20 Gottfried praises Hartmann for 'siniu cristallinen wortelin' (4629) which are clear and pure (4628), whereas Wolfram ('der maere wildenaere') cannot achieve words that are 'ebene unde sleht' (4661). Gottfried von Strassburg, *Tristan und Isold*, ed. F. Ranke (Dublin, 1967). All quotations from *Tristan* will be taken from this edition. This view is supported by James W. Marchand's interpretation of Gottfried's excursus which argues that Gottfried is attacking a poet (whom Marchand assumes is Wolfram) for using language which requires interpretation on a non-literal level, not for confused language, neologisms, etc. 'Tristan's *Schwertleite*: Gottfried's aesthetics and literary criticism', in *Husbanding the Golden Grain* (Ann Arbor, 1973), pp. 187-204.

21 Line 5,2 of the Heidelberg fragment reads: 'sin was solher spitze'. Both Petzet and Wolf accept Paul's suggestion that it should read 'sin sin'. See Petzet, p. 297.

22 The choice of words here ('ez gaebe stiure') echoes Albrecht's prologue stanza 59, which itself is a paraphrase of Wolfram's prologue to *Parzival* (2,5-9). See below pp. 198f. Schweikle, '*stiure* und *lere*. Zum "Parzival" Wolframs von Eschenbach', *ZfdA*, 106 (1977), pp. 183ff., has defined *stiure* as something the reader must bring to the work, rather than the other way around. Albrecht does

not interpret the *Parzival* passage in this way, removing support from what is otherwise an interesting discussion of how Wolfram challenges his audience. Albrecht's *stiure* clearly includes artistic guidance for the imitator as well as ethical for the reader or listener.

23 He refers both to listeners and readers (1663 etc.). For a compelling discussion of differences between works designed for oral delivery and those for a reader see Mohr, 'Fiktive und reale Darbietungs-zeit'. The change to written transmission is documented by Suchenwirt who holds it against Wolfram that he only *heard* his source (cited in Boesch, *Kunstanschauung*, p. 87). Wieland Schmidt, 'Vom Lesen und Schreiben im späten Mittelalter', *Beiträge* (Tüb.), 95 (1973), pp. 309-27, discusses the rise of reading and writing as 'Bildungsideale'. It is difficult to believe that Wolfram composed orally, but his tale is directed consistently to a listening audience. *Parzival* thus represents a transitional stage between oral and written (D. H. Green, 'Oral poetry and written composition', in Green and L. P. Johnson, *Approaches to Wolfram von Eschenbach* (Bern, 1978), pp. 180-9). Albrecht, though expecting his poem to be heard as well, seems mainly to be addressing readers.

24 It also reflects medieval rhetorical practice. See Edmond Faral, *Les arts poétiques du XIIe et du XIIIe siècle* (1924; rpt. Paris, 1962), especially the section of Matthieu de Vendome's *art poéti-que* on the form of words, p. 154.

25 Other examples occur in stanzas 5097, 5393; also 567, 650, 1250, 1974, E (p. 134) and in the *Verfasserfragment* 10. References to Ekunat contain numerous plays on 'blůmen' and 'wilde' (1879, 1881-2). I cannot agree with Brode's view of *blüemen* as applying only to the courtly language of Albrecht's characters and thus showing the 'Kraftlosigkeit des Höfischen' (pp. 172-4).

The term *blüemen* occurs fairly often in works of the classical era. Gottfried, for instance, uses it in his prologue in relation to *lob*:

> 23: swa er mit lobe geblüemet ist,
> da blüejet aller slahte list.

and in the 'excursus' discussion of *des hasen geselle* Wolfram (4646-52). It is clearly an aesthetic criterion for Gottfried and no doubt reflects his familiarity with Latin rhetorical terminology (*flores*). The expression becomes much more prevalent among the *Epigonen* who enthusiastically adopted it for the ornate language which they sought to master. That *geblümte kunst* became a sty-listic concept is clear, yet it was presumably not a *terminus techni-cus* but a rather generalised notion applied already in the thirteenth

233

century to the poetry of Wolfram, Gottfried, and even Hartmann as well as to other works. Ragotzky, pp. 34–6, gives some examples.

A now outdated discussion in the *Reallexikon*, I, 1926, 413–14, credits Albrecht with introducing the term *geblümte kunst* as a *terminus technicus*. In the new edition of the *Reallexikon* the subject will appear under 'Stil, geblümter' in vol. 4, not yet published. The classic discussion of *geblümter Stil* is Otto Mordhorst, *Egen von Bamberg und 'die geblümte Rede'* (Berlin, 1911). Also useful is Hans Pyritz's introduction to his edition of *Die Minneburg* (Berlin, 1950), especially lxxi–iii, which argues the need for more positive evaluation of such rhetorical flourishes. See also Nyholm, *Studien*, pp. 7–124 and his extensive bibliography. More recent still is Karl Stackmann, '*Redebluomen*. Zu einigen Fürstenpreisstrophen Frauenlobs und zum Problem des geblümten Stils', in *Verbum et Signum*, II, ed. Fromm et al. (Munich, 1975), pp. 329–46, who continues the efforts to define *geblümter Stil* and, though concluding this to be impossible, still finds the term useful. Also the massive undertaking by Frieder Schülein, *Zur Theorie und Praxis des Blümens* (Bern, 1976). These works attest to the recent flood of interest in this long-neglected stylistic mode.

26 Several studies of Wolfram have examined his descriptions of characters, landscape, geography, etc.: David Blamires, *Characterization and Individuality in Wolfram's 'Parzival'* (Cambridge, 1966); Rainer Gruenter, 'Zum Problem der Landschaftsdarstellung im höfischen Versroman', *Euphorion*, 56 (1962), pp. 248–78; Marianne Wynn, 'The poetic structure of Wolfram von Eschenbach's "Parzival". A study of the natural setting' (Diss., Cambridge, 1953/4) and related articles by the same author (see bibliography). Brode's study contains a short but typically dense section on descriptive technique (pp. 125–40). There is room for further consideration of the various categories he touches upon, such as armour, battles, characters, or landscape.

27 In his introduction (pp. xiv–xliii) Wolf discusses the major scholarly studies on Albrecht's Gral temple which include: Boisserée (1835); Ernst Droysen, *Der Tempel des heiligen Gral* (Bromberg, 1872); Friedrich Zarncke, 'Der Graltempel' (Leipzig, 1876); Blanca Röthlisberger, *Die Architektur des Graltempels im Jüngern Titurel* (Bern, 1917); Julius Schwietering, 'Mittelalterliche Dichtung und bildende Kunst, 2: Der Graltempel im Jüngeren Titurel', *ZfdA*, 60 (1923), pp. 118–27; Jost Trier, 'Architekturphantasien in der mittelalterlichen Dichtung', *GRM*, 17 (1929), pp. 11–24; Heinrich Lichtenberg, 'Die Architekturdarstellungen in der mittelhoch-

deutschen Dichtung', *Forschungen zur deutschen Sprache und Dichtung*, 4 (1931); Hans Sedlmayr, 'Die dichterische Wurzel der Kathedrale', *Mitteil. des österr. Instituts für Geschichtsforschung*, Ergänzungsband 14 (1939), pp. 275–87; Sedlmayr, *Die Entstehung der Kathedrale* (Zürich, 1950); and Lars-Ivar Ringbom, *Graltempel und Paradies* (Stockholm, 1951).

Numerous works on the history of architecture make reference to Albrecht's temple, see especially Paul Frankl, *The Gothic* (Princeton, 1960), pp. 167–93. Recent studies focusing on Albrecht include Karen-Maria Petersen, 'Zum Grundriß des Graltempels', in *Festschrift für K. H. Halbach* (Göppingen, 1972), pp. 271–306; and Gudula Trendelenburg, *Studien zum Gralraum im 'Jüngeren Titurel'* (Göppingen, 1972).

28 Those in Wolfram's audience familiar with the Perceval story of Chrétien could of course anticipate. Wolfram's text does not forewarn the audience, however. It is significant that Parzival is not actually lost at this point but hastening with single-minded purpose down a more-or-less straight path (Wynn, 'The poetic structure', pp. 63–5).

29 Quotes will be taken from Wolfram von Eschenbach, *Parzival*, ed. Lachmann, 6th edn (Berlin and Leipzig, 1926); *Willehalm* and *Titurel*, ed. Albert Leitzmann, 5th edn (Tübingen, 1963).

30 At Arthur's court he saw only a *palas* in the city of Nantes, and it is not described (147,11–14).

31 Chrétien de Troyes, *Le Roman de Perceval*, ed. W. Roach (Paris, 1959), lines 1321–51. All subsequent references to Chrétien's poem will be to this edition. Arthur T. Hatto, 'Two notes on Chrétien and Wolfram', *MLR*, 42 (1947), pp. 243–4, has shown how Wolfram used part of Chrétien's description (perhaps misunderstood) in a later imaginative passage. Max Wehrli, 'Wolfram von Eschenbach: Erzählstil und Sinn seines Parzival', in *Formen mittelalterlicher Erzählung* (Zürich and Freiburg, 1969), pp. 199–204, compares the approach to Gurnemanz's castle with the corresponding passage in Chrétien's *Perceval* as a prime example of Wolfram's intentional 'Zickzackbewegung'-technique.

32 In his excellent article on the depiction of landscape in courtly romances ('Landschaftsdarstellung' pp. 253f.), Gruenter criticises the perspective in this passage, finding the unclear space bothersome and demonstrating a change of perspective from Gawan to the narrator which he also finds disturbing. This view seems to over-emphasise the incongruities and misconstrue the listener's process of comprehension. On Gawan's and the audience's gradual realisation of identities in this scene see Sidney M. Johnson,

'Gawan's surprise in Wolfram's *Parzival*', GR, 33 (1958), pp. 285–92; and Mohr, 'Parzival und Gawan', *Euphorion*, 52 (1958), pp. 18–22.

33 Again some specific numbers are noted: 100 couches seating 4 knights each, i.e. 400 again. This kind of detail is not disruptive; it is to be interpreted as 'a great many', not as incongruous exactness.

34 Michael Curschmann, 'Das Abenteuer des Erzählens', DVjs, 45 (1971), pp. 636f., discusses this passage in light of what he sees as a developing intimacy between the narrator as 'armer Ritter' and his audience. Though Curschmann's points about the narrator's demands on the audience are convincing, I find his emphasis here exaggerates the disruptiveness of the narrator's role and overlooks his function as guide and surrogate. Also see Xenja von Ertzdorff, 'Typen des Romans im 13. Jahrhundert', *DU*, 20 (1968), pp. 85–6.

35 The vastness of the room is emphasised (231, 24), there are four walls (231, 28) and at least two doors, one of steel (231, 17 and 29; 232, 10).

36 Whenever Albrecht's spellings differ fairly consistently from Wolfram's, the different spellings will be used to distinguish the sources, i.e. Wolfram: Munsalvaesche, Jeschute, Lähelin; Albrecht: Munt Salvasch, Jescute, Lehelin.

37 Wolfram himself makes similar allusions in *Titurel*, echoes such as 39,4 and 72ff., references to characters and situations understood only through familiarity with *Parzival*, etc.

38 The reading of ms. X is more logical for the final line, since in fact Albrecht does not go on to describe the building: 'ain and' werch hie pawe   ich mûz da gen leb ich nv in grozzen vorchten'.

39 Albrecht similarly explains Parzival's reaction to Kundrie (who, in *Parzival* 314–18, accuses him repeatedly of *valsch*):

5532 Dort bi dem plimizole   mir durch kvndrien schelten.
Kintliche zornes dole   im fvgte leit des liez er got engelten.
Einvalticlichen aller valscheit ane.
Im was niht bezzers kunde   des ward er hoch an selden
sunder wane.

See Gruenter, 'Parzivals *einvalt*', *Euphorion*, 52 (1958), pp. 301–2, for a discussion of *einvalt* and *unbescheidenheit* and Albrecht's use of these terms.

40 In the JT the font is referred to only later by Titurel (552). Its absence in the original description may indicate Albrecht's use of a literary model for this passage.

41 Additional sources for Albrecht's description have been suggested, usually churches he may have seen (i.e. the Liebfrauenkirche in Trier, St Gereon in Cologne) or those he may have heard of (i.e. the Church of the Holy Sepulchre in Jerusalem). Borchling, Ringbom and Wolf believe Albrecht worked from a literary model as well. See the introduction to Wolf's edition for summaries of the various opinions. Albrecht himself compares the temple with Solomon's temple in Jerusalem (366, 3–4). According to Richard Krautheimer's discussion of medieval architectural description ('Introduction to an iconography of medieval architecture,' *Journal of the Warburg and Courtauld Institutes,* 5 (1942), p. 2) the possibilities for comparison would have been enormous, making a search nearly meaningless. He cites examples of churches that we know were copied from the Church of the Holy Sepulchre at Jerusalem (p. 7); the inexactness of the actual imitations reflects the inexactness of medieval architectural descriptions.

42 Dedicated by Bishop Penitenza. Sigune's hermitage (see pp. 36f.) is dedicated by Boniface. This emphasis shows Albrecht's doctrinaire view, as well as reflecting the importance of dedication in the medieval period. Krautheimer, pp. 15f.

43 Further examples of mechanical devices occur at stanzas 345, 392, 405, and the final wonder of fish swimming under the floor (436).

44 Some mss. read as high as 72 side-chapels (Trendelenburg accepts 72, pp. 90, 193–9), leading to fanciful but implausible reconstructions such as that of Boisserée. Such attempts also manifest the differences between medieval and modern conceptions of architecture. For the Middle Ages the religious implications of a building were uppermost, rather than the specifics of construction, and distinctions we find crucial (such as round or polygonal form) were not made in describing or even building. Krautheimer, pp. 1–7. Arguments based on Albrecht's Gral temple as a precise description are thus misleading, whereas Röll's decision for 22 side-chapels is based on a sound discussion of literary tradition which takes the symbolic aspects into account (pp. 109–11).

45 Similarly 383, 407, 416, 426, etc.

46 The emphasis is reminiscent of the importance of jewels on the leash (see Chapter 3). On the significance of jewels in MHG poetry including many references to Albrecht see the recent publication by Ulrich Engelen, *Die Edelsteine in der deutschen Dichtung des 12. und 13. Jahrhunderts* (Munich, 1978).

47 In the initial 23 stanzas there are numerous examples of intrusions:

237

336, 344, 345–6, 348–50, 357–64, 366–71. Neither Schwietering
('Mittelalterliche Dichtung') nor his student Lichtenberg was dis-
turbed by the lack of continuity in Albrecht's description, but saw
the temple as a 'mystisch versinnlichtes Raumerleben' or a 'besonders greifbar werdendes spezifisch gotisches Raumerleben'
(Lichtenberg, pp. 51 and 44). Space seems hardly one's first impression, yet such an enthusiastic view is a useful indication of earlier
admirers of Albrecht's temple, many of whom would have agreed
that it is 's i n n l i c h d u r c h f ü h l t und wirklich e r l e b -
n i s g e t r a g e n , individuell geprägt und in s u b j e k t i v
mystischem Herzensdrang vertieft, die persönlichste und wort-
künstlerisch bedeutendste Gestaltung des Sakralbaumotivs der Zeit'
(Lichtenberg's emphasis, p. 52).

48 This 42-stanza allegory further dissociates the temple from the
    story. In Wolf's edition, pp. 111–17, the verses form a prayer to
    the Virgin, in whose honour a temple of words is built. The authen-
    ticity of the *Marienlob* has been questioned, see especially Röll, pp.
    123–8, and Brode, p. 24. However, Nyholm, *Studien*, pp. 19ff.
    uses it for his discussion. A further allegorical exposition of the
    temple is contained in Titurel's retirement speech (500–76) which
    differs from its model in *Titurel* (1–10) in its Christian emphasis
    (compare JT 512 with *Titurel* 6) and its stress on didacticism
    (especially JT 575–6).

49 Schwietering and Lichtenberg saw the temple as Gothic in style
    and mystical in expression (see note 47 above). Röthlisberger saw it
    as late Romanesque. On its use as a model for actual buildings see
    Droysen, p. 40, and Frankl, pp. 12 and 186–7.

50 G. E. Lessing, *Laokoon oder Über die Grenzen der Malerei und
    Poesie* (Reclam edn, Stuttgart, 1964), p. 124.

51 Lessing, pp. 117 and 133. Compare Hartmann's description of
    Enid's horse in *Erec* (7286–766). Also see discussion of Jeschute
    in Chapter 2.

52 Another instance: whenever a priest celebrates mass he pulls a
    string (or according to some manuscripts a silken cord) and a
    mechanical dove descends from the vaulting with an angel.

53 Though clearly it has another level of significance. It is an 'allegory'
    more of the type discussed by Friedrich Ohly, 'Vom geistigen Sinn
    des Wortes im Mittelalter', *ZfdA*, 89 (1958–9), pp. 1–23.

54 This is not to deny the significance of the move as a comment on
    contemporary insecurity in western Europe. See Zatloukal.

55 Likewise Prester John's temple which appears in stanzas 6103–58.

For a discussion of Albrecht's tale in relation to general medieval interest in this utopian legend see Zarncke, 'Der Priester Johannes', *Abhandlungen der philolog.-hist. Classe der kgl. Sächsischen Ges. der Wiss.* (Leipzig), 7 (1879), pp. 827–1030, and 8 (1876), pp. 1–186. Leonardo Olschki, 'Der Brief des Presbyters Johannes', *Historische Zeitschrift*, 144 (1931), pp. 1–14, relates the popularity of the legend to the realities of contemporary Europe and a longing for the ideal. Zatloukal argues a similar point of view. For a summary and convincing harmonisation of current views see Charles E. Nowell, 'The historical Prester John', *Speculum*, 28 (1953), pp. 435–45.

Other examples of Albrecht's interest in architectural structures are Arabadille's tomb (4815–30) and Gamuret's tomb (990–1004). To the latter description in *Parzival* (107) Albrecht adds some details, notably four golden columns supporting an arched dome (995). Borchling, pp. 26 and 79, relates both descriptions to passages in Veldeke's *Eneit*.

56 Wolfram pauses to identify Sigune and to relate her history, which he has not yet done though Parzival has encountered her already twice (138ff. and 249ff.). A reference to Lunete of Hartmann's *Iwein* occurs in the second meeting (253, 10ff.), but the narrator stops himself from such talk and returns to the story. A similar pattern is followed here, but with more elaboration (436,4–25). Although this kind of interruption is discordant, drawing attention to the narrator as a distinct personality, the transitions are made easy by the continuity of the narrative matter. We see Parzival riding through a forest and espying a hermit's cell near a stream (435, 2–9); and after the aside this thread is swiftly picked up again at the same point (436, 26ff.). In fact, the two passages can be read contiguously and make perfect sense, suggesting the aside may be an afterthought on Wolfram's part.

57 There are still more paintings, but the narrator declines to describe them:

5492 Waz nu sigune mere   hiez in der klovsen malen.
     Al durch die gotes ere   des wil die auentevre fvrbaz twalen.

It is interesting to contrast the temple, where there are no paintings at all, though there are mosaics. In *Parzival*, paintings of the holy lamb are mentioned, 105, 22f.

58 Pyritz, p. lxxi, speaks of the drawing power of 'verrätselte Geheimsprache'.

CHAPTER 2

1 Albrecht's use of *Willehalm* is generally superficial, consisting mainly of lists of names or cursory remarks (Borchling, pp. 43–7 and 59–63). *Willehalm* himself is only mentioned briefly (JT 3623, 5910, 5929) as is Gyburc (5929–31). The JT is concerned with the sections of *Parzival* dealing with Parzival himself; Gawan is almost ignored (he is mentioned 1522 and 5636), though certain figures from his adventures are given more attention, for example Orgeluse, who appears in the account of her ill-fated relationship with Anfortas (1763ff. and 2012).

2 See especially Mohr's articles, 'Obie und Meljanz. Zum 7. Buch von Wolframs "Parzival"', in *Gestaltprobleme der Dichtung*, ed. R. Alewyn et al. (Bonn, 1957), pp. 9–20; and 'Zu den epischen Hintergründen in Wolframs *Parzival*', in *Mediaeval German Studies* (London, 1965), pp. 174–87. The general study of Wolfram's characterisation by Blamires treats only the major figures; for a critical reaction see L. P. Johnson, 'Characterization in Wolfram's *Parzival*', *MLR*, 64 (1969), pp. 68–83. Similarly Marion Gibbs, *Wiplîchez Wîbes Reht* (1972), focuses on interpretation of the more important female figures, though she does include Jeschute.

3 The exception is the excellent article by L. P. Johnson, 'Lähelin and the Grail horses', *MLR*, 63 (1968), pp. 612–17. Dietmar Peil treats them as well, *Die Gebärde bei Chrétien, Hartmann und Wolfram* (Munich, 1975).

4 L. P. Johnson, 'Lähelin', p. 612.

5 *Perceval*, lines 654–66. Peil offers a detailed comparison of Chrétien's and Wolfram's versions of this scene, pp. 171–2. Perceval's motivation is his wish to pray for food. That he mistakes the tent for a church is consistent with the comic aspect of his portrayal and with his very active imagination in identifying unknown things with those he has only heard about. Chrétien tells his tale from Perceval's perspective at times more consistently than Wolfram (Jean Frappier, *Chrétien de Troyes* (Paris, 1957), p. 174), but without Wolfram's irony.

6 The web of irony is being spun. Less than 60 lines earlier Herzeloyde told her son about his enemy Lähelin (128, 4), but no mention was made of Orilus in connection with him.

7 The imagery associated with Jeschute is remarkably consistent, coming from the realms of *minne*, sensuousness, and suggested religion. The term *got worht* (130, 23) is not used again except for the Gral kinship and Parzival. Schwietering, 'Natur und art', *ZfdA*,

91 (1961–2), p. 111: 'bei Wolfram [ist es] die Formel von der Schöpferkunst Gottes, die sich an der Schönheit Jeschutes mehr als an irgend einer anderen Stelle seiner Dichtung belebt'.

8 Jeschute's costume is not described, indeed it is not clear at first that she is wearing anything. Wolfram is being intentionally ambiguous, suggesting a high degree of déshabillé through references to her modesty (and her 'hüffelîn'), although later (136) it is clear that she is clothed.

9 On love and battle terminology see Erika Kohler, *Liebeskrieg* (Stuttgart, 1935). It is tempting to view Jeschute as a sleeping Venus or nymph, for there are similarities with the early semi-recumbent figure type. See Elisabeth MacDougall, 'The sleeping nymph: origins of a humanist fountain type', *Art Bulletin*, 57 (1975), pp. 357–65, especially pl. 3, p. 360, for a Roman statue surely reminiscent of Jeschute.

10 Evidence that others were moved by Wolfram's description of Jeschute's beauty is found following Wirnt von Gravenberc's much abbreviated paraphrase of the scene in *Wigalois* (6325–42) which inspires him to his famous lines:

> 6343 daz lop gît ir her Wolfram,
> ein wîse man von Eschenbach;
> sîn herze ist ganzes sinnes dach;
> leien munt nie baz gesprach.

Wirnt von Gravenberc, *Wigalois*, ed. J. M. N. Kapteyn (Bonn, 1926).

11 Although Haidu points out that the heightened description of nature at this point in *Perceval* is a sign of the presence of courtly love: *Aesthetic Distance in Chrétien de Troyes* (Geneva, 1968), p. 131.

12 Interpretations of this scene tend to claim Parzival's complete lack of response to Jeschute, seeing her ring as the only attraction for him (e.g. Gibbs, pp. 105f.). This overlooks the narrative point of view and Jeschute's sensuous appeal which are so important for the scene's effectiveness (similarly in the case of the pilgrim's daughters, see below pp. 122ff.) not only for the play between narrator and audience but in defining our response to an essential, and very positive, part of her nature and Parzival's.

13 The expression *an eines arme ligen* is elsewhere a synonym for *bî ligen* (Peil, p. 172).

14 In Chrétien's poem the unexpectedness is absent since we know of the hero's hunger from the beginning of the scene (see above n. 5) and the narrator repeats the reason for his hunger again before describing him reaching for food (734–7 and 745).

15 Similarly Wolfram protects Parzival's innocence on another level by keeping him unaware of his mother's collapse as he rides off (compare *Parzival* 128, 13ff. and *Perceval* 620ff.). Also see the discussion of *tumpheit* in Chapter 4.

16 *Perceval*, 544–56. *Parzival*, 127,26–128,2.

17 *Perceval*, 707–9. The manuscripts vary on the number of kisses, citing anywhere from 3 to 20. Mary A. Rachbauer, *Wolfram von Eschenbach* (1934; rpt. New York, 1970). Roach's edition reads 7.

18 Chrétien's duchess tells Perceval of the trouble he brings to her (729–33). In Wolfram's tale Jeschute does not mention her own misfortune except in her first words to Parzival, 'wer hât mich entêret?' (131,8). Parzival seems to have registered this comment, for he leaves to protect her *êre*.

19 Indeed, Wolfram's narrator says later it is his right (see below p. 63). J. Knight Bostock, '*Parzival* 264, 1–30', *Medium Aevum*, 21 (1952), pp. 34–5, discusses the legal aspects of Orilus's rights.

20 This is an especially interesting switch considering Wolfram's later emphasis on kisses. See below, pp. 63ff.

21 Michel Huby, 'Wolframs Bearbeitungstechnik im "Parzival" (Buch III)', in *Wolfram-Studien*, III, ed. W. Schröder (Berlin, 1975), pp. 49–50, argues that Jeschute's remark is part of Wolfram's 'höfische Bearbeitung' of Chrétien's text. I cannot agree, for as we have seen Wolfram's Parzival is less polite than Perceval and continues to be so (his reaction to the news of his mother's death shows his sensitivity, not his mastery of polite formulae). Emphasis on the courtly for its own sake here overlooks the emotional and psychological dimensions of the scene.

22 On the intricate complexities of the dragon image in *Parzival* see Hatto, 'Herzeloyde's dragon-dream', *GLL*, 22 (1968), pp. 18–31.

23 On the ironies involving Orilus see Green, 'Homicide and Parzival', in *Approaches*, pp. 46–9; and on dramatic irony in particular, L. P. Johnson, 'Dramatische Ironie in Wolfram's "Parzival"', in *Probleme mittelhochdeutscher Erzählformen*, ed. Ganz and Schröder (Berlin, 1972), pp. 133–52.

24 The same images (warmth, red lips, white skin) appear later as well (see below p. 57ff.). The repetition assures that we will recognise her when she reappears.

25 As Green shows ('Homicide and Parzival', pp. 47–9) Orilus represents the violent kind of knighthood, a dangerous aspect of which Parzival also participates in.

26 She pleads the cause of women, but to deaf ears (136, 16). Wolfram seems on her side, 137, 8–9.

27 For a discussion of the medieval use of direct dialogue see Eberhard

Lämmert, *Bauformen des Erzählens* (Stuttgart, 1955), pp. 204–11.
The distinctions Lämmert draws between 'Handlung *als* Dialog' and
'Handlung *und* Dialog' (pp. 223f.) seem to apply quite well to
Wolfram's and Albrecht's respective use of direct quotation. See
below Chapter 4.

28 Stephen C. Harroff, *Wolfram and his Audience* (Göppingen, 1974)
has coined the term 'quester audience', to point out this aspect of
Wolfram's approach.

29 Parzival learns of Orilus and his defeat of Schionatulander directly
after his encounter with Jeschute (141–2) and later hears of him
again (439–440) but does not make the connection. The narrator
names Orilus as the brother of Cunneware (152, 20), and Orilus
and
Jeschute are described at Arthur's court where Orilus goes to
pledge fealty to Cunneware and they are treated with courtesy
(275–6). Orilus's Gral horse is mentioned often (339, 27; 540, 30;
etc.). See Paul Salmon, 'Ignorance and awareness of identity in
Hartmann and Wolfram: an element of dramatic irony', *Beiträge*
(Tüb.), 82 (1960), pp. 95–115 (esp. p. 104).

30 This is especially apparent in the punning in the last lines of the
description (257, 21–5). There is also an intriguing similarity
between the description of Jeschute's breasts:

> 258, 24 al weinde diu frouwe reit,
>   daz si begôz ir brüstelîn,
>   als sie gedraet solden sîn.
>   diu stuonden blanc hôch sinewel:
>   jane wart nie draehsel sô snel
>   der si gedraet hete baz.

and Parzival's first view of the Gral castle:

> 226, 15 si stuont reht als si waere gedraet.

The legal and symbolic implications of Jeschute's ragged dress
are discussed by Hatto, 'Enid's best dress', *Euphorion*, 54 (1960),
pp. 437–8.

31 256, 15 'die er sach'; 257, 11 'dâ saher'; 257, 16 'er daz sach'.

32 This reading differs from Salmon's ('Ignorance and awareness', pp.
108–11), who argues that not only does Parzival not recognise
Jeschute, but neither would Wolfram's audience, suggesting that a
less attentive reader would only catch on when Parzival confesses.
The narrator does not tell us outright, it is true, but he certainly
gives us enough hints.

33 Horses have long been regarded as symbols of sex or 'the unre-
strained flesh' as D. W. Robertson Jr puts it, *A Preface to Chaucer*

(Princeton, 1963), p. 30. The Flemish miniature from *ca.* 1300 which he reproduces (pl. 8) offers an amusing parallel to the Parzival and Jeschute incident.

34 L. P. Johnson, 'Dramatische Ironie', pp. 140-1; and Mohr, 'Zu den epischen Hintergründen', pp. 183-5.

35 Hatto, 'Herzeloyde's dragon-dream', pp. 18-20, discusses the dragon as a symbol of kingship and empire and Orilus's excessive display of this device as an implication of his *unmâze.* Arthur B. Groos, '"Sigune auf der Linde" and the Turtledove in *Parzival*', *JEGP*, 67 (1968), p. 645, seems to give a too narrow and negative reading of the dragon symbol and of Orilus himself, who is said to bear the dragon emblem, a symbol of *malitia*, as an expression of his 'arrogant perversion of the knightly code which is revealed by his slaughter of all vanquished adversaries'.

36 There is remarkable similarity between Wolfram's description of this battle and interpolations (mss. H and P) of Chrétien's *Perceval.* See Rachbauer, pp. 182-7. Fourquet's discussion of this scene (*Wolfram d'Eschenbach*, pp. 124-8) is enlightening, yet typically goes too far in denying Wolfram a sense of irony and creative independence.

37 The unspoken irony would be evident to the perceptive audience who have learned Orilus's identity and connected him with his brother Lähelin and sister Cunneware. Thus Orilus offers Parzival's own lands to him as a bribe. Albrecht makes repeated use of the theme of offering lands and goods as attempted bribes. See Chapter 3, pp. 153-5.

38 In viewing Jeschute as symbolic of the physical versus Sigune as the spiritual, W. T. H. Jackson over-simplifies the depiction of Jeschute and Orilus, ignoring her sensitive characterisation and the subtlety of the lovers' reconciliation captured in the two kisses. Jackson renders this, 'Her reconciliation with Orilus is described entirely in physical terms and it is brought about by physical methods.' 'Faith unfaithful - the German reaction to courtly love', in *The Meaning of Courtly Love*, ed. Newman (Albany, 1968), p. 61. Rather, the physical gestures are symbols of the spiritual and legal reconciliation. See Hatto, 'Enid's best dress', p. 438; and Peil, pp. 206-7 and 173-4.

39 Mohr, 'Parzival and Gawan', p. 14. Mohr argues that in general Parzival and Gawan are distinguished in that Gawan has a humanising effect on the people he encounters, whereas Parzival tends to fumble things unintentionally and ineptly. His interaction with Jeschute and Orilus, however, offers an exception. He has brought out good qualities in Orilus and has finally produced a better situation than the original.

40 L. P. Johnson, 'Lähelin'.

41 The rich irony of this scene has been examined in detail. Most recently see Petrus W. Tax, 'Trevrizent. Die Verhüllungstechnik des Erzählers', in *Studien zur deutschen Literatur und Sprache des Mittelalters*, ed. Besch et al. (Berlin, 1974), pp. 119–34.

42 The JT can be said to have several major protagonists including Titurel and Parzival; but Tschinotulander is the primary one, and Jescute and Orilus are involved in his fate. A rough estimate of the percentage of text involving Orilus and Jescute reveals less than 4% in *Parzival* as opposed to about 10% in the JT.

43 Brode discusses Albrecht's depiction of time in some detail (pp. 141–53) and comes to the conclusion that the chronology is only clear in the middle section (i.e. Tschinotulander's adventures) and then only when the hero is successful.

44 This is clearly modelled on *Parzival*, 282. Albrecht makes extensive use of analogues in this way. See below, and 2404, 2527, 2589, 2610, 2761, etc.

45 Similarly Parzival, after his lonely night in the forest, is drawn unknowingly into battle with Arthur's knights who do not recognise him. In both poems the audience is cognisant of the identity of the combatants.

46 This is also similar to Parzival who as a youth (though before he is a knight) kills his opponent. Tschinotulander is not protected by references to *tumpheit* (see Chapter 4), but he refuses to lift a spear against relatives, although he does kill one unknowingly. Wolfgang Harms, *Der Kampf mit dem Freund oder Verwandten in der deutschen Literatur bis um 1300* (Munich, 1963), pp. 176–9.

47 This is consistent with the situation in *Parzival*. Also, the page's challenge to Orilus recalls Parzival's experience at Munsalvaesche (*Parzival*, 229). A further parallel exists in that Parzival, like Tschinotulander, is mistaken for Ither.

48 We are led to consider the ambiguities of who deserves to win (see above, pp. 63f.), but this adds to the tension.

49 Similarly one must view the leash as responsible for allowing Sigune to read the inscription to her heart's content, although Jescute – upon whose generosity such an opportunity would have to depend – is not mentioned (1868ff.). See also Chapter 3

50 The time element in the sequence involving the Baruch's messengers is especially confused. Borchling, p. 36.

51 There is no explanation given for the waning of the leash's effect, although its inscription has been read aloud once again, this time in full to Albrecht's audience as well (see Chapter 3).

52 Wolf's edition implies that Orilus must go to the east as well:

1945 Do liez er Lehelinen   ledic niht der verte
und den brûder sinen.

But Orilus is not bound to go, nor does he. It is better to read (with several manuscripts) *neve* here instead of *brûder*, since this in fact foreshadows another nephew's death. See below p. 85.

53 Albrecht is in some ways considerably more traditional than Wolfram. See Eugène Vinaver, *The Rise of Romance* (New York, 1971), esp. chapter 5, 'The poetry of interlace', pp. 68–98.

54 1979, 1; 2090, 4; 2199, 3; 2645, 1; 3581; 4137.

55 These epithets occur in the episode concerning the Bridge of Virtue. See Borchling, pp. 47ff. for a discussion of this motif.

56 As Tschinotulander considers his position with regard to Orilus and Lehelin (4437–42) we see a further build-up of the case against the brothers. They have wronged Tschinotulander in several ways: Orilus killed Galoes; he and Lehelin unjustly blame Tschinotulander for their nephews' deaths; Lehelin has forgotten that Tschinotulander saved his life; and they are attempting to take over the young hero's lands. His speech repeats points already made by the narrator. Orilus and Lehelin next manifest their unchivalrous aggression by besieging Kanvoleis and killing Turkentals (4452–3); this news arrives amid festivities at Arthur's court. Here the negative image of the brothers is strengthened by comparison with Clamide; the comparison serves to reinforce the interlocking elements of this plot with scenes from *Parzival*. Arthur and his troops nobly rush to help Tschinotulander defend the city. Albrecht reports that those fighting with Orilus and Lehelin are acting out of hatred and envy of Tschinotulander (4468–9), associating yet further injustice and petty jealousy with the brothers. After losing much of their army (4543), Orilus and Lehelin are forced to quit Waleis, but the respite is only temporary, for Tschinotulander almost immediately departs again, leaving his lands virtually undefended, and this time Orilus and Lehelin are successful in conquering them (this is reported later, 4652ff.). Tschinotulander himself realises the dangers in leaving (see 4562, 4574–6) but feels honour bound to aid Arthur who receives an unexpected challenge from Kaiser Lucius of Rome. The battle with Lucius is based on the *Historia regum Britanniae*. See Borchling, pp. 70–5.

57 The narrator points out that their joy is not to last, however (4860, 4). We are told in stanza 4859 that Orilus now rules Waleis and Lehelin Norgals.

58 Tschinotulander has voluntarily given up Gamuret's anchor until he can regain the lands that were entrusted to him.

59 Albrecht has not overlooked the kiss as a significant gesture between Orilus and Jescute. Reference to tent ropes alludes to *Parzival* (133, 1). The interrupted idyll also recalls the opening scene of *Titurel II*.

60 Compare above pp. 61ff. The humour of Orilus's unfortunate crash landing (4865) is also reminiscent of his predicament in *Parzival*, though sitting among the flowers is a fairly common image for the unhorsed warrior. Earlier in Wolfram's tale it is Parzival who in his clash with Ither sits thus (154, 29–30).

61 This magic gold, in the form of a ring and brooch, has been sent via a messenger from the Baruch to Tschinotulander. It is inadvertantly delivered to the 'herr des landes', Orilus, who upon receiving it is filled with sudden happiness (4886–9). Borchling, p. 81, discusses the motif. According to Albrecht, this is the same *fürspan* and *vingerlín* which Parzival takes from Jeschute at their first meeting (*Parzival*, 131, 16ff.). Although the scene between Parzival and Jescute is not related in the JT, Parzival himself makes the connection in a later discussion with Signe (JT 5451–2).

62 This logical explanation befits a tendency which Ragotzky illustrates (pp. 97–100) in comparing Wolfram's and Albrecht's versions of Herzeloyde hearing the news of her husband's death. Yet as we have seen, this is not a consistent feature of Albrecht's narrative mode.

63 The location of the Gral realm is intentionally ambiguous in *Parzival* (Wynn, 'The poetic structure', pp. 32–6). In the JT, Orilus and Jescute have put up their tent in a lonely area (5007–8) and Tschinotulander and Signe enter the woods 'precilie pretiment die kluse' (5009) in which they become lost and spend the night in the vicinity of the other couple. Albrecht demonstrates similar care later in explaining Signe's move 'zvr wilden laborie' where Kundrie helps her install herself and Tschinotulander in a linden tree (5100–9).

64 Quoted from Hahn. These stanzas and the following ones from this scene are also in Wolf's 1952 excerpted text edition.

65 Again underlining the similarities between Jescute and Signe. The scene is repeated later as Jescute faints (see below p. 104). Ragotzky, p. 109, associates Signe's fainting spell with Herzeloyde's reaction to the news of Gahmuret's death in *Parzival*.

66 Orilus's gesture of reviving Signe with water echoes *Parzival*, 109, 17–18. Signe at first mistakes Orilus for Tschinotulander (another parallel?) and then seeing clearly begs for her own death (5038–9).

67 The legend of the unicorn is told to Parzival by Trevrizent (*Parzival*, 482, 24ff.) though he offers no allegorical interpretation. The image also recalls the iconographic overtones of Wolfram's

247

depiction of Sigune with the dead Schionatulander in her arms in *Parzival* (in the JT 5107ff.). Herzeloyde compares herself to the Madonna as she suckles Parzival (*Parzival*, 113, 5–26).

68 Florence McCulloch, *Mediaeval Latin and French Bestiaries* (Chapel Hill, 1960), pp. 179–83.

69 See n. 61 above.

70 Ragotzky, p. 112.

71 The multiplication of the dragons is taken from *Parzival*, 263,16ff. in typically magnified form.

72 See Borchling, pp. 95–6 on the sword motif.

73 See 5829. Orilus is called *gehevre* (5805, 2); he is equally matched with Ekunat (5817,8); none is better at *ringen* (5820). It is implied that Ekunat wins only because of the magic sword (5798–9).

74 Walter J. Schröder's analysis of Wolfram's characters seems ironically appropriate here: 'Als durchgehender Wesenszug erscheint das Rollenmäßige der Figuren; sie handeln nicht aus dem Charakter, sondern ihrer Funktion im Grundplan entsprechend. Ob diese Funktion nun typologisch oder didaktisch ist: es steht nie ein wirklicher Mensch im Spiel sondern immer eine agierende Romangestalt. Wechselt die Funktion, spielt die Figur also eine doppelte Rolle, so tritt das Unlebendige, Maskenhafte besonders hervor.' 'Der dichterische Plan des Parzivalromans', *Beiträge* (Halle), 74 (1952), pp. 411–12. Schröder's conclusions here can be at least partly attributed to his desire to see an overriding form in *Parzival*; Wolfram's text must sometimes be forced to conform. The danger in stressing formal questions is of course likewise pertinent to the present study.

75 See Vinaver, chapter 6, pp. 99–122 for the uses of analogy in narrative to illuminate meaning and increase the impact of scenes. The recurrence of pattern is itself remarkable and heightens the significance and presence of both scenes.

CHAPTER 3

1 This is not to claim *Parzival* for a modern *Entwicklungsroman*, though there are certainly similar elements. Wehrli's judgement seems to the point, viewing Parzival's story as both the 'Konstituierung eines Ich' and 'eine romanhafte Analogie zur Heilsgeschichte' (pp. 212–13).

2 I cannot agree with James Poag's interpretation that Wolfram's use of *dinc* reveals his sense of humour; '*Diu verholnen maere umben grâl*', in *Wolfram-Studien*, II, ed. W. Schröder (Berlin, 1974), p. 74.

3 Sigune appears vindictive in this scene, which contradicts her

248

image of pious devotion. There is some logical inconsistency in her delay in enquiring if Parzival asked the question. She first tells of the Gral kingdom and some of the Gral's powers, identifies herself, gives the details of the magic sword, and only then enquires about Parzival's success, the latter being the crucial issue judging from her reaction. The dialogue flows so naturally, however, that one hardly notices this emphasis.

4 Neither does Cundrie allude to Parzival's genetic bond with Anfortas, though she does reveal Parzival's name to Arthur and his court, mentioning his parents as well as his half-brother Feirefiz. Her general purpose, however, is to curse Parzival.

5 In his detailed description of Cundrie's physical appearance Wolfram deviates from his model, Chrétien, and from traditional patterns of Latin rhetoric. See Salmon, 'The wild man in "Iwein" and medieval descriptive technique', *MLR*, 56 (1961), pp. 520–8. Wolfram's description may demonstrate his ignorance of Latin rhetorical practice as Salmon suggests (p. 523), but his changes can be appreciated as indications of his gift for dramatic presentation, animating a visual image through a very natural impressionistic perspective. Thus the listener experiences this apparition with the court, seeing first her mule, then her clothes (as Salmon points out 'logically enough, since they would be visible from a greater distance', p. 523), her head, the scourge, and then the ugly hand that holds it. These images seem the more powerful by their connection with a natural system of observation, the grotesque claw grasping the *geisel* (314, 2–9) vividly culminating the description – an image which captures the impact of Cundrie in terms as expressionistic as they are descriptive. Similarly Wolfram's description of Jeschute concentrates on those aspects of her appearance which best reflect the psychological impact of the scene.

6 Naturally the Gral ceremony itself constitutes a high point, yet within Wolfram's carefully developed plot Sigune's and Cundrie's speeches increase the tension as Parzival's life becomes entangled with the Gral image.

7 The court are more responsive to Kingrimursel's challenge (322–5). Their interest in Parzival seems limited to his lineage (325, 17–326, 4). Green, 'Irony and medieval romance', in *Arthurian Romance*, ed. Owen (New York, 1970), pp. 59–61, interprets the lack of curiosity as irony of values, whereby the court accept Parzival as a hero when we, the audience, know he has failed at Munsalvaesche. Thus their response to Cundrie's announcement demonstrates that their chivalric criteria are not of the highest order. This is a compelling view, though it is difficult to prove such

Ironic intent on Wolfram's part. In any case this passage is another example of Wolfram's subtle engagement of the reader in Parzival's experiences and confusion, avoiding the necessity of explaining anything until the proper moment.

8 Wynn has discussed the 'narrative reciprocity' of Gawan and Parzival with great sensitivity and compares this scene with Chrétien's poem where the woman's speech is more polite and Perceval's reaction less severe. 'Parzival and Gâwân – hero and counterpart', *Beiträge* (Tüb.), 84 (1962), pp. 145–8. She points out that Gawan – falsely accused of a knightly transgression – remains calm, while Parzival – attacked as a human being – is plunged into despair. Parzival does, however, manage to aid Clamide and interrogate the heathen woman.

9 Herzeloyde's answer advised trust in God's help:

> 119, 17 'ôwê muoter, waz ist got?
> 'sun, ich sage dirz âne spot.
> er ist noch liehter denne der tac,
> der antlitzes sich bewac
> nâch menschen antlitze.
> sun, merke eine witze,
> und flêhe in umbe dîne nôt:
> sîn triwe der werlde ie helfe bôt.
> sô heizet einr der helle wirt:
> der ist swarz, untriwe in niht verbirt.
> von dem kêr dîne gedanke,
> und och von zwîvels wanke.'

The nearly literal repetition of the question serves to recall the earlier passage and to show Parzival's continued lack of understanding about God. He has progressed from a literal reading of his mother's description to a view of God as a feudal lord. He does not follow Herzeloyde's advice but must come to learn its truths through his own experience. The black and white symbolism is a recurrent theme in both *Parzival* and the JT.

10 This is the third time he sets off alone. The first chapter of his life closed when he left his mother and his carefree youth behind and departed to enter the courtly realm (128, 13ff.). Having succeeded in that world, he once more leaves a beloved behind and rides off alone, this time to enter physically the world of the Gral:

> 223, 29 von allen sînen mannen
> schiet er al eine dannen.

Only after a further chapter, one of great struggle, will he be able to re-enter that realm both physically and spiritually, thereby re-uniting the former realms he had left behind.

11 The technique of interlace is typical of medieval formats. William W. Ryding, *Structure in medieval Narrative* (Paris, 1971), esp. 139ff.; and Vinaver, pp. 68ff. Inheriting the juxtaposed Parzival and Gawan stories from his model, Wolfram integrates the tales of his two heroes with remarkable formal expertise. For detailed analyses of the parallel yet different structures of the Parzival and Gawan sections see, Wynn, 'Parzival and Gâwân'; and Mohr, 'Parzival und Gawan'. Also of interest here is Hans-Hugo Steinhoff, *Die Darstellung gleichzeitiger Geschehnisse im mittelhochdeutschen Epos* (Munich, 1964), esp. pp. 47-58.

12 The wood is not named by Wolfram but called merely 'ein walt'. For a discussion of a similar passage in the Gawan section see, L. P. Johnson, 'Characterization', p. 72.

13 See especially the recent article by Tax.

14 Wynn, 'Scenery and chivalrous journeys in Wolfram's *Parzival*', *Speculum*, 36 (1961), pp. 405-6.

15 Hugh Sacker, *An Introduction to Wolfram's 'Parzival'* (Cambridge, 1963), pp. 90-2.

16 As in her interpretation of Jeschute (see Chapter 2, n. 12), Gibbs minimises the sensuality in Wolfram's depiction of these young girls (pp. 144-5). She argues that it is their spirituality and love of God that make them the 'epitome of Womanhood' for Wolfram. I would certainly not deny the importance of their devotion, but would argue that they represent a very real, warm, *human* encounter which touches Parzival and leads to a realisation of his loneliness and isolation from human love as well as from God's love. It seems undeniable that Wolfram's vision of the epitome of womanhood includes an erotic, physical aspect. Hermann J. Weigand, 'Courtly love in Wolfram's *Parzival*', in *Wolfram's Parzival* (Ithaca and London, 1969), p. 170, remarks on their sex appeal but finds it 'incongruous'.

17 I would disagree with W. T. H. Jackson who sees the throwing of the reins purely as a challenge and consequently feels Parzival's vices are at their peak when he meets Trevrizent. 'The progress of Parzival and the Trees of Virtue and Vice', *GR*, 33 (1958), pp. 121-2.

18 See below pp. 135f. The truth of Wolfram's claims is not important here, nor is it important whether he is responding to actual criticisms. What matters is the placement of this insert. It occurs in Book 9 where Parzival finally learns about the Gral; thus the climax is at the same point for the audience and the hero.

19 Pp. 65–78.

20 The gesture provides a nice illustration for Green's recent proposal that *âventiure* for Wolfram means a meeting point between knightly endeavour and divine guidance: 'The concept *âventiure* in *Parzival*', in *Approaches*, pp. 136–7. Parzival surrendered his horse and knightly accoutrements on his first visit to the Gral as well, but as Green has pointed out ('Irony', p. 63), Parzival mistakenly thought he was still experiencing a knightly adventure.

21 Mohr, 'Hilfe und Rat in Wolframs *Parzival*', in *Festschrift für Jost Trier*, ed. Benno von Wiese and Karl H. Borck (Meisenheim, 1954), pp. 173–97, has shown how intricately the leitmotif of *hilfe* is woven into Parzival's story, and how Parzival as well as the audience is led to a changed understanding of its meaning. The links are omnipresent. In the earlier scene with the pilgrims he was offered a cloak to warm himself, but could not yet forfeit his independence.

22 There are many ambiguities in the interpretation of this passage. See Tax, pp. 130–2; and Bumke, *Wolfram-Forschung*, pp. 263ff.

23 Unlike Sigune. Opinions differ on whether or not Trevrizent recognises Parzival at once. Tax argues that Trevrizent believes the stranger to be Lähelin and is thus especially kind, convinced he can never return to the Gral, whereas Weigand most recently ('Spiritual therapy in Wolfram's Parzival', GQ, 51 (1978), pp. 444–64) argues that Trevrizent knows Parzival's identity all along and treats him therefore with great psychological insight. Henry Kratz, *Wolfram von Eschenbach's 'Parzival'* (Berlin, 1973), p. 309, sees Trevrizent as an 'aging, somewhat reluctant recluse who has found a sympathetic ear'. Bernd Schirok, 'Trevrizent und Parzival. Beobachtungen zur Dialogführung und zur Frage der figurativen Komposition', in *Amsterdamer Beiträge*, 10 (1976), pp. 54–60, posits that Trevrizent, suspecting his guest to be either Lähelin or Parzival, seeks through carefully chosen comments to draw out the truth. Schirok offers a *Forschungsbericht* on views of the composition of Book 9 as well.

24 See Benedikt Mockenhaupt, *Die Frömmigkeit im Parzival Wolframs von Eschenbach* (Bonn, 1942), pp. 91–112 for a detailed discussion of the religious content of Trevrizent's lessons.

25 See n. 10 above. His departures from Jeschute and Gurnemanz also fit into this pattern.

26 For a convincing reading of Cundrie's words see L. P. Johnson, '*ungenuht al eine (Parzival* 782,23)', in *Probleme mittelhochdeutscher Erzählformen*, pp. 49–66.

27 On the jewels see Engelen.

28 For a penetrating discussion of the theme of questioning in *Parzival* and of Parzival's variation on the final question – to which he

already knows the answer – see Ruth K. Angress, 'Interrogation in Wolfram's *Parzival*', GQ, 62 (1969), pp. 1–10. Harroff, p. 78, rightly stresses the importance of kinship recognition in Parzival's variation of the wording but overlooks other aspects pointed out by Angress.

29 And by fighting. See Chapter 4, n. 54.

30 The details of the scene shed light on Wolfram's views of love and Christian salvation. As the Gral is carried forward, Feirefiz admits that he cannot see it (810, 10–14). This admission is followed by a long discussion (*ca.* 60 lines) of his overwhelming love for Repanse, with no note taken of the Gral's invisibility by any of the assembled Gral family or by Wolfram's narrator. Anfortas mentions it again (813, 9–11) and an explanation is offered by Titurel (813, 17–22): heathens cannot see it. Feirefiz is willing to be baptised, but his primary concern is love:

> 814, 1 'Ob ich durch iuch ze toufe kum,
> ist mir der touf ze minnen frum?'

Feirefiz's consuming longing for Repanse is amusing and, one feels, slightly misdirected. Should he not be longing for the Gral? Isn't his attitude sacrilegious? There are several responses to this. First of all, in the Middle Ages, ceremony in and of itself was much more valued than today: baptism made one automatically a Christian – one could *learn* about Christianity any time. This is of course contradicted by Parzival's long struggle towards a more perfect relationship with God, but Parzival can be viewed as an exception. Feirefiz himself exhibits an abundance of Christian traits already, and is clearly a Christian in spirit if not in education (as was his mother Belakane, *Parzival* 28, 10–20). Secondly, Wolfram's insistence on the mundane side of Feirefiz's wish for conversion can also be understood from a different angle: a disinclination on the part of the poet to enter into a weighty discussion of the Gral. Feirefiz's initial reaction to his newly acquired Christianity is a logical continuation of his yearning for Repanse (818, 15–19), like Gyburc's love of God and Willehalm. Neither is Parzival's love for Condwiramurs lessened by his Christian awakéning – on the contrary. Although from our contemporary point of view this may seem unsatisfying, for Wolfram's audience the union of these two people would be seen as wonderful in itself and as a symbol and proof of the power of God. Wolfram has carefully overshadowed the object of the Gral with this dramatic episode, for it is mentioned only in passing (818, 20–3).

31 Albrecht similarly concentrates the ending of his poem. See above p. 11.

32 It seems that Parzival must overcome a few inherent weaknesses, especially *unmâze* in the courtly realms of knightly endeavour and love. S. M. Johnson, 'Herzeloyde and the Grail', *Neophilologus*, 52 (1968), pp. 148-56, offers some credible insights. In contrast, Gertrude J. Lewis, 'Die unheilige Herzeloyde. Ein ikonoklastischer Versuch', *JEGP*, 74 (1975), pp. 465-85, goes much too far in attributing excessive passion and selfishness to Herzeloyde. On Gahmuret see the readable overview by Kratz, pp. 191-8. Also see Bumke, *Wolfram-Forschung*, pp. 175-6.

33 See Fourquet, *Wolfram d'Eschenbach,* for a discussion of the probable order of Wolfram's original composition.

34 For bibliography on the complex discussions centered on Kyot see Bumke, *Wolfram-Forschung*, pp. 243-50. More recently, Lofmark, 'Zur Interpretation der Kyotstellen im "Parzival"', in *Wolfram-Studien*, IV (Berlin, 1977), pp. 33-70.

35 There is a surprising similarity between Wolfram's method of unfolding a plot and W. P. Ker's description of the method of narration in Icelandic sagas: 'The story for them [the Icelandic authors] is not a thing finished and done with; it is a series of pictures rising in the mind, succeeding, displacing, and correcting one another; all under the control of a steady imagination, which will not be hurried, and will not tell the bearing of things until the right time comes.' *Epic and Romance, Essays on Medieval Literature* (2nd edn, 1922; rpt. New York, 1957), p. 237.

36 The opening section tells the history of the Gral kinship, the story of Titurel and the building of the Gral temple. The closing relates Parzival's adventures and the final history of the Gral (see Chapter 1, n. 12). For a summary of Albrecht's rendition of the Gral see Wolf, 'Wer war der Dichter', pp. 338-9.

37 Tschinotulander's relationship to Munt Salvasch is never made clear. The strict boundaries of the realm do not exist for him, since he plans to accompany Sigune there, and it is suggested that he is worthy to be of the Gral kinship (5396ff.). Albrecht simply does not cope with this touchy subject. One wonders, for instance, why Tschinotulander never searches for the Gral.

38 For a discussion of Sigune's guilt in this light see, Wolff, pp. 124-5; and Bernhard Rahn, *Wolframs Sigunendichtung. Eine Interpretation der 'Titurelfragmente'* (Zurich, 1958), pp. 78ff. Joachim Heinzle, *Stellenkommentar zu Wolframs Titurel: Beiträge zum Verständnis des überlieferten Textes* (Tübingen, 1972), pp. 212ff., offers an overview of scholarly opinion, concluding that Sigune's guilt cannot be established, nor wholly denied. Green, 'Homicide and Parzival', p. 60, sees 'superfluous futility' in Schionatulander's search for a leash as the cause of tragedy and argues that this

reflects a changed attitude in Wolfram, expressing in *Titurel* elegiac regret for the death of knighthood.

39   I.e. 1184 describes the hound further; 1189 adds to the list of jewels.

40   See Chapter 2. Keie's scorn for the hero is expected behaviour from that pompous knight and puts Tschinotulander in the good company of Iwein and others as well as Parzival. Tschinotulander, thus slandered, gains in righteousness when he returns.

41   Tschinotulander does not know of the connection between Ekunat and the hound because he has not yet read the inscription and apparently Sigune has given him no more than a cursory description of its contents (see *Titurel*, 164–5).

42   This recalls the court's singular lack of interest in Parzival's experiences, see above p.116.

43   See Chapter 2, n. 43.

44   This same attention and memory is required of Albrecht, who occasionally 'nods'. Borchling, p. 39.

45   The narrator's guidance is an essential aid. See Chapter 4.

46   The original goal of winning Sigune, subtly augmented by the moral symbolism of the dog's name and the inscription, merges into the goal of perfect Christian knighthood. Ohly, 'Die Suche in Dichtungen des Mittelalters', *ZfdA*, 94 (1965), pp. 179–80, interprets Tschinotulander's goal as a quest not for the leash but for 'Lebenswahrheit' and the leash itself as a catechism for 'Lebensführung'. Indeed, the leash does formally symbolise a certain ideal code, but this is not integrated so neatly into the narrative.

47   See Ragotzky, p. 121.

48   Sigune began reading on the collar and continued on the leash itself until she reached the point at which it was knotted. In untying the knot to read further she made it possible for the hound to escape. The stanzas she read then do not seem to fit in with the inscription presented here (from the *seil*) and Albrecht does not tie the two together.

49   These stanzas seem clearly based on the information contained in bestiaries, but Albrecht's hybrid approach makes a specific source difficult to identify. Ernst Hermann, *Die Inschrift des Brackenseils: Wandlungen der höfischen Weltanschauung im Jüngeren Titurel* (Marburg-Lahn, 1939), p. 19, says Albrecht's references are from *Physiologus* but cites nothing specific. Leckie, '"Bestia de funde"', pp. 275–7, concludes that Albrecht drew from 'popular' medieval learning, especially the *Physiologus* tradition, for his scientific information, often creating imaginative composites. See also, Leckie, '"Gamaniol"', esp. p. 141.

50   Parzival, 502,7ff. Also see JT 1884–90. Hermann, pp. 24–33, gives

a detailed analysis of the inscription as an expression of Albrecht's personal *Weltanschauung*.

51 They are: 'belde', 'küsche', 'milt', 'triwe', 'maz', 'sorge', 'scham', 'bescheiden', 'staete', 'diemüte', 'gedulde', 'minne'. It is interesting to note that the virtue of *mâze*, not included in the preceding section, is here given five stanzas (1914–18).

52 This, the concluding stanza of the JT, is considered by many to be the work of a redactor. There are certainly similarities with Albrecht's commentary on Wolfram (see above p. 13) and with the words of Wirnt von Gravenberc (Chapter 2, n. 10). Keie comments on the leash's purpose, referring to the 'loik der lere' (1870, 3–4).

53 Sigune's original wish to finish a good story has been lost in a symbolic network, the theme of completion transmuted to a new level. Jescute's tenacity concerning the leash is never explained but presented as self-evident.

54 The powerful effect is not solely a magical one from the jewels as Hermann (p. 12) suggests, but the jewels symbolise the power of the word.

55 Sigune argues that she and Tschinotulander should be joined in marriage, if not for their own sakes then for the sakes of their children and the welfare of their respective lands which would then have rulers. Borchling, p. 55, argues that Albrecht has based this on Herzeloyde's reasons for not taking her own life.

56 He does go into Arthur's failing on this score at some length (2492–2518).

57 This is now his main goal, and until the vengeance is complete he assumes Gamuret's name.

58 See above pp. 85ff. That Lehelin is never shown to respond to the Baruch's direct statement is further evidence that the scene is not intended to portray a dramatic encounter but serves to reintroduce the leash.

59 Occasionally one also wonders whatever happened to the hound! This 'disappearance' does not seem to have bothered Albrecht's readers over the centuries, however.

60 Ragotzky, p. 115, interprets this as an expression of the 'tragische Widersprüchlichkeit der irdischen Welt'. Tschinotulander's behaviour is never connected with the *vervaren* against which the closing two stanzas of the inscription warn. Engelen, pp. 403–6, is too narrow in seeing Tschinotulander's *unmâze* as a major fault which causes his ruin and relieves Sigune of guilt.

61 The complex arguments concerning Wolfram's bow metaphor have failed to provide a conclusively sound reading, and in fact such may be impossible. For bibliography see Bumke, *Wolfram-Forschung*,

256

pp. 82-3 and 294-7. Groos, 'Wolfram von Eschenbach's "bow metaphor" and the narrative technique of *Parzival'*, *MLN*, 87 (1972), pp. 391-408, relates the metaphor to medieval Bible exegesis where the image represents the relationship between Old and New Testaments. Though there are clearly parallels, this analogy does not account for the significant aspects of Wolfram's narrative technique, namely that he is defending his own (and Chrétien's) method of maintaining interest and suspense by engaging the audience as partners in the hero's gradual enlightenment. Wolfram does not first tell the bow (Old Testament) and then make it intelligible (New Testament). Secondly, Wolfram, far from excusing himself for straying from his sources (also Bertau, *Deutsche Literatur im Europäischen Mittelalter*, vol. 1 (Munich, 1972), p. 779), in fact defends the general arrangement of disclosure he inherited from Chrétien. The parallels to *heilsgeschichtliche Struktur* and to *ordo artificialis* cannot be denied, yet in essence Wo metaphor to describe the natural development of his narrative as it follows his hero. The complexity of Wolfram's juggling – withholding information and revealing it – is captured in Curschmann's discussion, pp. 639-41. Eberhard Nellmann, *Wolframs Erzähltechnik* (Wiesbaden, 1973), pp. 90ff., sees the bow metaphor as a positive defence of Wolfram's narrative technique, but in suggesting that the information withheld is supplied as early as the Sigune scene misconstrues the significance of the metaphor as an image of Wolfram's essential mode of narration. Harroff's interpretation, pp. 79-86, reinterpreting certain lines as expressing Wolfram's attitude towards open didacticism, is intriguing but unconvincing.

CHAPTER 4

1 Since 1970 when this study was undertaken, numerous scholars have focused on Wolfram's narrative technique and his narrator, a topic still rich with possibilities. The notes which follow here are intended to support the particular needs of my discussion and do not attempt to survey the considerable literature which has appeared since 1974 when this study was originally completed.

2 George Kane, *The Autobiographical Fallacy in Chaucer and Langland Studies* (London, 1965), p. 15.

3 For a study of the narrator in modern fiction see Wayne C. Booth, *The Rhetoric of Fiction* (Chicago, 1961), especially chapters VI, VII, and VIII with enlightening discussions of the subtleties in defining the narrator's relation to the author and the audience. Many of the distinctions Booth draws are clearly relevant to

Wolfram's narrator, and Booth's terminology is adopted in my discussion. See Pörksen for a discussion of aspects of the narrator in medieval German literature.

4 Pörksen's findings on this subject are summarised pp. 200ff. The historical development of poets' self-awareness is discussed also by Fritz Tschirch, 'Das Selbstverständnis des mittelalterlichen deutschen Dichters', in *Beiträge zum Berufsbewußtsein des mittelalterlichen Menschen*, ed. P. Wilpert (Berlin, 1964), pp. 239–85. See also Olive Sayce, 'Prolog, Epilog und das Problem des Erzählers', in *Probleme mittelhochdeutscher Erzählformen*, pp. 63–72.

5 I.e. *Perceval* 3277ff. Vinaver, pp. 34ff., discusses Chrétien's comments on narrative technique in *Eric et Enide*. That Chrétien was sophisticated in his awareness of literary tradition is seen in *Cligès* where he plays with conventions.

6 W. H. Jackson's analysis of the narrator in Hartmann's *Iwein* seems very appropriate to the varied functions of Wolfram's narrator ('Some observations on the status of the narrator in Hartmann von Aue's "Erec" and "Iwein"', *Forum for Modern Language Studies*, 6 (1970), pp. 65–82, esp. p. 72). To try to separate the narrator fully from the author, as Nellmann does especially pp. 18–20 and 26–7, leads to misinterpretation. Curschmann's article captures the complexities in the varied roles of Wolfram's narrator.

7 Though he seems to have been accused of too much imaginative fancy by Gottfried, Wolfram has been criticised in the twentieth century for stupifying naïveté in his attempts to follow Chrétien's every word (Fourquet, *Wolfram d'Eschenbach*, p. 184). A correct assessment, I think, should commend Wolfram for both his orthodox adherence to his model's material and his imaginative interpretation and elaboration of it. For a well-balanced discussion of the poet's duty in these respects see Lofmark, 'Der höfische Dichter als Übersetzer', in *Probleme mittelhochdeutscher Erzählformen*, pp. 40–62. On Hartmann's struggles to remain true to the *maere* while altering the interpretation see Wolfgang Dittmann, '"Dune hâst niht wâr, Hartman!" Zum Begriff der *wârheit* in Hartmanns *Iwein*', in *Festgabe für U. Pretzel*, ed. W. Simon et al. (Berlin, 1963), pp. 150–61.

8 See Fourquet, 'La structure du *Parzival*', in *Les romans du Graal aux XIIᵉ et XIIIᵉ siècles* (Paris, 1956), pp. 201–5, on the interlaced structure of Chrétien's poem and Wolfram's handling of it.

9 It is likely that Wolfram paused after the sixth book (see Bumke, *Wolfram-Forschung*, pp. 26–7). In this case the opening of Book 7 would have served as a sort of prologue and would have offered the opportunity for Wolfram to defend himself against criticism

engendered by the earlier books (i.e. 3-6). It is possible that Wolfram also had in mind the pro-Gawan factions in his audience whose existence is registered through such works as Heinrich von der Türlin's *Krône*.

10 For scholarship on the prologue see Bumke, *Wolfram-Forschung*, pp. 275-86, on the 'Selbstverteidigung' pp. 288-90, and on the feud with Gottfried pp. 81-8. More recently, Hatto has discussed the probable order of appearance of *Parzival* and the implications for the Gottfried-Wolfram feud, in 'Wolfram von Eschenbach and the Chase', in *Et multum et multa* (Berlin, 1971), pp. 105ff. See also n. 74 below.

11 Jaeger, 'The "strophic" Prologue to Gottfried's *Tristan*', GR, 47 (1972), pp. 5-19.

12 In his humorous rendition of Segramor's ill-fated charge towards the entranced Parzival Wolfram utters a similar remark: 289, 11-12.

Albrecht's attitude towards *lob* (see also p. 10 above) is intriguingly reminiscent of Gottfried's in the *Tristan* prologue.

> 13 Ez zimet dem man ze lobene wol,
> des er iedoch bedürfen sol,
> und laze ez ime gevallen wol,
> die wile ez ime gevallen sol.

Albrecht would agree with Gottfried that it is the discerning critic's duty to give praise where it is due, and in the *Verfasserfragment* he acknowledges the value of *lob* with a similar circularity of argument, admitting that the winning of just praise was one reason for writing his poem in Wolfram's name:

> VF 5 Un waer aber iemen lebende,   so cluoc an richer witze,
> dem waer doch niemen gebende   daz zehende lop.

Albrecht's poem is itself a work of praise to Wolfram, and, he implies, it could not be greater even if Wolfram had appeared as an angel sent directly from heaven (VF 13)! The apparent sarcasm of this passage no doubt indicates Albrecht's bitterness over his own difficulties in finding proper recognition for his work, especially support to finish it. For, as he goes on to say, Wolfram was not an angel, and others too are capable of great art:

> VF 14 Er was in menschen modele   und niht ein engel heilic.
> gots gebe ze mangem rodele   ist noch vil richer kunst
>   mit witzen teilic.

13 This motif is imitated in the JT 4019 where the discussion is of *minne*. Wolfram himself varies it (*Parzival* 593, 14-18. See below

p. 176) with Orgeluse entering Gawan's heart as *nieswurz* enters the nose! See Ohly, 'Cor amantis non angustum', in *Gedenkschrift für W. Foerste* (Cologne/Vienna, 1970), pp. 454-76, on the motif of the heart as a place to be entered.

14 Groos's view ('Bow metaphor') that Wolfram rearranged the traditional order of narration according to the rules of *ordo artificialis* seems a misrepresentation; see Chapter 3, n. 61 above.

15 For a concise list of Wolfram's source references and a useful discussion of their general lack of 'authenticity' see, Lofmark, 'Wolfram's source references'. Pörksen discusses the formulaic nature of such references to truth, pp. 75-83.

16 Albrecht's adaptation of this passage is quite aggressive:

3307, 4 swer mir des nicht geloubet,   dem brich ich uf der
                                            herpfen ouch di seiten,
3308   Daz im sin spil verworren   get als mir daz mine.

17 The formulaic *welt ir* (639, 2) can be seen on the edge of this category. Also 349, 28-30; 381, 28-30; similarly 257, 26.

18 It is not clear in Chrétien's text that the food comes miraculously from the Graal, though it could easily be interpreted as such. There is a similar twisting of an argument in a discussion between Gawan and Orgeluse (*Parzival*, 524, 2-6) in which he turns her own mockery back onto her.

Fourquet's position (*Wolfram d'Eschenbach*, pp. 159-61) that the narrator's interruptions are later interpolations by Wolfram and not in the original passage (which reads consistently without them), does not change the implications of Wolfram's manner of interruption. In addition this point of view supports the analysis of Wolfram's narrative technique as a consistent, dramatic unrolling of the scene before Parzival and the audience simultaneously by explaining the intrusions as later additions.

19 On this passage see Walter J. Schröder, 'Über Ironie in der Dichtung. Der Teufel am Sakrament', *Akzente*, 2 (1955), pp. 568-75; Curschmann, p. 638; and Nellmann, p. 69. Lofmark, 'Wolfram's source references', p. 827 sees this passage as an example of Wolfram's disguised independence and thus as jocular and simultaneously an attempt 'to deceive critics rather than to make fun of the rules of source adaptation'.

20 For example: 63, 10-11; 74, 10-15; 75, 11; 207, 4-5; 337, 23-30; 397, 7-11; 399, 1-10; 401, 5 - 402, 6; 403, 10-11; 443, 2-5; 516, 3-14; 532-5; 624, 20-7; 637, 1-4; 642, 10-13; 678, 28-30, etc.

21 For example: 74, 10-15; 82, 16-20; 534, 1-8; 631, 22; 682, 2-7;

734, 15-26; 737, 25-7; 738, 11-12; etc. Albrecht plays with this same idea, see below pp. 217ff.

22 For example: 130, 14-16; 287, 12-18; 291-3; 450, 1-8; 638, 25-30.

23 See Chapter 2. A similar interruption occurs in the midst of Gawan's perilous battle with the lion (572, 8-10).

24 'ir ladet ûf herze swaeren soum'. A *soum* is the load carried by lowly beasts of burden.

25 Herbert Kolb, 'Die Blutstropfen-Episode bei Chrétien und Wolfram', *Beiträge* (Tüb.), 79 (1957) pp. 363-79 compares the two scenes, though his conclusions about Wolfram's view of *minne* are too negative. Gerhard Bauer, 'Parzival und die Minne', *Euphorion*, 57 (1963), pp. 92-4 is more to the point in recognising that Parzival's love goes beyond courtly conventions (*Parzival* 302, 2-5) – only the magical effect is stopped when the blood drops are covered. But that Parzival's love keeps him from the Gral seems fundamentally wrong; his love supports him and makes his ultimate success possible. See Carl Wesle, 'Zu Wolframs Parzival', *Beiträge* (Halle), 72 (1950), pp. 1-38.

26 Humphrey Milnes, 'The play of opposites in *Iwein*', *GLL*, 14 (1960/1), pp. 241-56, has demonstrated a similar kind of tension between ideals and social norms in Hartmann's poem. Also see Weigand, 'Courtly love', pp. 194-8; and Curschmann, pp. 643ff. who discusses the narrator's attitude towards *minne* conventions at some length, concluding that Wolfram is proclaiming the value of his own method of 'Frauenlob' as opposed to Minnesang or to other courtly romances.

27 Other examples: 584-8; 598. 5-12.

28 Although inheriting the figure of Antikonie from Chrétien, Wolfram seems to have added a level of ironic ambiguity to her depiction. For an extreme view see Poag, 'Wolfram von Eschenbach's Antikonie', *GR*, 41 (1966), pp. 83-8. Sacker's discussion is more reasonable, pp. 79-86.

29 Also: 201, 20-30; 257, 29-30; 551, 20-30; 167, 27-30.

30 See above p. 44. The metaphor of love as a battle has a long tradition. On its development in MHG poetry from the classical *militat omnis amans* see Kohler (on *Parzival*, pp. 94ff.). The contest between the virtues and vices in Prudentius was a strong influence, as were conceptions of spiritual *vs.* profane love. In Chrétien love is seen as the opponent of reason (see p. 175 for a variation of this motif in *Parzival*). In Wolfram's poem other examples are seen in the imagery of the narrator's address to Frou Minne (292-3) and in depictions of Herzeloyde. Similarly *Titurel* 74, 4 and 75, 4. Even

Trevrizent uses this image as he politely accuses *minne* of *unêre* (478, 10–12). Albrecht occasionally reflects this (*minne* with *zange*, 1806, 2536).

31 Malcreatiure's ugliness is due to women: 520, 1–2. Trevrizent too blames women in the form of Eve (463, 19–22). H. B. Willson, 'Wolfram's self-defence', *MLR*, 52 (1957), pp. 572–5 has associated Trevrizent's statement with the 'self-defence' which he sees aimed specifically at Eve as the prototype of *valsch* (rather than at Isolde). Expressive of a patriarchal society, the serpent too is identifiably female in many medieval and Renaissance pictorial representations of the Fall.

32 Gibb's study shows Wolfram's female figures conforming to an ideal. Extreme views, either finding hidden criticism (Gertrude Lewis) or positive symbolism (Willson, who compares Herzeloyde and the Virgin Mary) seem to cancel each other out.

33 *Minne* is not discussed with levity in *Titurel* (see 48–51); its mystifying power is presented in oxymorons (49–50). There is a certain melancholy in Wolfram's tone here which is suited to the tragic outcome of the young lovers' tale. There is not, however, the unambiguously positive attitude discussed by Werner Simon, 'Zu Wolframs *Titurel*', *Festgabe für U. Pretzel* (Berlin, 1963), p. 190, who sees a mellowing of Wolfram's attitude in *Titurel*, a return of the ageing poet to a praise of *minne* as good, even when it comes too soon and ends tragically. Instead the tone suggests criticism of chivalric love. See W. T. H. Jackson, 'Faith unfaithful', pp. 60ff.; and Groos, 'Sigune', pp. 631–43 who argues that Sigune is shown in a linden tree as a sign that courtly love is the cause of her suffering. See also Heinzle, pp. 81–2.

34 See 436, 8–33 on Lunete. Wolfram also inserts other remarks on constancy more or less in passing, i.e. 311, 23–4.

35 Curschmann, pp. 633, 649–50, 652 and 658. Also, Karl Kurt Klein, 'Wolframs Selbstverteidigung', *ZfdA*, 85 (1954–5), pp. 158–9; and Poag, 'Heinrich von Veldeke's *minne*; Wolfram von Eschenbach's *liebe* and *triuwe*', *JEGP*, 61 (1962), pp. 721–35.

36 The narrator often admits the possibility of goodness in women within his negative diatribes: 334, 26–30; 551, 29–30. A positive judgement is also implicit in his laments over lack of success with females.

37 'Zu den epischen Hintergründen', p. 177. Mohr consistently points out Wolfram's humanising gifts (see the well-deserved praise granted this scholar by Bumke, *Wolfram-Forschung*, p. 194). Wolfram's habit of both revealing and concealing has been recently analysed in Harroff's perceptive study.

38 For example: 13, 2–15 on Gahmuret's virtues; 43, 5–8; 568, 1–14; 656, 3–5; 710, 15–18. Pörksen, esp. pp. 162–83, notes Wolfram's striving for a positive view in *Willehalm*.

39 In both cases Wolfram is annotating his source which does not proffer such excuses. The defence of Keie has been interpreted by Curschmann, pp. 644–5, as referring specifically to contemporary events.

40 For example: Gawan sinned in not revealing his identity (636, 6–8); Keie's negative role leads to a discussion of disloyal friends (675, 15–676, 2); and the dubious presentation of Antikonie (above p. 176). Nellmann, p. 134, judges Wolfram's criticism of protagonists 'eine wichtige Form des Wolframschen Erzählerkommentars', yet he lists only a few references (which are not necessarily criticisms as such) and later (p. 152) seems to contradict himself in discussing the unusually positive attitude of Wolfram's narrator.

41 Quoted from Hartmann von Aue, *Iwein*, ed. G. F. Benecke, K. Lachmann and L. Wolff, 7th edn (Berlin, 1968). Pörksen, pp. 177–83 discusses the traditional emphasis on *laus* in rhetoric; also pp. 153–4. In discussing the criticism of Antikonie, Curschmann (pp. 664–5) points out that the rule applies less to men than to women characters: 'Fürstenschelte' is fair game (*Parzival*, 410, 16f.). Wolfram says he could criticise Orgeluse but won't (516, 3ff.).

42 A fourth occasion might be Parzival's departure from his mother, which in Chrétien's poem is represented as a sin in that Perceval sees his mother collapsed on the ground and pays no heed. However, in Wolfram's version Parzival is ignorant of her fate, and the narrator does not comment on his deed but rather on Herzeloyde (128). That her death counts as a sin within the context of Book 9 (499, 20–2) has been pointed out by Hatto, 'On Chrétien and Wolfram', *MLR*, 44 (1949), p. 384, yet this opinion is not expressed by the narrator in Book 3 who instead calls on all loyal women to wish the hero well (129, 2–4). This seems to be a further example of the narrator's care in presenting his hero's innocence (see below pp. 183ff.). I would disagree with W. T. H. Jackson's implications that Parzival is directly responsible for her death because 'he never even looks back on leaving', *The Literature of the Middle Ages* (New York, 1960), p. 119, also p. 131; and with Huby who sees Perceval's action as 'unhöfisch'.

43 For summaries see Bumke, *Wolfram-Forschung*, under 'Parzivals Schuld' in the *Sachregister*; and Kratz, pp. 497–513.

44 In his excellent article Rupp does make a distinction between the

author and the characters, 'Die Funktion des Wortes *tump* im *Parzival* Wolframs von Eschenbach', *GRM*, 38 (1957), pp. 97–106. Haas, *Parzivals tumpheit bei Wolfram von Eschenbach* (Berlin, 1964). Christa Ortmann, *Die Selbstaussagen im 'Parzival'* (Stuttgart, 1972), n. 50, pp. 106–7 analyses *tumpheit* according to a fourfold exegetical mode and provides some insight into problems in Haas's approach.

45 Hans G. Welter, 'Zur Technik der Wortwiederholungen in Wolframs Parzival', *ZfdPh*, 93 (1974), pp. 34–42 analyses Wolfram's use of *Wâleis* in reference to Parzival's *tumpheit*. Walter K. Francke, 'The Function of "wis" in the Characterization of Gahmuret, Gawan and Parzival', *MLN*, 87 (1972), pp. 409–18 has shown that the use of *wîs* is likewise not arbitrary (as opposed to Rupp's view, p. 97).

46 See Haas, pp. 16–23 for definitions of *tump, tor, witze, wîs, sin,* etc.

47 There is a similar use of *tump* in the *Titurel* fragments (48; see p. 178 above) which clearly does not imply guilt.

48 In Book 3 the references are (N = narrator's comment):

121, 5		toersche Wâleise
121, 9		toerscher
124, 16	N	knappe der vil *tumpheit* wielt
124, 20		ob du mit witzen soldest lebn
126, 19	N	*tump*
126, 26		tôren kleider
127, 5	N	tôren kleit
129, 13	N	alsez sînen witzen tohte
131, 25		waert ir ze frumen wîse
132, 7	N	gescheiden von den witzen
133, 16		tôr
138, 9	N	toerscher knabe
139, 14	N	*tumpheit*
142, 13	N	der *tumpheit* genôz
144, 11	N	der knappe an witzen laz
149, 6	N	*tumb*
155, 19	N	*tumbe*
155, 28	N	wîsheit der umberuochte
156, 10	N	*tumber* nôt
156, 24	N	*tumpheit*
161, 6	N	*tumben* Parzival
161, 17	N	*tumbe* man
161, 19	N	(ez hete lân) ein blôz wîser
161, 25	N	*tumben*

162, 1	N	*tumbe* man
162, 28	N	*tumbe* witzen
163, 21	N	*tumpheit*
167, 9	N	witze ein weise
167, 11	N	*tumpheit*
169, 15	N	der helt mit witzen kranc
171, 24	N	
175, 6	N	(Gurnemanz's advice will make Parzival wise)

The word *tump* also appears twice in Book 4 in the narrator's commentary (179, 23 and 188, 17), once in Book 14 (689, 26), and once in Book 15 (744, 18). See Rupp's discussion of these passages.

49 Wolfram stresses Parzival's simplicity much more than Chrétien. Perceval's mother is distressed that he looks so foolish (607-11), and she does not warn him against dark fords, so Perceval, unlike his German counterpart, does not ride for a full day afraid to cross a shallow stream. Huby has recently pointed out Wolfram's increased emphasis on the hero's *tumpheit*, but in seeing Wolfram's changes as a scheme to render Parzival more courtly, Huby misses the point. For Wolfram is showing his hero instead as more natural, ultimately more sensitive. See above pp. 47ff.

50 Parzival's beauty is recognised by Ither and by Arthur's court. See the recent article by L. P. Johnson, 'Parzival's beauty', *Approaches,* pp. 273-91, who also points out the emphasis on Ither's beauty which heightens the serious implications of his slaying (pp. 275-6).

51 See especially Mohr's excellent article, 'Parzivals ritterliche Schuld', *WW,* Sammelband II (1962), pp. 196-208. Also Werner Schröder, 'Parzivals Schwerter', *ZfdA,* 100 (1971), pp. 113-17 on the significance of Ither's sword for Parzival's state of sin or potential sin.

52 Hatto, 'Archery and chivalry: A noble prejudice', *MLR,* 35 (1940), pp. 40-54 discusses the implications of death by such ignoble means as a javelin, and points out how Wolfram in contrast to Chrétien leaves his hero ignorant of the javelin's lowly position, thereby making Parzival innocent of malicious intent. Again we see how carefully Wolfram prepares Parzival's innocence.

53 See above pp. 165ff. It is useful at this point to look at Chrétien's version of Perceval's deeds. He mentions the hero's foolishness in not being able to remove the Red Knight's armour ('Molt grief chose est de fol aprendre', 1173). However, the sin is diminished because the Red Knight is depicted as evil and a great enemy of Arthur. Neither is Perceval blamed by Gornemant (1364ff.) who instead teaches the youth correct knightly skills and sends him on

his way with the advice to discontinue citing his mother as an authority:

> 1682 Car se vos plus le disiiez,
> A folie le tenroit l'en.

Chrétien's most frequent tag for Perceval's foolishness is *nice* (Haidu, *Aesthetic Distance*, p. 124), but the epithets stop with the Gornemant episode. The Graal episode is presented less ambiguously by Chrétien who repeats at several points the reason for Perceval's silence: his strict adherence to Gornemant's advice. The damning judgement is left to the maiden. As Perceval begins his lonely adventures he does not denounce God but simply forgets him (6217ff.). The hermit then tells him of his sin (*pechiez*, 6393) in his mother's death, which is cited as the cause of his failure at the Graal. No mention is made of the slaying of the Red Knight. As narrator Chrétien remains generally silent.

54 'Parzivals ritterliche Schuld'. There is a further dimension to Parzival's simplicity in that he does not know Ither's identity. On the conflict between Christianity vs. knighthood see Mockenhaupt, pp. 32–5, 179–85. Wolfram's attitude towards fighting has been further explored by Herta Zutt, 'Parzivals Kämpfe', in *Festgabe für F. Maurer* (Düsseldorf, 1968), pp. 178–98, who exaggerates the negative in Wolfram's views. A more balanced account is offered by Martin H. Jones, 'Parzival's fighting and his election to the Grail', *Wolfram-Studien*, III (Berlin, 1975), pp. 52–71, who goes perhaps too far in the opposite direction in evaluating *erstrîten*. Wolfram is ultimately ambiguous, for he does not deny the good of knightly valour and the chivalric code, but warns against believing it to be all, or perfect. Wolfram is not putting forth an alternative profession (the choices were limited for a knight, after all) but is pointing out that knighthood is a tempting opportunity for man to express his inherent sinfulness. Thus one's conduct must be leavened with faith and humble trust in God. Parzival is called to Munsalvaesche through an act of grace, yet his continued *erstrîten* (with a new attitude) has not kept him from it but been part of the proof of his deservedness. Man must make an effort; the world of chivalry offers one valid if dangerous way. See Green, '*âventiure*', pp. 135–7, on *âventiure* as the meeting point between knightly endeavour and divine guidance; and 'Homicide and *Parzival*', pp. 58–60.

55 Harms and Mockenhaupt see *triuwe* as the central issue.

56 Mohr ('Parzivals ritterliche Schuld', p. 205) points out the irony in that Parzival's killing of Ither makes him a knight and therefore in

a position to repeat such a deed. Parzival is twice called *der tumbe man* by the narrator following Ither's death but before Gurnemanz's instruction. He is now a *man* but still *tump* until properly trained. When the narrator mentions Parzival's *tumpheit* much later, it is again in reference to Ither, reminding us of the *reroup* and reassuring us that God will no longer allow Parzival to slip into the disasters chivalry repeatedly sets up for him.

57 Sigune, 255, 1–20; Cundrie, 316. For Albrecht's analysis of Parzival's silence see above p. 24.

58 *Scham* is stressed again later (321, 28ff.); also in the opening of Book 7 and in the prologue.

59 Rupp lists these passages.

60 Pp. 101–3. Even if Trevrizent is ignorant of Parzival's identity throughout the first part of their conversation (Tax, see Chapter 3 n. 23) this does not alter the significance of his use of the word *tump*. He uses it later as well and his final statement on *tumpheit* clearly reveals the difference between his interpretation and that of the narrator in Book 3. Trevrizent speaks of a *tumpheit* not necessarily concurrent with immaturity and lack of experience, but found in men of all ages (489, 5–12).

Chrétien refers only once to the concept of folly in the corresponding scene. The hermit says it was foolish not to ask the question (6413f.). Also see Haas on the different levels of *tumpheit*.

61 Parzival has already confessed his sin against Ither with similar words:

> 475, 5 genam ich ie den rêroup,
>
> sô was ich an den witzen toup.

62 Blanka Horacek, 'Zur inneren Form des Trevrizentbuches', *Sprachkunst*, 3 (1972), p. 224.

63 Tax (pp. 124–5) suggests the confession is delayed to synchronise with Christ's death *ad horam nonem* (see 485, 25). Wolfram's narrator apologises for his flippancy, reminiscent of when he stops himself from discussing joy in Sigune's presence (436, 23–5). On a similar contrast see Weigand, 'A jester at the Grail castle in Wolfram's *Parzival*?', in *Wolfram's Parzival*, pp. 75–119.

64 Parzival is called *wîgant* seven times, the last being 459, 10 in Book 9: 'do entwâpent sich der wîgant'. This may document a change in Wolfram's use of Germanic vocabulary, but it might also suggest that Parzival has risen above a certain level of the warrior state.

65 This term is used by V. A. Kolve in discussing the function of the *Expositor* or *meneur du jeu* in medieval drama: *The Play Called Corpus Christi* (Stanford, 1966), p. 27. There is intriguing similarity

between some aspects of the narrator in *Parzival* and these 'characters' in medieval plays.

66 See Bumke, *Wolfram-Forschung*, esp. pp. 275-86.

67 1, 15 - 2, 12. The usage implies a definition of *tump* closer to Trevrizent's than to that expounded by the narrator in Book 3. His words apply to both aesthetic and moral issues. Albrecht picks this up (VF 7-9 and 'Hinweisstrophen' A and B, p. 133).

68 Albrecht's narrator mentions as his contemporaries: her Walter (607, 2); Hartman von Owe (2402, 1; 4539, 1; 5094, 1); herre von Veldek (4831, 1) and Nithart (p. 134, E, 4). See Borchling, pp. 177-8. The one notable exception is Richard of Cornwall (2946) who died in 1272 (see n. 1, p. 259 in Wolf's edition).

69 Mankind is envisioned in Albrecht's prologue as situated between heaven (*tugend*) and hell (*untugend*) and choosing between. For a detailed summary of the contents of Albrecht's prologue see Hennig Brinkmann, 'Der Prolog im Mittelalter als literarische Erscheinung. Bau und Aussage', *WW*, 14 (1964), pp. 12-13, whose interpretation of the *Parzival* prologue is similar to Albrecht's, i.e. a general lesson on moral tenets based on rhetorical models and not specifically tied to the contents of the story. Also see Ragotzky's enlightening discussion, pp. 102-7. Albrecht's meaning seems that of Hartmann in *Gregorius*. For arguments on the meaning of *zwîvel* in *Parzival* and *Willehalm* (1, 24) see Bumke, *Wolfram-Forschung*, pp. 99-100, 126, 165, 282-3.

70 Vinaver, pp. 17-21.

71 Brode (pp. 25-8) argues that Albrecht's stanza form is especially suited to his repeated 'lehrhafte Hinwendungen' to his audience.

72 See *Parzival* 1, 6 and 119, 19. See JT 24-6, 31, 47-9, 58, 2791, and the *Verfasserfragment* 8.

73 See above p. 284. There are many similarities with the medieval *ars praedicandi* in Albrecht's approach, as well as a specific analogy to one of St Bernard's sermons which he begins by defending his exposition of the Song of Songs against criticisms from the quick-witted among his listeners who might be impatient at the slow pace: 'I also have a duty towards slower people, and indeed especially towards them; for I am not concerned nearly so much to explain words as to influence hearts. My duty is both to draw water and to give it to people to drink, and this is not to be done by discussing things hastily and cursorily, but by careful commentary and frequent exhortation.' Quoted from Spearing, p. 125.

74 Among the many articles on this problem see Frederick Norman's recent summary of opinion, 'Meinung und Gegenmeinung: die literarische Fehde zwischen Gottfried von Strassburg und Wolfram

von Eschenbach', *Miscellanea in Orore di B. Tecchi* (Rome, 1969), pp. 67–86. Also David Dalby, *'Der maere wildenaere'*, *Euphorion*, 55 (1961), pp. 77–84; and Wolfgang Monecke, *Studien zur epischen Technik Konrads von Würzburg, Das Erzählprinzip der 'wildekeit'* (Stuttgart, 1968), esp. chapter 1. W. T. H. Jackson, 'The literary views of Gottfried von Strassburg', *PMLA*, 85 (1970), pp. 992–1001 denies that Gottfried is engaging in literary criticism in his excursus, a compelling perspective if not totally convincing. Gerhild Geil, *Gottfried und Wolfram als literarische Antipoden* (Cologne/Vienna, 1973) offers an 80-page Forschungsbericht. Her limited conclusion is that the idea of a feud was the outgrowth of nineteenth-century morality.

75 Ragotzky, p. 103 etc., argues that the audience was totally familiar with Wolfram's poetry and assumes a verbatim knowledge of his prologue.

76 At one point (5091–5) Albrecht's narrator reflects on his treatment of women in an exchange with Frou Aventiure. He, 'vil edel ritter von esschenbach', defends his own slight criticisms by comparing himself to Ovid and Hartmann who treated women very badly. This passage clearly alludes to *Parzival*. Also see below.

77 The only references I have found are: Ysalde: 1640; Isalde: 1814, 1971, 5706. Tristram: 2034, 2162. Also Morolt: 1402, 1971, 2161–3, 3726ff.; and King Mark: 117, 1565, 1737, 1753, 1971, 2161–3.

78 The discussion of vices could have been left out on the grounds that it was clear in itself and not in keeping with Albrecht's *tugende lêre*. Albrecht's narrator does suggest an atmosphere of rivalry when he refers to the supreme position of *Parzival* among its *gesinde*, using metaphors from knightly contests to describe the competition (61). However, the reference is not to a specific rival but rather to *Parzival's* pre-eminence among courtly romances. Following this, the narrator muses over his task and his determination to carry on, mentioning his patrons ('fursten drin', 64, 1) and, in imitation of Wolfram's narrator, alluding to his duties as a knight. Walter Haug, 'Rudolfs "Willehalm" und Gottfrieds "Tristan": Kontrafaktur als Kritik', in *Deutsche Literatur des späten Mittelalters*, ed. Harms et al. (Berlin, 1975), pp. 83ff., points out that already near contemporaries of Wolfram and Gottfried failed to distinguish the two poets' styles or to recognise a feud. He suggests rather that the two were seen as similar on a certain level of aesthetic principle: 'beide Dichter setzen ihr Werk zu einem elitären Hörerkreis in Beziehung, bei beiden entscheidet sich die Zugehörigkeit zu diesem Kreis durch die Teilhabe an einem durch das Werk vermittelten

Erfahrungsprozeß, und bei beiden bedeutet dieser Prozeß ein Selbststverständnis über einen Sinnzusammenhang, der sich in der Dialektik zwischen Fiktion und Faktizität öffnet' (p. 84). Burghart Wachinger, *Sängerkrieg* (Munich, 1973), discusses various MHG literary feuds and concludes that many are 'Gelehrtenphantasie' (p. 105), though *Spruchdichtung* contains relatively many polemics. Wachinger ties this to the 'neue Literatenbewußtsein der Berufsdichter' (p. 309).

79 His relationship with Frou Aventiure is not at all consistent in this respect, see below pp. 217ff.

80 See above pp. 144–6 and 150ff. *Tugende* are discussed repeatedly in the JT, and allegories of virtue occur in the temple description as well as in the *brackenseil* inscription. Also 5887ff.

81 In the prologue the Trinity is compared to a fountain, 26–48, and in 16 stanzas (67–83) Albrecht names 12 biblical figures. On the fountain metaphor see Kern. Albrecht's description of the power of water recalls the short passage in *Parzival* describing Feirefiz's baptism (817, 4–30). Albrecht's penchant for supporting his statements with learned references is discussed by Wolf, 'Wer war der Dichter', p. 330. Wolfram's use of exempla in *Willehalm* includes only secular references (Pörksen, pp. 117–20). On Albrecht's references see also the articles by Leckie; and Wolf, 'Der Vogel Phönix'.

82 The lines quoted below (stanza 68) and a later stanza (4832) are based on the narrator's words in *Willehalm* (2, 19–22) which though ambiguous seem to claim a lack of formal education. Albrecht's narrator makes instead a qualitative remark on his relative lack of expertise, wound into an expression of his humble consciousness of God's power. The word *sin* refers in the JT passages to the reasoning power of man which can recognise though not understand God's infinite *kraft*. It does not seem to connote spiritual inspiration. See Boesch, *Kunstanschauung*, pp. 169ff. On *kunst* and *sin* see Ohly, 'Wolframs Gebet an den Heiligen Geist im Eingang des Willehalm', in *Wolfram von Eschenbach*, ed. Rupp (Darmstadt, 1966), pp. 455–509 and 'Nachtrag 1965', pp. 510–18; Hans Eggers, 'Non cognovi litteraturam (Zu *Parzival* 115, 27)', in *Wolfram von Eschenbach*, ed. Rupp, pp. 533–48; and Werner Schröder, '*kunst* und *sin* bei Wolfram von Eschenbach', *Euphorion*, 67 (1973), pp. 219–43, who rejects Ohly's interpretation.

83 Wolf's notes show some manuscripts with 4 instead of 9 here, though the latter seems preferable because of its symbolic potential. See *Parzival* 4, 2–8 for Wolfram's version ('nu lât mîn eines wesen drî') and a similar passage in Gottfried's *Tristan*, 4604ff., which may well be another reflection of the feud between the two poets.

84 In general Albrecht gives a straightforward chronological account. He seems to run out of steam with Titurel and has him live 900 years, so he does not need to invent further ancestors. He also interrupts his story to insert earlier anecdotes, i.e. Arthur's previous lack of moderation (2498–2518).

85 Albrecht continually draws attention to the burden of his task in carrying out the orders of Frou Aventiure. See below pp. 217ff.

86 Albrecht is extremely fond of this metaphor and uses it repeatedly in his introductory section: 101, 105–8, 143–6, 158.

87 Borchling lists these, pp. 170–1, though his interpretation of their effect and significance is mistaken: 'Der Dichter denkt sich bei der Abfassung seines Gedichtes stets unter eine Menge von Zuhörern, die seinen Worten lauschen.'

88 Other examples: 101, 149, 153, 158.

89 Brode, pp. 108 and 198, sees the JT as a denial of chivalric values. Rather, the chivalric system is presented as a worldly Christian ideal. See Ragotzky, pp. 101–2.

90 Wolfram's poem contains three realms – west, east and Gral – which remain separate, with the Gral world in a kind of fourth dimension (Fourquet, 'La structure du *Parzival*', pp. 203–4). Feirefiz and Parzival finally link them in Book 16. There are otherwise few suggestions of crossing borders: in Arthur's words to Segramors (286, 1–14); Arthur is camped on the outskirts of Terre de Salvaesche, partly on Gral territory (see Wynn, 'Geography of fact and fiction in Wolfram von Eschenbach's "Parzival"', *MLR*, 56 (1961), pp. 34–5); Trevrizent's hermitage is visited regularly by the pilgrims, and Orilus and Parzival go there (though this is not all the way to Munsalvaesche). The exception of Lähelin is not explained.

In the JT the boundaries between the Gral and Arthurian worlds are also vaguely defined, yet potentially crossable. Tschinotulander himself can go to Munt Salvasch (he intends to do so with Sigune, 4983ff.); Tschinotulander is one of the greatest knights (5687) and deserves to be called to the Gral (5396ff.); Arthur gives advice to Anfortas, etc. (see 1769, 5851, 5875, 5080). For further instances see Ragotzky, pp. 113f. There is a sense of free-flowing exchange between the realms both of which seem to exist on the same plane.

91 Wolf offers a different reading in his notes which alters the meaning. A similar joy-bringing effect is described, 4190; also 918. The JT, like *Willehalm*, is much bloodier than *Parzival*. See Henry Lee Tapp, 'An investigation of the use of imagery in the works of Wolfram von Eschenbach', Diss. Yale, 1953, pp. 255ff.; Pörksen, pp. 175ff. See JT 3720–1, 3539, 3763–4, 4190, 3877, 3978. An intriguing reflection of Albrecht's attitude towards killing is seen in

his preoccupation with the importance of burial rites: 672, 679, 989, 1024, 1081, 1705, 2667, 2762, 3657, 4306, 4370, 4551, 5374. This is of course a reflection of his emphasis on Christian sacrament as well.

92 Marc Bloch, *Feudal Society*, II (Chicago, 1961), pp. 305 and 318. Bloch also quotes a song presumably by Bertrand de Born in praise of battle (p. 293): 'I love the gay Eastertide, which brings forth leaves and flowers; and I love the joyous songs of the birds, re-echoing through the copse. But also I love to see, amidst the meadows, tents and pavilions spread; and it gives me great joy to see, drawn up on the field, knights and horses in battle array; and it delights me when the scouts scatter people and herds in their path . . . Maces, swords, helms of different hues, shields that will be riven and shattered as soon as the fight begins; and many vassals struck down together; and the horses of the dead and the wounded roving at random.' On the other hand, jousting was forbidden by the Church as early as 1130 (Weigand, 'Courtly love', p. 166).

93 These lines are reminiscent of the prologue to *Tristan*, though without the ambiguity (see above p. 168 and n. 12):

> 177 wan swa man hoeret oder list,
> daz von so reinen triuwen ist,
> da liebent dem getriuwen man
> triuwe und ander tugende van.

In *Titurel* Wolfram speaks of the importance of seeing ('erspehent') good examples in learning to be a knight (40, 4), i.e. the value of experience and action, not words.

94 *Parzival* 115, 29-116, 4:

> disiu âventiure
> vert âne der buoche stiure.
> ê man si hete für ein buoch,
> ich waere ê nacket âne tuoch,
> sô ich in dem bade saeze,
> ob ichs questen niht vergaeze.

See Curschmann, pp. 660-1; and Chapter 1, n. 23.

95 There are similarities with several Christian stories: Samson's birth (Borchling, p. 9), John the Baptist, or even Christ.

96 Typically, in *Parzival* the description occurs at a natural point in the tale, just as the knights themselves look carefully at him and are struck by his perfection. See also a description of Gamuret, JT 4352.

97 The occurrences of direct quotation are:

162–4   Annunciation
174   Titurel is named
190–6   Titurel and his teacher discuss *minne* (exchange)
240–6   'Wolfram' and Frou Aventiure (exchange)
266   'Wolfram' and Frou Aventiure (exchange)
280   Titurel consoles his parents
283–92   continued consolation and praise of God
295–6   his parents bid farewell

98 Reminiscent of the *brackenseil* inscription.
99 Jescute and Orilus are similarly valuable as presentation-pieces (see Chapter 2, above). As Ragotzky has pointed out, Tschinotulander's story is essentially 'eine Kette von Bewährungssituationen' (pp. 113 and 121–2).
100 In the JT both Tschinotulander and Sigune are well-educated (4270, 5450). See also 4832, 5057, 5231, etc.
101 The narrator summarises in conclusion:

197 Sust mŭst er in bewisen   der minne gar ein ende,
wie eine paradisen   kan, und di ander bŏse missewende
der sele git. di wolt er gerne vliehen
und sich mit ritterschefte   von der valschen zŭ der
waren ziehen.

A similar method of presentation was used in relating the leash inscription, see above Chapter 3. *Minne* is discussed at various points throughout the text: 187ff., 1275, 1906, 4575ff., 4606, 5429; *ware minne* leads to God, 555; *minne* is next to God in power, 2633–5; love of God is greatest love, 2636, 2148f., 5470, 5478–9; *unminne*, 193, 186, 4023–5 (compare *Parzival*, 291, 28–30).
102 Parzival's youth is depicted in Book 3 in vignettes where little dialogue is used but the actions are specifically described and unadorned with commentary. In the JT depiction of Titurel's youth there are two specific and humorously worldly exceptions to the rule of generalised states of perfection. These are Elizabel's desire that her son be kept ignorant of *minne* (186), and Titurel's habit of crossing himself fearfully whenever the word *minne* is uttered in his presence (187). Both of these are variations on incidents in Parzival's youth, emphasising Titurel's similarity with that hero and affirming his piety and innocence.
103 See the image of a blind man in *Titurel*, 49 and a similar image JT 2953–4.

104 See *Parzival* 502, 4–12 and JT 197, 1887, 1909, 1910, 6034, 6098.
105 Zatloukal, p. 407, n. 18 notes that Albrecht does not blame women or horses.
106 See Borchling, p. 173.
107 Brode, pp. 182f.
108 See 665–8, 2290, 3598–9, 2688, 5019–30, 5233–9 (a similar image of following a path). She also offers explanations for the story's course, i.e. that Tschinotulander loses to Orilus only because of the magic gold (5019ff.).
109 See above, pp. 194ff. In her spiritedness Albrecht's Frou Aventiure is reminiscent of Hartmann's Frou Minne.

CONCLUSION

1 See Chapter 1.
2 Dr H. Sparnaay, *Karl Lachmann als Germanist* (Bern, 1948), p. 109.
3 *Quoted from* Gerhard Kozielek, ed., *Mittelalterrezeption* (Tübingen, 1977), p. 20.
4 Sparnaay, p. 110. Bodmer, who rediscovered *Parzival* in 1753, admired the work, but felt the Gral to be the only point of interest, claiming: 'Von der Einheit der Handlung hatte der Dichter keine Idee' (quoted from Helmut Brackert, 'Eine romantische Parzival-Allegorese', in *Festschrift G. Weber* (Bad Homburg/Berlin, 1967), p. 239). Brackert quotes other early criticisms of *Parzival* which from a contemporary viewpoint seem more appropriate to the JT.

BIBLIOGRAPHY

Angress, Ruth K. 'Interrogation in Wolfram's *Parzival*', *GQ*, 62 (1969), 1–10.

Bauer, Gerhard. 'Parzival und die Minne', *Euphorion*, 57 (1963), 67–96.

Becker, Peter J. *Handschriften und Frühdrucke mittelhochdeutscher Epen.* Wiesbaden, 1977.

Bertau, Karl. *Deutsche Literatur im Europäischen Mittelalter.* 2 vols. Munich, 1972 and 1973.

— and Rudolf Stephan. 'Zum sanglichen Vortrag mhd. strophischen Epen', *ZfdA*, 87 (1956–7), 253–70.

Blamires, David. *Characterization and Individuality in Wolfram's 'Parzival'.* Cambridge, 1966.

Bloch, Marc. *Feudal Society.* 2 vols. Chicago, 1961.

Boesch, Bruno. *Deutsche Literaturgeschichte in Grundzügen.* Bern, 1946 (English edn, *German Literature. A Critical Survey.* London, 1971).

— *Die Kunstanschauung in der mittelhochdeutschen Dichtung.* Bern and Leipzig, 1936; rpt. Hildesheim and New York, 1976.

Boisserée, Sulpiz. 'Über die Beschreibung des Tempels des heiligen Grales in dem Heldengedicht: Titurel Kap. III', *Abhandlungen der philos.-philolog. Classe der könig. bayer. Ak. der Wiss.*, I (1835), 307–92.

Boor, Helmut de. 'Drei Fürsten im mittleren Deutschland', *Beiträge* (Tübingen), 95 (1973), Sonderheft, *Festschrift für Ingeborg Schröbler*, 238–57.

Booth, Wayne C. *The Rhetoric of Fiction.* Chicago, 1961.

Borchling, Conrad. *Der Jüngere Titurel und sein Verhältnis zu Wolfram von Eschenbach.* Göttingen, 1897.

Bostock, J. Knight. '*Parzival* 264, 1–30', *Medium Aevum*, 21 (1952), 34–5.

Brackert, Helmut. 'Eine romantische Parzival-Allegorese', in *Festschrift für Gottfried Weber*, ed. H. O. Burger et al., Bad Homburg/Berlin/Zurich, 1967, 237–54.

Brinkmann, Hennig. 'Der Prolog im Mittelalter als literarische Erscheinung. Bau und Aussage', *WW*, 14 (1964), 1–21.

Brode, Hanspeter. 'Untersuchung zum Sprach- und Werkstil des "Jüngeren Titurel" von Albrecht von Scharfenberg'. Diss., Freiburg i. B., 1966.

Bumke, Joachim. Review of the Marburg *Willehalm* edition, *Euphorion*, 64 (1970), 423–31.

'Titurelüberlieferung und Titurelforschung. Vorüberlegungen zu einer neuen Ausgabe von Wolframs Titurelfragmenten', *ZfdA*, 102 (1973), 147–88.

'Zur Überlieferung von Wolframs Titurel. Wolfram's Dichtung und der Jüngere Titurel', *ZfdA*, 100 (1971), 390–431.

Wolfram von Eschenbach. Stuttgart, 1964.

Die Wolfram von Eschenbach Forschung seit 1945. Munich, 1970.

Curschmann, Michael. 'Das Abenteuer des Erzählens. Über den Erzähler in Wolframs "Parzival"', *DVjs*, 45 (1971), 627–67.

Dalby, David. '*Der maere wildenaere*', *Euphorion*, 55 (1961), 77–84.

Dittmann, Wolfgang. ' "Dune hâst niht wâr, Hartman" '; Zum Begriff der *wârheit* in Hartmanns *Iwein*', in *Festgabe für Ulrich Pretzel,* ed. W. Simon et al., Berlin, 1963, 150–61.

Droysen, Ernst. *Der Tempel des heiligen Gral nach Albrecht von Scharfenberg.* Bromberg, 1872.

Eggers, Hans. 'Non cognovi litteraturam (Zu *Parzival* 115, 27)', in *Festgabe für Ulrich Pretzel,* ed. W. Simon et al., Berlin, 1963, 162–72 (= in *Wolfram von Eschenbach,* ed. H. Rupp, Darmstadt, 1966, 533–48).

Ehrismann, Gustav. *Geschichte der deutschen Literatur bis zum Ausgang des Mittelalters.* 4 vols. Munich, 1922–35.

Engelen, Ulrich. *Die Edelsteine in der deutschen Dichtung des 12. und 13. Jahrhunderts.* Munich, 1978.

Ertzdorff, Xenja von. 'Typen des Romans im 13. Jahrhundert', *DU*, 20 (1968), 81–95.

Faral, Edmond. *Les arts poétiques du XIIe et du XIIIe siècle.* Paris 1924; rpt. Paris, 1962.

Fechter, Werner. *Das Publikum der mittelhochdeutschen Dichtung.* Frankfurt, 1935 and 1966; rpt. Darmstadt, 1972.

Fourquet, Jean. 'La structure du *Parzival*', in *Les romans du Graal aux XIIe et XIIIe siècles.* Paris, 1956, 119–209.

Wolfram d'Eschenbach et le 'Conte del Graal', 2nd edn, Paris, 1966.

Francke, Walter K. 'The function of "wis" in the characterization of Gahmuret, Gawan and Parzival', *MLN*, 87 (1972), 409–18.

Frankl, Paul. *The Gothic.* Princeton, 1960.

Frappier, Jean. *Chrétien de Troyes.* Paris, 1957.

Geil, Gerhild. *Gottfried und Wolfram als literarische Antipoden.* Cologne/Vienna, 1973.

Gibbs, Marion E. *Wîblîchez Wîbes Reht. A Study of the Women Characters in the Works of Wolfram von Eschenbach.* Pittsburgh, 1972.

Green, D. H., 'Irony and medieval romance', in *Arthurian Romance*, ed. D. D. R. Owen, New York, 1971 (= *Forum for Modern Language Studies*, 6 (1970), 49–64).

Green, D. H. and Johnson, L. P. *Approaches to Wolfram von Eschenbach. Five Essays*. Bern, 1978.

Groos, Arthur B. '"Sigune auf der Linde" and the Turtledove in *Parzival*', *JEGP*, 67 (1968), 631–46.

'Wolfram von Eschenbach's 'bow metaphor" and the narrative technique of *Parzival*', *MLN*, 87 (1972), 391–408.

Gruenter, Rainer. 'Parzivals *einvalt*', *Euphorion*, 52 (1958), 297–302.

'Zum Problem der Landschaftsdarstellung im höfischen Versroman', *Euphorion*, 56 (1962), 248–78.

Haas, Alois M. *Parzivals tumpheit bei Wolfram von Eschenbach*. Heft 21, *Philologische Studien und Quellen*. Berlin, 1964.

Haidu, Peter. *Aesthetic Distance in Chrétien de Troyes: Irony and Comedy in Cligès and Perceval*. Geneva, 1968.

'Introduction' to 'Approaches to Medieval Romance', *Yale French Studies*, 51 (1976), 3–11.

Harms, Wolfgang. *Der Kampf mit dem Freund oder Verwandten in der deutschen Literatur bis um 1300*. Munich, 1963.

Harroff, Stephen C. *Wolfram and his Audience. A Study of the Themes of Quest and of Recognition of Kinship Identity*. Göppingen, 1974.

Hatto, Arthur T. 'Archery and chivalry: a noble prejudice', *MLR*, 35 (1940), 40–54.

'On Chrétien and Wolfram', *MLR*, 44 (1949), 380–5.

'Enid's best dress. A contribution to the understanding of Chrétien's and Hartmann's *Erec* and the Welsh *Gereint*', *Euphorion*, 54 (1960), 437–41.

'Herzeloyde's dragon-dream', *GLL*, 22 (1968), 18–31.

'Two notes on Chrétien and Wolfram', *MLR*, 42 (1947), 243–6.

'Wolfram von Eschenbach and the chase', in *Et multum et multa. Festgabe für Kurt Lindner*. Berlin, 1971, 101–12.

Haug, Walter. 'Rudolfs "Willehalm" und Gottfrieds "Tristan": Kontrafaktur als Kritik', in *Deutsche Literatur des späten Mittelalters*, ed. W. Harms and L. P. Johnson, Berlin, 1975, 83–89.

Heinzle, Joachim. *Stellenkommentar zu Wolframs Titurel: Beiträge zum Verständnis des überlieferten Textes*. Tübingen, 1972.

Hermann, Ernst. *Die Inschrift des Brackenseils: Wandlungen der höfischen Weltanschauung im Jüngeren Titurel*. Marburg-Lahn, 1939.

Horacek, Blanka. 'Zur inneren Form des Trevrizentbuches', *Sprachkunst*, 3 (1972), 214–29.

Bibliography

Huby, Michel. 'Wolframs Bearbeitungstechnik im "Parzival" (Buch III)', in *Wolfram-Studien*, ed. W. Schröder, III, 1975, 40-51.

Huschenbett, Dietrich. 'Albrecht, Dichter des "Jüngeren Titurel"' and 'Albrecht von Scharfenberg' in the *Verfasserlexikon*, I, 1977, 158-73 and 201-6.

Albrechts 'Jüngerer Titurel'. Zu Stil und Komposition. Munich, 1979.

Review of Ragotzky, *Studien zur Wolfram-Rezeption*, in *Anzeiger*, 87 (1976), 114-22.

Jackson, W. H. 'Some observations on the status of the narrator in Hartmann von Aue's "Erec" and "Iwein"', in *Arthurian Romance*, ed. D. D. R. Owen, New York, 1971 (= *Forum for Modern Language Studies*, 6, I (1970)), 65-82.

Jackson, W. T. H. 'Faith unfaithful – the German reaction to courtly love', in *The Meaning of Courtly Love*, ed. F. X. Newman, Albany, 1968, 55-76.

'The literary views of Gottfried von Strassburg', *PMLA*, 85 (1970), 992-1001.

The Literature of the Middle Ages. New York, 1960.

'The progress of Parzival and the Trees of Virtue and Vice', *GR*, 33 (1958), 118-24.

Jaeger, C. Stephen. 'Der Schöpfer der Welt und das Schöpfungswerk als Prologmotiv in der mittelhochdeutschen Dichtung', *ZfdA*, 107 (1978), 1-18.

'The "strophic" Prologue to Gottfried's *Tristan*', *GR*, 47 (1972), 5-19.

Johnson, L. P. 'Characterization in Wolfram's *Parzival*', *MLR*, 64 (1969), 68-83.

'Dramatische Ironie in Wolframs "Parzival"', in *Probleme mittelhochdeutscher Erzählformen*, ed. P. F. Ganz and W. Schröder, Berlin, 1972, 133-52.

'Lähelin and the Grail horses', *MLR*, 63 (1968), 612-17.

'*ungenuht al eine (Parzival 782, 23)*', in *Probleme mittelalterlicher Überlieferung und Textkritik*, ed. P. F. Ganz and W. Schröder, Berlin, 1968, 49-66.

Johnson, Sidney M. 'Gawan's surprise in Wolfram's *Parzival*', *GR*, 33 (1958), 285-92.

'Herzeloyde and the Grail', *Neophilologus*, 52 (1968), 148-56.

Jones, Martin H. 'Parzival's fighting and his election to the Grail', *Wolfram-Studien*, ed. W. Schröder, III, Berlin, 1975, 52-71.

Kane, George. *The Autobiographical Fallacy in Chaucer and Langland Studies.* London, 1965.

278

Bibliography

Ker, W. P. *Epic and Romance. Essays on Medieval Literature.* 2nd edn, 1922; rpt. New York, 1957.

Kern, Peter. 'Der Kommentar zu "Parzival" 1, 13f. im Prolog des "Jüngeren Titurel"', in *Studien zur deutschen Literatur und Sprache des Mittelalters,* ed. Besch et al. (= *Festschrift für Hugo Moser*), Berlin, 1974, 185–99.

Klein, Karl Kurt. 'Wolframs Selbstverteidigung', *ZfdA,* 85 (1954–5), 150–62.

Kohler, Erika. *Liebeskrieg. Zur Bildersprache der höfischen Dichtung des Mittelalters.* Stuttgart, 1935.

Kolb, Herbert. 'Die Blutstropfen-Episode bei Chrétien und Wolfram', *Beiträge* (Tübingen), 79 (1957), 363–79.

Kolve, V. A. *The Play Called Corpus Christi.* Stanford, 1966.

Kozielek, Gerhard, ed. *Mittelalterrezeption. Texte zur Aufnahme altdeutscher Literatur in der Romantik.* Tübingen, 1977.

Kratz, Henry. *Wolfram von Eschenbach's 'Parzival'. An Attempt at a total Evaluation.* Berlin, 1973.

Krautheimer, Richard. 'Introduction to an iconography of medieval architecture', *Journal of the Warburg and Courtauld Institutes,* 5 (1942), 1–33.

Kuhn, Hugo. *Minnesangs Wende.* 2nd edn, Tübingen, 1967.

Lachmann, Karl. *Kleinere Schriften.* Berlin, 1876; rpt. Berlin, 1969.

Lämmert, Eberhard. *Bauformen des Erzählens.* Stuttgart, 1955.

Leckie, R. William. 'Albrecht von Scharfenberg and the "Historia de Preliis Alexandri Magni"', *ZfdA,* 99 (1970), 120–39.

'"Bestia de funde": Natural science and the Jüngerer Titurel', *ZfdA,* 96 (1967), 263–77.

'"Gamaniol, der Vogel": Natural science and the Jüngerer Titurel II', *ZfdA,* 98 (1969), 133–44.

Lessing, G. E. *Laokoon oder Über die Grenzen der Malerei und Poesie.* Reclam edn, Stuttgart, 1964.

Lewis, C. S. *The Discarded Image.* Cambridge, 1964.

Lewis, Gertrude Jaron. 'Die unheilige Herzeloyde. Ein ikonoklastischer Versuch', *JEGP,* 74 (1975), 465–85.

Lichtenberg, Heinrich. 'Die Architekturdarstellungen in der mittelhochdeutschen Dichtung', *Forschungen zur deutschen Sprache und Dichtung,* 4, Münster, 1931.

Lofmark, Carl J. 'Der höfische Dichter als Übersetzer', in *Probleme mittelhochdeutscher Erzählformen,* ed. P. F. Ganz and W. Schröder, Berlin, 1972, 40–62.

'Zur Interpretation der Kyotstellen im "Parzival"', in *Wolfram-Studien,* ed. W. Schröder, IV, Berlin, 1977, 33–70.

'Wolfram's source references in "Parzival"', *MLR*, 67 (1972), 820–44.

Maak, Hans-Georg. 'Zu Füetrers "Fraw Eren Hof" und der Frage nach dem Verfasser des Jüngeren Titurel', *ZfdPh*, 87 (1968), 42–6.

McCulloch, Florence. *Mediaeval Latin and French Bestiaries*. Chapel Hill, 1960.

MacDougall, Elisabeth B. 'The sleeping nymph: origins of a humanist fountain type', *Art Bulletin*, 57 (1975), 357–65.

Marchand, James W. 'Tristan's *Schwertleite*: Gottfried's aesthetics and literary criticism', in *Husbanding the Golden Grain. Studies in Honor of Henry W. Nordmeyer*. Ann Arbor, 1973, 187–204.

Mertens, Volker, 'Zu Text und Melodie der Titurelstrophe *Iamer ist mir entsprungen*', in *Wolfram-Studien*, ed. W. Schröder, I, Berlin, 1970, 219–39.

Milnes, Humphrey. 'The play of opposites in *Iwein*', *GLL*, 14 (1960–1), 241–56.

Mockenhaupt, Benedikt. *Die Frömmigkeit im Parzival Wolframs von Eschenbach*. Bonn, 1942; rpt. Darmstadt, 1968.

Mohr, Wolfgang. 'Zu den epischen Hintergründen in Wolframs *Parzival*', *Mediaeval German Studies*. Presented to F. Norman. London, 1965, 174–87.

'Fiktive und reale Darbietungszeit in Erzählung und Drama', *Volksüberlieferung, Festschrift für Kurt Ranke*, ed. F. Harkort et al., Göttingen, 1968, 517–29.

'Hilfe und Rat in Wolframs *Parzival*', *Festschrift für Jost Trier*, ed. B. v. Wiese and K. H. Borck, Meisenheim, 1954, 173–97.

'Obie und Meljanz. Zum 7. Buch von Wolframs "Parzival"', in *Gestaltprobleme der Dichtung, Festschrift für Günther Müller*, ed. R. Alewyn et al., Bonn, 1957, 9–20 (= in *Wolfram von Eschenbach*, ed. H. Rupp, Darmstadt, 1966, 261–80 and 'Nachtrag 1965', 280–6).

'Parzival und Gawan', *Euphorion*, 52 (1958), 1–22 (= in *Wolfram von Eschenbach*, ed. H. Rupp, Darmstadt, 1966, 287–318).

'Parzivals ritterliche Schuld', *WW*, Sammelband II (1962), 196–208.

'Zur Textgeschichte von Wolframs "Titurel"', in *Wolfram-Studien*, ed. W. Schröder, IV, Berlin, 1977, 123–51.

Monecke, Wolfgang. *Studien zur epischen Technik Konrads von Würzburg. Das Erzählprinzip der 'wildekeit'*. Stuttgart, 1968.

Mordhorst, Otto. *Egen von Bamberg und 'die geblümte Rede'*. Berlin, 1911.

Nellmann, Eberhard. *Wolframs Erzähltechnik*. Wiesbaden, 1973.

Norman, Frederick. 'Meinung und Gegenmeinung: die literarische

Fehde zwischen Gottfried von Strassburg und Wolfram von Eschenbach', in *Miscellanea di Studi in Onore di Bonaventura Tecchi*. Rome, 1969, 67–86.

Nowell, Charles E. 'The historical Prester John', *Speculum*, 28 (1953), 435–45.

Nyholm, Kurt. *Albrechts von Scharfenberg 'Merlin'*. Abo, 1967.

Review of Röll, *Studien zu Text und Überlieferung*, in *Beiträge* (Tübingen), 87 (1965), 442–60.

Studien zum sogenannten geblümten Stil. Abo, 1971.

Nykrog, Per. 'Two creators of narrative form in twelfth century France: Gautier D'Arras – Chrétien de Troyes', *Speculum*, 48 (1973), 258–76.

Ohly, Friedrich. 'Cor amantis non angustum', in *Gedenkschrift für W. Foerste*. Cologne and Vienna, 1970, 454–76.

'Vom geistigen Sinn des Wortes im Mittelalter', *ZfdA*, 89 (1958–9), 1–23.

'Die Suche in Dichtungen des Mittelalters', *ZfdA*, 94 (1965), 171–84.

'Wolframs Gebet an den Heiligen Geist im Eingang des Willehalm', *ZfdA*, 91 (1961–2), 1–37 (= in *Wolfram von Eschenbach*, ed. H. Rupp, Darmstadt, 1966, 455–509 and 'Nachtrag 1965', 510–18).

Olschki, Leonardo. 'Der Brief des Presbyters Johannes', *Historische Zeitschrift*, 144 (1931), 1–14.

Ortmann, Christa. *Die Selbstaussagen im 'Parzival'. Zur Frage nach der Persongestaltung bei Wolfram von Eschenbach*. Stuttgart, 1972.

Peil, Dietmar. *Die Gebärde bei Chrétien, Hartmann und Wolfram*. Munich, 1975.

Petersen, Karen-Maria. 'Zum Grundriß des Graltempels', in *Festschrift für K. H. Halbach*, Göppingen, 1972, 271–306.

Petzet, Erich, 'Über das Heidelberger Bruchstück des Jüngeren Titurel', *Sitzungsberichte der Münchener Akad. d. Wiss., philos.-hist. Klasse* (1903), 287–320.

Pickering, F. P. *Literature and Art in the Middle Ages*. London, 1970.

Poag, James F. 'Heinrich von Veldeke's *minne*; Wolfram von Eschenbach's *liebe* and *triuwe*', *JEGP*, 61 (1962), 721–35.

'*Diu verholnen maere umben grâl*', in *Wolfram-Studien*, ed. W. Schröder, II, Berlin, 1974, 72–83.

'Wolfram von Eschenbach's Antikonie', *GR*, 41 (1966), 83–8.

Pörksen, Uwe. *Der Erzähler im mittelhochdeutschen Epos. Formen seines Hervortretens bei Lamprecht, Konrad, Hartmann, in Wolframs Willehalm und in den 'Spielmannsepen'*, Berlin, 1971.

Rachbauer, Mary Aloysia. *Wolfram von Eschenbach. A Study of the*

Bibliography

Relation of the Content of Books III–VI and IX of the 'Parzival' to the Crestien Manuscripts. 1934; rpt. New York, 1970.

Ragotzky, Hedda. *Studien zur Wolfram-Rezeption. Die Entstehung und Verwandlung der Wolfram-Rolle in der deutschen Literatur des 13. Jahrhunderts.* Stuttgart and Berlin, 1971.

Rahn, Bernhard. *Wolframs Sigunendichtung. Eine Interpretation der 'Titurelfragmente'.* Zurich, 1958.

Richey, Margaret F. 'The "Titurel" of Wolfram von Eschenbach: structure and character', *MLR*, 56 (1961), 180–93.

Ringbom, Lars-Ivar. *Graltempel und Paradies. Beziehungen zwischen Iran und Europa im Mittelalter.* Stockholm, 1951.

Robertson, D. W. Jr. *A Preface to Chaucer.* Princeton, 1963.

Röll, Walter. *Studien zu Text und Überlieferung des sogennanten Jüngeren Titurel.* Heidelberg, 1964.

Röthlisberger, Blanca. *Die Architektur des Graltempels im Jüngern Titurel.* Bern, 1917.

Rupp, Heinz. 'Die Funktion des Wortes *tump* im *Parzival* Wolframs von Eschenbach', *GRM*, 38 (1957), 97–106.

'Rudolf von Ems und Konrad von Würzburg. Das Problem des Epigonentums', *DU*, 17 (1965), 5–17.

Ryding, William W. *Structure in medieval Narrative.* Paris, 1971.

Sacker, Hugh. *An Introduction to Wolfram's 'Parzival'.* Cambridge, 1963.

Salmon, Paul. 'Ignorance and awareness of identity in Hartmann and Wolfram: an element of dramatic irony', *Beiträge* (Tübingen), 82 (1960), 95–115.

'The wild man in "Iwein" and medieval descriptive technique', *MLR*, 56 (1961), 520–8.

Sayce, Olive. 'Prolog, Epilog und das Problem des Erzählers', in *Probleme mittelhochdeutscher Erzählformen*, ed. P. F. Ganz and W. Schröder, Berlin, 1972, 63–72.

Schirok, Bernd. 'Trevrizent und Parzival. Beobachtungen zur Dialogführung und zur Frage der figurativen Komposition', in *Amsterdamer Beiträge*, 10 (1976), 43–71.

Schmidt, Wieland. 'Vom Lesen und Schreiben im späten Mittelalter', *Beiträge* (Tübingen), 95 (1973), Sonderheft, *Festschrift für Ingeborg Schröbler*, 309–27.

Schröder, Walter J. 'Der dichterische Plan des Parzivalromans', *Beiträge* (Halle), 74 (1952), 160–92, 409–53.

'Über Ironie in der Dichtung. Der Teufel am Sakrament', *Akzente*, 2 (1955), 568–75.

Schröder, Werner. '*kunst* und *sin* bei Wolfram von Eschenbach', *Euphorion*, 67 (1973), 219–43.

282

Bibliography

'Parzivals Schwerter', *ZfdA*, 100 (1971), 111–32.

Schülein, Frieder. *Zur Theorie und Praxis des Blümens. Untersuchungen zur Sprachästhetik in der deutschen Literatur des 13.–15. Jahrhunderts.* Bern/Frankfurt/Munich, 1976.

Schweikle, Günther, ed. *Dichter über Dichter in mittelhochdeutscher Literatur.* Tübingen, 1970.

'*stiure* und *lêre.* Zum "Parzival" Wolframs von Eschenbach', *ZfdA*, 106 (1977), 183–99.

Schwietering, Julius. 'Mittelalterliche Dichtung und bildende Kunst, 2: Der Graltempel im Jüngeren Titurel', *ZfdA*, 60 (1923), 118–27.

'Natur und *art*', *ZfdA*, 91 (1961–2), 108–37.

Sedlmayr, Hans. 'Die dichterische Wurzel der Kathedrale', *Mitteilungen des österr. Instituts für Geschichtsforschung*, Ergänzungsband, 14 (1939), 275–87.

Die Entstehung der Kathedrale. Zurich, 1950.

Simon, Werner. 'Zu Wolframs *Titurel*', in *Festgabe für Ulrich Pretzel*, ed. W. Simon et al., Berlin, 1963, 185–90.

Sparnaay, Dr H. *Karl Lachmann als Germanist.* Bern, 1948.

Spearing, A. C. *Criticism and Medieval Poetry.* London. 1972.

Springer, Otto. 'Etymologisches Spiel in Wolframs Parzival', *Beiträge* (Tübingen), 87 (1965), 166–81.

'Playing on words: a stylistic note on Wolfram's *Titurel*', *Research Studies* (= Albert W. Thompson Festschrift), 32 (1964), 106–24.

Stackmann, Karl. '*Redebluomen.* Zu einigen Fürstenpreisstrophen Frauenlobs und zum Problem des geblümten Stils', in *Verbum et Signum*, vol. 2, ed. H. Fromm et al., Munich 1975, 329–46.

Stammler, Wolfgang. 'Ideenwandel in Sprache und Literatur des deutschen Mittelalters', *DVjs*, 2 (1924), 753–69.

Steinhoff, Hans-Hugo. *Die Darstellung gleichzeitiger Geschehnisse im mittelhochdeutschen Epos.* Munich, 1964.

Tapp, Henry Lee. 'An investigation of the use of imagery in the works of Wolfram von Eschenbach'. Diss., Yale, 1953.

Tax, Petrus W. 'Trevrizent. Die Verhüllungstechnik des Erzählers', in *Studien zur deutschen Literatur und Sprache des Mittelalters. Festschrift Hugo Moser*, ed. Besch et al., Berlin, 1974, 119–34.

Trendelenburg, Gudula. *Studien zum Gralraum im 'Jüngeren Titurel'.* Göppingen, 1972.

Trier, Jost. 'Architekturphantasien in der mittelalterlichen Dichtung', *GRM*, 17 (1929), 11–24.

Tschirch, Fritz. 'Das Selbstverständnis des mittelalterlichen deutschen Dichters', in *Beiträge zum Berufsbewußtsein des mittelalterlichen Menschen*, ed. P. Wilpert, Berlin, 1964, 239–85.

Vinaver, Eugène. *The Rise of Romance.* Oxford, 1971.

283

Bibliography

Wachinger, Burghart. *Sängerkrieg. Untersuchungen zur Spruchdichtung des 13. Jahrhunderts*. Munich, 1973.

Wehrli, Max. 'Wolfram von Eschenbach. Erzählstil und Sinn seines Parzival', in *Formen mittelalterlicher Erzählung*, Zurich and Freiburg, 1969, 195-222 (=*DU*, 6 (1954), 17-40).

Weigand, Hermann J. 'Spiritual therapy in Wolfram's Parzival', *GQ*, 51 (1978), 444-64.

Wolfram's Parzival. Five essays with an Introduction, ed. Ursula Hoffmann. Ithaca and London, 1969.

Welter, Hans Günther. 'Zur Technik der Wortwiederholungen in Wolframs Parzival', *ZfdPh*, 93 (1974) 34-63.

Wesle, Carl. 'Zu Wolframs Parzival', *Beiträge* (Halle), 72 (1950), 1-38.

Willson, H. B. 'Wolfram's self-defence', *MLR*, 52 (1957), 572-5.

Wolf, Werner. 'Zu den Hinweisstrophen auf die Wolframfragmente in der kleinen Heidelberger Handschrift des Jüngeren Titurel', *ZfdA*, 82 (1948-50), 256-64.

'Der Jüngere Titurel, "das Haubt ob teutschen Puechen"', *WW*, 6 (1955-6), 1-12.

'Nochmals zum "Ehrenhof" im Jüngeren Titurel', *ZfdA*, 85 (1954-5), 311-13.

'Zur Verskunst der Jüngeren Titurel-Strophe', in *Festschrift für F. R. Schröder*, ed. W. Rasch, Heidelberg, 1959, 163-77.

'Der Vogel Phönix und der Gral', in *Studien zur deutschen Philologie des Mittelalters*, F. Panzer dargebracht, ed. R. Kienast, Heidelberg, 1950, 73-95.

'Wer war der Dichter des Jüngeren Titurel', *ZfdA*, 84 (1952-3), 309-46.

Wolff, Ludwig, 'Wolframs Schionatulander und Sigune', in *Studien zur deutschen Philologie des Mittelalters*, F. Panzer dargebracht, ed. R. Kienast, Heidelberg, 1950, 116-30 (= in *Wolfram von Eschenbach*, ed. H. Rupp, Darmstadt, 1966, 549-69).

Wynn, Marianne. 'Geography of fact and fiction in Wolfram von Eschenbach's "Parzival"', *MLR*, 56 (1961), 28-43.

'Parzival and Gâwân - hero and counterpart', *Beiträge* (Tübingen), 84 (1962), 142-72.

'The poetic structure of Wolfram von Eschenbach's "Parzival". A study of the natural setting'. Diss., Cambridge, 1953/4.

'Scenery and chivalrous journeys in Wolfram's Parzival', *Speculum*, 36 (1961), 393-423.

Zarncke, Friedrich. 'Der Graltempel. Vorstudie zu einer Ausgabe des Jüngern Titurel', *Abhandlungen der philol.-hist. Classe der kgl. Sächsischen Ges. der Wiss.*, vol. 7 (1876), 375-554.

Bibliography

'Der Priester Johannes', *Abhandlungen der philol.-hist. Classe der kgl. Sächsischen Ges. der Wiss.*, vol. 7 (1879), 827-1030; vol. 8 (1876), 1-186.

Zatloukal, Klaus. 'India – ein idealer Staat im "Jüngeren Titurel"', in *Strukturen und Interpretationen, Studien zur deutschen Philologie für Blanka Horacek*, ed. A. Ebenbauer et al., Vienna, 1974, 401-45.

Zutt, Herta. 'Parzivals Kämpfe', in *Festgabe für F. Maurer*, ed. Besch et al., Düsseldorf, 1968, 178-98.

CRITICAL EDITIONS CITED

Albrecht von Scharfenberg. *Albrecht von Scharfenberg. Der Jüngere Titurel.* Ausgewählt und herausgegeben von Werner Wolf (Altdeutsche Übungstexte, 14). Bern, 1952.

Albrechts von Scharfenberg Jüngerer Titurel, ed. Werner Wolf. 2 vols. (Deutsche Texte des Mittelalters, 45 and 55/61). Berlin, 1955 and 1968.

Der Jüngere Titurel, ed. K. A. Hahn. Quedlinburg and Leipzig, 1842.

Chrétien de Troyes. *Le Roman de Perceval ou le Conte du Graal*, ed. William Roach. Paris, 1959.

Gottfried von Strassburg. *Tristan und Isold*, ed. Friedrich Ranke. Dublin, 1967.

Hartmann von Aue. *Iwein*. 7th revised edn, ed. G. F. Benecke, Karl Lachmann and L. Wolff. Berlin, 1968.

Die Minneburg, ed. Hans Pyritz (Deutsche Texte des Mittelalters, 43). Berlin, 1950.

Wirnt von Gravenberc. *Wigalois. Der Ritter mit dem Rade*, ed. J. M. N. Kapteyn. Bonn, 1926.

Wolfram von Eschenbach. *Wolfram von Eschenbach*, ed. Karl Lachmann. Berlin, 1833.

Parzival, ed. Karl Lachmann. 6th edn, Berlin, 1926. Rpt. 1965.

Titurel, ed. Albert Leitzmann (Altdeutsche Textbibliothek, 16). 5th edn, Tübingen, 1963.

Willehalm, ed. Albert Leitzmann (Altdeutsche Textbibliothek, 15 and 16). 5th edn, Tübingen, 1963.

INDEX

Albrecht, 2-4
attitude towards: chivalric code, 152-3, 206-8, 210-11, 214; courtly love, 211-14; sources, 7-10, 12-15, 221, 223; women, 200, 215-16; literature, 9, 151-2, 200, 208, 211
concern with completeness, 9-11, 15, 103, 152
consciousness: as follower, 7-10, 13, 259 n12; of narrative technique, 195-202, 217-19
emphasis on written word, 14-16, 75, 151-2, 160, 196, 205
moral stance, 22, 195-6, 198-200, 206, 222
narrator persona as Wolfram, 7-8, 10, 194-5, 201-2
patrons, 3, 10-11, 269 n78
allegory, 22-3, 25, 32-3, 103, 106, 147, 150, 175, 201, 238 n48
Anfortas, 19-20, 26, 68, 112, 114, 127, 132-3, 135, 189-90, 240 n1, 253 n30, 271 n90
Antikonie, 176, 182, 263 n40
Arbidol, 72-3, 78, 85, 142
âventiure, 144, 151, 170, 181, 201, 219, 223, 252 n20
Frou Aventiure: in the JT, 98, 201, 204, 216-19, 269 n76, 273 n97; in Parzival, 118, 136, 161, 169, 171, 191

Bernhard, St, 268 n73
Berthold von Regensburg, 3
blüemen, 14-15, 40, 196, 220
bow metaphor, 12-13, 111, 135-6, 161-2
brackenseil
in the JT, 15, 79-86, 88, 103-4, 107-9, 132, 136-7, 140-62, 222, 237 n46; as pawn, 92-4, 153, 155, 158; inscription, 15, 80-1, 141, 143-53, 155-7, 160-1, 203, 255 n41, 270 n80, 273 nn98, 101

in Parzival and Titurel, 69-70, 137-9, 149, 155, 255 n41; inscription, 137-9
bribery, 63, 82, 84, 101, 153-5, 158
bǔch, 151, 208, 213

Chrétien de Troyes
Cligès, 258 n5
Eric et Enide, 258 n5
Perceval, 17, 43, 45, 47-50, 52, 60, 63-5, 120, 135, 164-6, 169, 175, 230 n11, 235 n28, 241 n14, 242 n21, 244 n36, 249 n5, 250 n8, 257 n61, 260 n18, 261 nn28, 30, 263 n42, 265 nn49, 52, 53, 267 n60
Clauditte, 69, 143-4, 149, 155
Condwiramurs, 79-80, 114, 117, 119, 130, 134, 176, 178, 181
Cundrie, 26, 35, 114-15, 117, 119-20, 130-1, 182, 187, 249 n7; see also Kundrie
Cunneware, 52, 243 n29, 244 n37

dedication fragment, see Verfasserfragment
dialogue, use of
Albrecht, 93-5, 209-13, 217-18
Wolfram, 55, 93-5
didacticism
Albrecht, 39, 157, 197, 202, 208, 211, 216, 238 n48; in the leash inscription, 145, 150, 160
Wolfram, 169, 180-1, 192, 203, 219, 257 n61
see also lêre, tugende lêre
dragon, 52, 62, 74, 104

Ekunat, 69, 78-82, 87, 102, 104, 106, 142-4, 146, 149, 159, 230 n12
Enite, 52, 96-7
Epigone, 9, 232 n16, 233 n25
Erec, 51-2, 96
Erec, see Hartmann von Aue
eroticism, 43-8, 59-61, 121-4

Index

Feirefiz, 26, 116, 130, 132-4, 249 n4, 270 n81, 271 n90
Fontane la Salvatsche, 36, 124, 129, 188, 190-1, 271 n90
Frou Aventiure, see *âventiure*
Frou Minne, see *minne*

Gahmuret, 104, 109, 134, 247 n65, 263 n38
Gamuret, 86, 154-5, 239 n55, 246 n58, 272 n96
Gardeviaz, 69, 138
Gardivias, 71, 78, 142-3, 149
Gawan
  in the JT, 240 n1
  in *Parzival*, 71, 78, 129-30, 153, 165, 169-70, 175-6, 179, 235 n32, 251 n12, 259 n9, 260 n18, 261 n23, 263 n40; parallels with Parzival, 18, 66, 115-17
geblümte kunst, see *blüemen*
Gottfried von Strassburg: *Tristan*, 13, 167-8, 199-200, 229 n4, 233 n25, 258 n7, 270 n83, 272 n93
Gral
  in the JT, 2, 8, 21, 23, 31, 34, 217, 230 n12; castle, 22-4; kinship, 22, 204; realm, 22, 206, borders with courtly realm, 271 n90; sword, 104, 230 n12; temple, 9, 36, 38-40, 160, 208, 221-2, 254 n36, 270 n80, architecture of, 16, 24-34
  in *Parzival*, 15, 20, 25, 66, 109-37, 140-7 *passim*, 160-1, 170-2, 191-2; castle, 17, 23, 118, 182, 243 n30; horse, 67-8, 112, 120, 243 n29; kinship, 112, 114, 134-5, 137, 240 n7; knight, 68, 118, 120, 124, 132, 191; realm, 16, 68, 96, 109-33 *passim*, 179, 187, borders with courtly realm, 112, 114, 119, 134, 271 n90; sword, 111-12, 249 n3; temple, 25-6
Grey Knight, *see* pilgrim family
Gurnemanz, 17-18, 184-5, 187-8, 213, 252 n25

Hartmann von Aue, 13, 234 n25, 268 n68, 269 n76, 274 n109
Erec, 52, 238 n51
Gregorius, 268 n69

Iwein, 182, 239 n56, 258 nn6, 7, 261 n26
Heinrich von Veldeke, 213, 239 n55, 268 n68
Herzeloyde, 59, 87, 109, 134-5, 178, 240 n6, 248 n67, 261 n30, 263 n42
  advice to Parzival, 45, 47, 68, 116, 129, 213
  reaction to Gahmuret's death, 104, 247 nn62, 65, 256 n55
Hinweisstrophen, 2, 227 n10, 268 n67
hüte wol der verte, 149-50, 160; *see also*, Gardeviaz

irony
  Albrecht, 73, 82, 92, 97, 143, 145, 150, 158, 218-19
  Wolfram, 6, 164, 168, 171-5, 177, 181-2, 193, 200, 249 n7, 261 n28; related to Jeschute and Orilus, 46-8, 52, 55-6, 62-4, 67, 240 nn 5, 6, to Parzival, 46-8, 120, 125, 127, 187, to Sigune, 138-9, and to Trevrizent, 127, 245 n41
Isolde, 179, 262 n31, 269 n77
Ither
  in the JT, 73, 142
  in *Parzival*, 182-7, 247 n60, 267 n61

Jeschute, 41-67, 70-1, 133, 170, 207, 252 n25
  appearance, 43-6, 55, 57-60, 79, 84, 122, 173, 249 n5
  encounters with Parzival: first, 43-9, 55-6, 66-7, 70, 96-7, 122, 173-4, 184; second, 57-67, 76-7, 92-5
  relationship to Orilus, 42, 49-55, 60, 63-6, 90-1, 94-5
Jescute, 69, 78-9, 85, 104-8, 162, 273 n99
  appearance, 79-80, 83-4
  encounters with Parzival: first, 96-7, 101-3; second, 103
  fate, 103, 105-7, 230 n12
  and leash, 147, 155-6, 158; possessiveness towards, 80, 87-8, 108, 143, 156, 256 n53; reading inscription of, 81, 143-6
  parallels with Sigune, 97-8, 104-6, 108
  relationship to Orilus, 83, 89-97

For EU product safety concerns, contact us at Calle de José Abascal, 56–1°, 28003 Madrid, Spain or eugpsr@cambridge.org.

www.ingramcontent.com/pod-product-compliance
Ingram Content Group UK Ltd.
Pitfield, Milton Keynes, MK11 3LW, UK
UKHW010347140625
459647UK00010B/894